A Generation of Seekers

A Generation of Seekers

THE SPIRITUAL JOURNEYS OF THE BABY BOOM GENERATION

Wade Clark Roof

With the Assistance of Bruce Greer, Mary
Johnson, Andrea Leibson, Karen Loeb,
and Elizabeth Souza

HarperSanFrancisco
A Division of HarperCollinsPublishers

FIRST HARPERCOLLINS PAPERBACK EDITION
PUBLISHED IN 1994

**An Earlier Edition of This Book Was Cataloged as
Follows:**
Roof, Wade Clark.
     A generation of seekers : the spiritual journeys of
the baby boom generation / Wade Clark Roof ; with
the assistance of Bruce Greer . . . [et al]. —1st ed.
          p.   cm.
     Includes bibliographical references and index.
     ISBN 0–06–066963–2 (cloth)
     ISBN 0–06–066964–0 (pbk)
     1. Baby boom generation—United States—
Religious life.   2. United States—Religion—1960-
I. Title.
BL2525.R65   1993
248.8'4—dc20   92–53920
                                                          CIP

94 95 96 97 98 ❖ HAD 10 9 8 7 6 5 4 3 2

We shall not cease from exploration

And the end of all our exploring

Will be to arrive where we started

And know the place for the first time.

T. S. Eliot,
"LITTLE GIDDING"

Contents

Contents

Acknowledgments

In a study as large and ambitious as this one, there are many whose help made the project possible. Major funding came from the Lilly Endowment, Inc., a private foundation interested in the study of religion. Robert Wood Lynn, then Vice President for Religion at Lilly, encouraged the research with the awarding of a grant in 1988; his successor, Craig Dykstra, and Lilly colleagues Fred Hofheinz, Jim Lewis, and Dorothy Bass, have generously supported the project with supplementary grants. To the Endowment and its staff, my great appreciation.

Many people deserve mention for their help, of one sort or another: David Roozen, Jackson W. Carroll, and William McKinney for advice in designing the research in the early planning stages; Phillip E. Hammond for collaboration on a survey yielding a portion of the data; Steven M. Tipton for consultation on interviewing methods; Barbara G. Wheeler for encouraging me to study congregations as part of this project; and Marilyn Metcalf-Whitacker for assistance with the North Carolina interviews. Others, too numerous to mention by name, have responded to lectures and speeches on boomers, and thereby helped to bring focus and direction to the work.

I am especially grateful to my research team, without whose help this project could not have been carried out on so grand a scale: Bruce Greer, Sr. Mary Johnson, Andrea Leibson, Karen Loeb, Elizabeth Souza, all of the University of Massachusetts at Amherst. All baby boomers themselves, they were a great working group in the early phases of this project. Together we conducted telephone interviews, and then face-to-face interviews in various locations across the country. As a team we spent many hours reading and discussing the interviews. We continued our work together even after I moved across the country to Santa Barbara, California, in late 1989. For all these reasons, even though I am responsible for the writing, I have opted to write using the comradely "we" in appreciation for their assistance.

Mary Johnson, Martha Finch-Jewell, Julie Ingersoll, and Jeff Graver read the manuscript and offered helpful comments. Terry Potter Roof not only read it but also discussed (and debated!) the contents with me at great length. As usual, I benefited from her insights. And thanks to Jezebel, my cat. Her amusements with my keyboard, as she sat on the edge of my desk while I wrote much of this, kept me entertained and never let me forget life's simple pleasures.

John Loudon, Joann Moschella, and all the people at Harper San Francisco have been a pleasure to work with. An author could not have asked for a better support team.

Finally, thanks again to the boomers themselves, who opened up their lives to us.

Introduction

This is a book about the religious and spiritual lives of baby boomers: their experiences and struggles with religion, their search for meaningful spiritual styles, and how this generation is altering the religious landscape of America in the 1990s. Admittedly, this is a big undertaking. Given the size of this population— 76 million—baby boomers defy easy generalizations about their beliefs and practices. This generation, born over the span of years from 1946 to 1964, includes men and women who grew up in very different decades: the turbulent 1960s, in the Age of Aquarius; the mid- to late 1970s, a time of evangelical and charismatic revival; and the 1980s, with its smorgasbord of New Age spiritualities. Trying to grasp the religious and spiritual gestalt of any generation is difficult, and possible only in some relative sense; but for this generation it is especially tough, given its immense size and diversity.

Virtually all aspects of the lives of baby boomers—their family styles, moral values, work habits, political views—defy simple generalizations. There are many white, upscale boomers, but there are also millions of blue-collar, minority, single-parent, and poor boomers. Polls show they are tolerant in matters of lifestyle and committed to women's issues, yet many call for a return to traditional family values. They cherish the freedom of individual expression, yet agree there should be greater respect for authority. Aside from whatever unites them as a generation, they are divided along lines of age, education, economic class, gender, and lifestyle, making them anything but a monolith.

Partly for this reason, the boomers are an easy target for caricature. At various times they have been called the Pepsi Generation, the Rock Generation, the Love Generation, the Now Generation, the Me Generation. Labels come and go, but some kind of label always seems to pop up. As Paul C. Light has observed, "The baby boomers have always been known by a handful of stereotypes—hippies in the 1960s, yuppies in the 1980s. Ask the average American to define the baby

1

boomer of today, and he or she will likely think of yuppies or grumpies on Wall Street, or Dinks in the suburbs, long before remembering the real people just down the street."[1]

In this book we have tried to get beyond stereotypes to the real people. Over the past four years we have interviewed hundreds of boomers on the telephone. We have gone out and met scores of them, asking about their experiences and life histories. We have visited churches and synagogues, conducted group interviews, and talked to them in more casual settings—at folk festivals and retreat centers, in seminaries, on airplanes, at bars. Everywhere we have gone—primarily in California, Massachusetts, North Carolina, and Ohio—we have listened to their stories. While our aim was to learn as much as possible about their religious and spiritual biographies, we have found out a great deal as well about their work and careers, their marriages and families, their visions of the country and its future, their hopes and dreams.

Many of the people we interviewed asked us two questions: "Why are you studying boomers?" and "Why are you asking questions about religion and spirituality?" Boomers are keenly aware they are one of the most studied, analyzed, and watched-over generations in history—hence the curiosity about yet another inquiry into their lives.

Why talk to baby boomers? One answer is because there are so many of them. Roughly one-third of the nation's population, they are a much larger birth cohort than either those born during the Depression cohort of the 1930s before them, or the baby bust that followed them in the 1970s.[2] Size alone makes them the "lead cohort" in the country today, setting trends in American life—in consumption patterns, television programming, housing construction, and political party affiliation. Market researchers and political analysts monitor them closely to detect changes in their tastes and preferences, in what they purchase, and how they vote. We cannot really understand contemporary America without some appreciation for this group and its values, beliefs, and opinions.

Because of their numbers, the boomers have of course long been in the spotlight. Since the time they were children, they were told they were a special generation. As children they had an enormous impact on society in the 1950s—on the construction of new schools, on the creation of child-centered families, and on child-rearing philosophies. As they move through life, they create a bulge in the population structure—like a "pig in a python," as demographers say—forcing society to adjust and accommodate their needs. At every stage in the life cycle, then, this generation has had a dominating influence on how Americans live and think and believe.

But more than just numbers, they constitute a "generation" in the broader social sense. Many years ago sociologist Karl Mannheim wrote about generations and their importance in bringing about social change.[3] In times of social upheaval and cultural discontinuity especially, generations tend to become more sharply set off from one another. In Mannheim's phrase members of the same generation share "a common location" in the social process. More than just an aggregate of individuals of a similar age, a generation thus tends to have common, unifying social experiences and to develop a collective sense of identity. Members of one age group define themselves in relation to other cohorts by rejecting or reaffirming one or another set of cultural values, beliefs, and symbols; in this way a generation comes to have its own distinctive "historical-social" consciousness. This is likely to occur in late adolescence and early adulthood—the formative years for the shaping of a distinct outlook.

The notion of a generation implies that members' experiences in the formative years exert a strong, often lasting influence on their lives. That is to say, people carry their memories from the past into the present —memories that continue to shape how they perceive the world and how they relate to it. Research shows that Americans of all ages, when asked about important events, recall as especially important memories of events and changes that refer back largely to a time when they were in their teens or early twenties.[4] These memories have largely to do with the social and political world beyond the family and personal relationships— wars, assassinations, social upheavals, economic depression, environmental disasters, terrorism, space exploration. As developmental psychologists since Mannheim have come to recognize, the years of youth and early adulthood are a critical period for learning about the larger society; memories arising out of the intersection of personal and national history during these years live on in our lives. Thus because they have quite differing pasts, the generations see and act toward the world differently: A Depression generation is frugal, a Vietnam generation is wary of war.

Timing is right for a look at the boomers. The oldest members of the generation are now in their forties, many of them are in their mid- to late thirties. Today, they are reshaping our national life: As in the past they altered the meanings of childhood and youth, now they define what is meant by adulthood. The great majority are now in the prime child-rearing years: With so many of them having children, they shape family and parenting styles. They enjoy enormous social and economic influence: They now own small businesses, occupy seats on corporate boards, and are rapidly moving into the front offices, taking on leadership and power

3

positions. Across the country they are the volunteers filling posts in civic and community organizations. With the election of Bill Clinton and Al Gore, baby boomers now occupy the nation's highest offices. In Annie Gottlieb's words, now is the time of their "second coming," when they have another chance to have an impact on the world.[5]

And while this is happening, the 1960s—as a decade, a movement, a moment in history—is up for reappraisal. Historians and sociologists are taking a fresh look at the era that gave birth to this generation and inspired its way of life. Both nostalgia and cynicism are found in these accounts of the decade, which makes for considerable debate over how best to interpret the period.[6] Those who celebrate the decade point to a more egalitarian, more tolerant, richer way of life since midcentury; they point to ecology, peace, civil rights, the women's movement, and quality of life as outgrowths. Those who criticize its darker side see the breakdown of authority and the family and epidemics of crime, drugs, and AIDS all traced to the period. Some of the labels they use are "destructive," "narcissistic," "greedy," and "materialistic."

But whether nostalgic or cynical, commentators agree that baby boomers came of age in a time of increased choices and optimistic dreams. The 1960s were an era of expanding horizons. Opportunities opened up for people growing up then that were far greater than anything their parents had known—career options, changing gender roles, new family types, choice of lifestyles. But it was also an era of disappointments and disillusionments—of shattered dreams, of encounters with war, injustice, and corruption in high places, of having to scale down material expectations. The 1970s, with its recessions, environmental disasters, and long gas lines, tempered their optimism. The era as a whole produced a distinctive boomer ethos, one that is not easily defined but is reflected in many ways—for example, in the topics addressed in Anna Quindlen's newspaper column, in the themes covered in the *Utne Reader,* and in the style of Dave Barry's humor.

Why ask about religion and spirituality? Because there is widespread ferment today that reaches deep within their lives. Members of this generation are asking questions about the meaning of their lives, about what they want for themselves and for their children. They are still exploring, as they did in their years growing up; but now they are exploring in new, and, we think, more profound ways. Religious and spiritual themes are surfacing in a rich variety of ways—in Eastern religions, in evangelical and fundamentalist teachings, in mysticism and New Age movements, in Goddess worship and other ancient religious rituals, in the mainline churches and synagogues, in Twelve-Step recovery groups, in concern about the environment, in holistic health, and in personal and social transformation. Many within this generation who dropped out of churches and synagogues years ago are now shopping around for a congregation. They move freely in and out, across religious boundaries; many combine elements from various traditions to create their own personal, tailor-made meaning systems. Choice, so much a part of life for this generation, now expresses itself in dynamic and fluid religious styles.

Religion and spirituality, of course, are an integral part of human culture, or the web of meanings that inform people's lives. Culture has to do with making sense out of life and formulating strategies for action; and the ideas and symbols that people draw on in these fundamental undertakings are, implicitly if not explicitly, saturated with religious meaning. Religion is itself a set of cultural symbols. As Andrew M. Greeley observes, "Religion is an imaginative 'cultural system'—a collection of directing 'pictures' through which humans organize and give meaning to the phenomena that impinge on their consciousness, especially insofar as these phenomena require some explanation of the ultimate purpose of life."[7] It is these "pictures" as expressed in symbol and metaphor, as Greeley notes, that explain what life is about and shape human response to life. These pictures are the foundations on which all worldviews rest—whether religious or secular. Hence in this study we have tried to be sensitive to the phenomenological worlds in which people live, and to what they view as the governing forces shaping their lives. We have sought to be empathetic listeners to what they are saying are their deepest concerns, about what gives meaning and purpose to their lives, about what is sacred.

Again, timing is right. Many boomers are now approaching middle age, or that stage of life often talked about as midlife. "Forty is the old age of youth and the youth of old age," so the adage goes. However one cares to view it, reaching forty marks a significant passage in life's journey. Midlife is popularly thought of as a time of crisis, but it is more appropriately viewed as a time of transition. Developmental psychologists describe it as a transition from early adulthood into later adulthood, a juncture when people often reexamine their lives, their past and anticipated future, their most cherished values and commitments.[8] This can be a period of uncertainty and emotional strain, but it can also be highly challenging and self-enriching. It is a time when adults experience a capacity for growth and maturity, which potentially can occur at any life stage but is especially likely at midlife.

Boomers are now experiencing, as is common in life's passages, a sense of aliveness and freshness, an openness to new spiritual sensitivities. They are at a critical juncture of affirming life's meanings and fundamental values and of dealing with spiritual voids, of looking back upon their lives as a means of preparing to move forward. Psychologist John Roschen speaks of a "second journey into self." He points out that many young Americans are inwardly appraising self but are also moving outward toward others. In this second journey of self, they are revising their notions of who they are as their lives spiral outward to spouses, to families, to the wider communities. Boomers are no longer, if ever most of them were, to be thought of as the "Me Generation" caught up in their own selfish pursuits; instead, this is a maturing generation of individuals concerned not just with their inner lives, but with their outer lives. We sense that they are reaching out to commit themselves to something of importance, yearning for relationships and connections, longing for more stable anchors for their lives. To quote Roschen:

> This balanced care for self and others brings out the virtues of connectedness, intimacy, love, fairness, a sense of justice, and commitment to duty which yearn to be reclaimed in the lives of many in the baby-boom generation. Fulfillment versus responsibility, and individual ambition versus the needs of others are at the crux of the baby-boomers' midlife dilemma.[9]

How the boomers deal with their lives at midlife is important, not just for themselves, but for the country. American culture as a whole could be profoundly affected in the years ahead.

Hence our concerns are similar to those of Robert Bellah and his associates in *Habits of the Heart*.[10] These commentators concentrate primarily on white, middle-class Americans, looking at their individualism and struggles to commit themselves across many sectors of personal and public life. The analysis is framed broadly in terms of the nation's moral cultures, and of public discourse about what it means to be a responsible American today. We have been inspired by their work, yet our focus differs in three important ways: One, we look only at religion and spirituality and thus are more concerned with what is happening within this particular realm. Two, by examining a broad cross section of the boomer population, we explore more the diversity, the strains, and tensions surrounding religious belief and practice in America today. Three, given our concern with generations, we are interested in how boomers may be transforming religious and spiritual life. Put simply, ours might be thought of as an exploration into a generation's culture, inquiring into how its members relate to the sacred and what this might mean for future religious trends.

A word about method. The people we talked to were part of a large representative survey conducted by a polling firm. After a telephone interview, we obtained from them a more in-depth interview. In this way we have combined two research methods—the large-scale survey and life-history interviews—believing that by integrating survey findings with biographies we have a much richer data base for describing the religious and spiritual qualities of this generation. (See the Appendix on Data and Methods for a more detailed explanation.) The two methods are complementary, each offering strength where the other is weak: Surveys allow us to generalize on a wide range of questions but are unable to do much more than scratch the surface of people's lives; biographies, or the stories people tell about their lives, may or may not be representative in any way of the generation, but they offer richness and nuance—what Robert Coles describes as the "complex, ironic, inconsistent, contradictory nature of human character, and too, of faith and doubt."[11] It is this balance of generalizability and thick description of people's lives that we have sought.

The book consists of four parts. Part One, consisting of chapters 1 and 2, tells the stories of seven people we interviewed and describes how events and experiences during the sixties shaped their lives. Together, these two chapters set the context for the themes dealt with in the remainder of the book. These themes are hardly exhaustive of a complex set of experiences, but they are among the most important in helping us to grasp the religious and cultural changes now underway. Part Two looks at spirituality in its many forms and explores issues of authority, belief, and belonging that divide the boomers. We look carefully at both the differences and the unities in the boomer culture, in an attempt to show the influences on this generation and how individuals have responded in organizing their religious and spiritual lives. Part Three focuses on institutional trends in religion. Here we look at the return to religious involvement of those who dropped out, the subcultures that are emerging within the boomer population, the qualities of congregations that attract returning boomers, and the struggles individuals have within religious institutions. Part Four reflects on the implications of the trends as a whole for the American religious future and offers a concluding comment about our seven representative boomers.

However elusive it may be, we are convinced that there is something that can be called a "boomer culture"—including a search for a spiritual style. "We're like everybody else. Some go to church, some don't," said one respondent we talked to at a Jesus Day festival in Chicago. He then quickly added, "But maybe we are different in that so many of us don't go even if at heart, deep down, we are very religious." His comment captures what this book aims to get at—a generation's own experience and search for a spiritual style.

This is a generation of seekers. Diverse as they are—from Christian fundamentalists to radical feminists, from New Age explorers to get-rich-quick MBAs—baby boomers have found that they have to discover for themselves what gives their lives meaning, what values to live by. Not since the cataclysm of World War II have most of us been able simply to adopt the meanings and values handed down by our parents' religion, our ethnic heritage, our nationality. Rather, what really matters became a question of personal choice and experience.

Our aim has thus been to portray the baby boom generation's search for meaning and value in an increasingly complex, uncertain, and fast-changing world. We draw on the life stories of prototypical boomers to attempt to reveal the soul of the generation that now comprises the bulk of our new leaders (in politics, business, education, religion, and so on), of the prime consumers, of parents. Through our research and the individual accounts, which put flesh on the bones of our statistical findings, there emerges a generation of diverse seekers who share surprising commonalities. They value experience over beliefs, distrust institutions and leaders, stress personal fulfillment yet yearn for community, and are fluid in their allegiances—a new, truly distinct, and rather mysterious generation. Beginning to understand what makes them tick seems vital to every segment of our society. Now it's time to meet them, and most likely ourselves.

PART ONE

Stories

CHAPTER 1

The Lives of Seven Boomers

Let us begin with introductions to seven people whose lives we will follow throughout this book. The seven are Barry Johnson, Linda Kramer, Pam Fletcher, Sonny D'Antonio, Oscar Gantt, Mollie Stone, and Carol McLennon. All are actual people, but names and incidental details have been changed to protect their privacy.

BARRY JOHNSON

"I guess it was through my kids," replies Barry Johnson when asked about why he started going to church again. An engineer, forty-two years old, earning a good salary, he is now a member of a progressive Southern Baptist church in the Research Triangle area of North Carolina. Like many boomers who have looked around for a congregation, he was concerned to find one that fits the family. He likes the church because it doesn't have rigid beliefs or guidelines and encourages people to think for themselves about the big questions of life and death and why things happen as they do. It's the kind of place where he's happy to have his children get involved.

But he didn't always think this way. Like most boomers, he dropped out of church in his late teen years. He grew up in the South in an upper middle-class, Presbyterian family and attended a conservative state university. In engineering school, however, he found himself becoming more and more opposed to the Vietnam War as it lingered on. For the first time in his life, he came to realize what it was like to hold views at odds with majority opinion—to be a "duck out of water." Unable to discuss the war with his parents and many of his friends, he became very frustrated. This experience had a powerful effect on him: It galvanized his radical views and taught him to think and to believe for himself—in short, he found out what it was like to be marginal in a conformist culture.

As he looks back on those days, the 1960s and early 1970s were the worst of times and the best of times. Definitely the worst of times: assassinations, the civil rights struggles, environmental destruction, the loss of confidence in the government and in social institutions—including organized religion. He became politically involved, supporting McGovern for president in 1972; but after the Nixon election, he became deeply skeptical and disillusioned with the political process.

Yet they were also the best of times:

> There were some beautiful things that occurred. People became aware of things other than themselves . . . people were looking outside of themselves . . . what happened in the sixties . . . was a rejection of a lot of the old values and growing into looking outside of oneself to the rest of the world. Being conscious of a global point of view and not just me or . . . my neighborhood.

It was a time when people awakened and came to their senses. The earth required stewardship, the nation needed integrity, the South needed healing from its racial crisis.

At the time Barry questioned his belief in God and wondered if there was meaning in the midst of so much chaos and tragedy. He recalls thinking, "Where is God? This world is really screwed up." But after years as a religious skeptic, he has come to look on things differently. How could he explain his father's slow and painful death to his children? Even if he was "pissed off" with God, shouldn't his kids know about God? And as he has grown older, has he not learned that life poses new mysteries and challenges?

Along with his wife and children, he credits M. Scott Peck's *The Road Less Traveled* as helping him to resolve his spiritual questions. Peck's book begins with the sentence, "Life is difficult," a point not wasted on Barry: He believes that once a person accepts the fact that life is difficult, then paradoxically life becomes less difficult. Back during the Vietnam years, he didn't really understand the point about life's difficulties; midlife brought him to this insight—the understanding that personal doubts and struggles can be a source of spiritual growth. He continues to have doubts concerning God and what life is about, doubts in a big way; but he also believes in a big way. Struggle, doubt, faith—they all go together.

Barry feels that much of what was learned from the 1960s and 1970s got lost in the 1980s, with people so "concerned about their well-being and when the big bucks are going to be coming in and when I am going to be able to buy my big house." But now he sees some hopeful signs that his generation is moving beyond the "me-first" yuppie ethic—toward greater responsibility, toward concern for the environment, toward relationships with people. His skepticism about institutions is still with him. "I wouldn't class myself as a rebel or anything, but I think it is healthy to have some skepticism about accepted institutions." For this reason he insisted on carefully choosing the congregation the family attends and required that it must be one that encourages an open and exploring stance toward faith and allows the individual to develop spiritually. He tries not to be anti-institutional, for he recognizes the great importance of structures; yet never again—whether in church, in the government, or in war—will he be a blind follower. He is committed to his congregation but is determined that it not stifle his need to find God outside its walls—in nature, in jogging, in people. He insists on some "space" of his own.

LINDA KRAMER

Ask Linda Kramer about her faith, and she'll tell you she believes that Jesus Christ saved her through faith, that heaven awaits her in the life to come, and that the Bible teaches you what is right and wrong. Unlike Barry Johnson, who struggles with his faith and his church, Linda speaks with much greater assurance and confidence. Linda is one among many boomers today who have turned to an evangelical faith in search of clearer religious and moral guidelines. An active churchgoer all her life, a strong faith has become more important to her as she has become older. Now forty-two, she is a housewife and mother of two children and lives in a midwestern city.

Life seems so different now from what she remembers as a child. Drugs, infidelity, pornography, abortion, materialism, greed, and selfishness are rampant today—all signs, for Linda, of a corrupt and fallen world. It bothers her that people do not even know what the Ten Commandments are anymore, much less try to follow them. But it was not always that way. When she was growing up, she remembers happy times with her parents and sisters. In her little rural community in Ohio, people knew and cared for one another. Kids respected their parents. Families went to church. It was as if the 1960s didn't happen. "I didn't know anybody who took drugs," she said, thinking back to her high school years. "I knew a couple of guys who drank beer once in a while from my class."

QUESTION: Did you rebel as a teenager?

ANSWER: I really don't think I did rebel much. Tried a few cigarettes when I was out on my own. I was pretty sheltered, I guess, growing up.

She wasn't totally sheltered, of course. She remembers enjoying the music very much. She wore beads and had long straight hair for a while. And the Vietnam War touched her: She was married at nineteen, and three months later her husband went off to the war. When he returned, he was like a different person. They were soon divorced. Then she was married for a second time and was divorced again by her midtwenties. The women's movement has also touched her: She worked to support herself during those difficult years and learned that a woman has to look out for herself. Linda knows from experience that life has plenty of hard knocks.

After moving to the city and attending business school, she left behind her Methodist heritage and joined a Baptist church. Going to church, she thought, ought to be more than a "rote thing," as it had been growing up with her parents. And finding herself living among hippies and strangers who didn't live or believe as she did, it was necessary more than ever to have a Bible-based faith. She checked out several differing congregations, looking to find a church that would help her to grow as a Christian and make her feel welcome in its fellowship. Denomination is not important; all that really counts is if Christ is present.

Today she is a member of a huge megachurch, where three thousand people show up on a Sunday morning—a "new-style" evangelical congregation that combines Bible preaching, modern sound technology, and popular psychology. Her congregation is made up largely of lower middle-class and working-class members; its emphasis is on people, on family life, on the power of love. It offers lots of music, stage productions, a huge library of books, films and cassette tapes to help people in Christian growth, programs and activities for every age, dozens of prayer and interest groups, a growing Christian school, and a parking lot that covers ten acres. She describes the church as follows:

People are concerned about you as a person. I met my husband through the singles group that's here. They also have a group for single parents. They have a group for those that are widowed. They have young married or newly engaged groups. They have groups for young families. They have a choir. They have an orchestra. So whatever your interests and wherever your talents lie, you can get involved with a small group. And they become like a family to you. There is a lot of love.

She enjoys listening to the popular family counselor Dr. James Dobson on the radio. His program gives her advice on marriage, on rearing children to respect parents, and on how to deal with children and drugs. She finds his authoritative approach to raising children and support of anti-abortion and pro-family concerns much needed in today's world. She likes very much his patriotic messages about America; and though she doesn't say much about it, she is fascinated with what he has to say about "growth" as a person and about "finding happiness" in life.

But the Bible is her main source for Christian living—her "rule-book and guidebook." It offers clear guidelines, even on abortion:

> It sure does, for me. . . . The Bible speaks of God knowing us in our mother's womb and planning our whole lives ahead of us before we were even born. I think for a woman just to think that she is in control of her own body and not to consider the life within her is making the wrong decision.

Linda worries about what she sees happening around her. Women having abortions, drugs in the schools, and the whole country, it seems, straying from God's ways. She wonders what might lie ahead for a nation that has broken its covenant with God. "People disregard God's laws . . . the country is in a downward spiral . . . things are going to get worse . . . a huge monetary collapse is coming." In her view America has been great because people have loved God and tried to walk in his ways, but she worries: How long will his mercies last?

PAM FLETCHER

"When your number is up, your number is up," Pam Fletcher exclaims, in what is for her a quasi-religious philosophy about life and death. She admits it's a fatalistic view and prefers not to think about what it means. She grew up in an educated, middle-class Pennsylvania household that was very open and talked freely about things. Her family insisted that your religious views are whatever you choose and not to be imposed by parents. Her mother was Jewish, her father a New England WASP. Attending neither synagogue nor church, she grew up "nonsectarian." Now thirty-seven years old, she and her husband (reared Congregationalist) are not involved at all with a congregation; they have two children and live comfortably on the Massachusetts South Shore.

Pam recalls a happy youth that was not greatly affected by the sixties' culture. Her years growing up, and later at college, were pretty mild compared to the lives of many around her. "I didn't do drugs or sex," she insists, in her way of setting herself apart from so many of her generation who tested the limits. But unlike Linda Kramer, it was not that Pam didn't know what was going on: "We were inexperienced. We were not naive. There is a difference." She attributes her good years growing up to the wonderful relationship she had with her parents. They were model parents—the "best"—and from an early age she and her siblings had many conversations around the dinner table concerning politics, Watergate, Woodstock, drugs, sex. Anything the kids wanted to talk about was discussed in an open, permissive atmosphere.

She is pleased to have been raised "nonsectarian." Her parents were nondogmatic, very liberal-minded. Like other boomers who grew up in a more secular environment, she sees religion as a very private matter, and as something that ought not to interfere in any way with family relations. For Pam and her siblings, family was and still is of utmost concern. So strong were her ties to her parents that she speaks of them in an unusual way: "They were our religion." She still has a very close relationship with them and speaks of a good family as doing for you just about everything religion does: "You have people when things get upset or things don't work out, they turn to religion. They go to church. It never even occurs to us. I go to my parents."

Organized religion has no real place in her life. Even personal faith and practice seem not to be of great concern to her. When asked about belief in God, she is uncertain. Her father's Protestant heritage is of little significance to her. Occasionally, she reads about Judaism, her mother's background, but the religious aspects of the tradition are of no particular interest to her. As a child she attended a few Passover *seders,* but she cannot imagine getting actively involved in a synagogue or church today. It doesn't bother her very much if her children go to the local Sunday school once in a while, but she certainly doesn't encourage it. She worries that her children could come under the influence of "born-again Christians," which would be awful. She would probably be appalled at Linda Kramer's determined efforts to make sure that her children do not stray from the evangelical faith. Being married to someone who is not a churchgoer helps Pam reinforce the family's noncommittal stance toward religion. As did her parents, she and her husband practice a secular style of tolerance and are agreed that religion is a purely private matter.

From time to time, pressure arises from her Congregationalist in-laws about the children and church. When the first daughter was born, the question came up about whether the baby would be baptized. She told her husband they could do it if it was meaningful to him, since he was the one who had gone to church at one time in his life:

> I said it has no meaning to me. I said I would feel very hypocritical. Stand up there and go through this charade, because that's what it would be. It doesn't mean anything to me. If it's important to you, it's your upbringing. He said, "Pam, I couldn't care less."

The issue of the children and religion is not fully resolved, but she and her husband are agreed to let the children decide about it for themselves when they are old enough.

Pam thinks mainly in practical terms of everyday life and tries not to think too much about the big metaphysical questions. She wants mainly to be comfortable and to have a "nice, ordinary, pleasant, happy family." She hopes that all will be "healthy," and that "we don't have any tragedies." Not an unreasonable wish, yet she knows there are no assurances. Is there any kind of ultimate meaning in life? Does it all add up in the end? Can you ever really know? She prefers not to think about such things.

> I want a guarantee that I am going to live and my kids are going to live and my husband is going to live. But there is no such thing. That's why I don't think about it. You could get depressed. . . . Are they going to make it? Are they going to live? Are they going to get hit by a car?

But since there are no guarantees, what are you left with? There are some choices in life, but some things seem already planned, beyond human control.

> I guess I believe in fate . . . a religion in its own sort of way . . . when your number is up, your number is up. I just don't want my number to be up.

SONNY D'ANTONIO

"Absolutely not," exclaims Sonny D'Antonio, when asked if the Catholic church has anything to offer him today. A machine operator with a ninth-grade education, Sonny grew up in an Italian Catholic family in Massachusetts. He stopped going to mass or having anything to do with the church many years ago. "Some people go to church, some people don't . . . whatever makes your boat float. If that's what somebody believes, that's fine, but all I ask is, don't push it off on me." Like Pam Fletcher he wants nothing to do with priests, preachers, and rabbis; but unlike her Sonny holds dearly to some traditional religious values. God, country, family, and the American way of life are all deeply important. Not unlike many others of his generation, he is a "believer but not a belonger." He is thirty-six, married with two young daughters, and lives in a working-class Boston suburb.

To hear Sonny tell it, the sixties didn't influence him very much. Hippies with long hair, demonstrators turning their backs on the country, crazy college students—he wanted little to do with them. He did worry a lot about being drafted. His father had fought in World War II, and he felt that maybe he too should fight for his country. He struggled with himself over Vietnam, knowing his life was in the hands of fate—the lottery. In the end he didn't have to go, but he still gets emotional when he thinks about the war:

> I was very confused about why we were in Vietnam and I certainly didn't want to die for something I wasn't clear about. . . . It's not that I am against killing—if someone came to my door and wanted to harm my family, I'd kill them and feel no remorse. But I didn't want to kill some stranger for a reason that was never clear to me and still isn't to this day. . . . As it turned out, I had a high number in the lottery so it didn't matter.

Sonny has a lot of anger toward the church. Though he was raised in a Catholic school, he insists it had no influence on him. His parents did not attend mass regularly, and he grew up without having to feel he had to be there every Sunday. The "material parts of the church," he says, "turned me off." He remembers priests who were always after him for money and is still angry about the way the church treated his sister. His sister was a devoted Catholic all her life. Then she met a man who was divorced, and they wouldn't allow her to be married in the church. "Somebody that devoted . . . they slammed the door in her face, they just slammed it. . . . you can go out and kill somebody and be forgiven for that. And you can't be forgiven for . . . I mean, he's a human being."

Though he has abandoned the church, there's much Sonny hasn't given up of his Italian Catholic heritage. He wears a St. Anthony medal around his neck. He believes in God and in heaven. He talks to his kids about these things. He even prays occasionally, as he did when his father had a triple bypass. "At that point you're totally helpless . . . there is absolutely nothing that you can do as an individual to help, other than pray." And there are times when he feels a need for direction, and he'll pray: "Like I may be confused about something, and I'll just pray to him and say, y'know, jeez, I'm confused . . . just whatever's right, let it happen . . . that type of thing." If things turn out bad, then he knows that was the way things were meant to be. He is curious, too, about the Bible. Sometimes when he and his friends go on a fishing trip, he'll pick up a Bible in the motel and read a bit. "What's in this book that people are reading that's so damn interesting?" he asks. Only when he's alone does he do this, " 'Cause I'd get beat on if I ever got caught with a Bible in my hand. . . . They'd call me Rev. Sonny."

"My home is my church," he says. His wife, children, and parents are the significant others in his life, followed, perhaps, by his fishing buddies; they are the people he feels most obligated to help. The fishing buddies are important partly because they attend the same Alcoholics Anonymous group as does Sonny; a heavy drinker since his twenties, he has been in and out of AA ever since. Relationships are important, almost sacramental. His private religious world is shaped around them, and especially around the family:

> I don't have to dig in my pocket and give to the church every day. I sit here, I can believe in God, I can go through my routine of prayer, my wife can go through her routine of prayer, my kids know about God, we don't harm anybody, we mind our own business, if somebody needs help, we're there to help them, somebody breaks down in the street, I'll help 'em. I've picked people up off the middle of the street.

He does this not out of religious motivation, he says, but because there's "a human being that needs help."

OSCAR GANTT

Having "roots" gives you an identity. Oscar Gantt, thirty-nine and a skilled machine operator, grew up in the African Methodist Episcopal Church in western North Carolina and is steeped in his religious tradition. His life is intimately bound up with the history and destiny of the African-American people. His church is so much a part of this experience that he could not imagine "walking away from those roots."

Oscar knows all too well the struggles against racism. It was during the 1960s racial revolution that his roots became meaningful to him. Segregation between the races was crumbling everywhere in the South as the civil rights movement, under the leadership of Dr. Martin Luther King, Jr., inspired blacks in a struggle for their rights. North Carolina was the scene of the first major desegregation efforts. "We were beginning to stand up," says Oscar, "and say that we would not accept life that way anymore." King's philosophy of nonviolence was a powerful, liberating force for religious people who had been taught that the Bible called for obedience, even to racist masters. The life and teachings of the man helped many young blacks especially, to feel they could express their anger without venting hatred:

> I think his example led me not to dwell on hatred. . . . And it was very easy for me to feel that way. Want to strike out. But I met his courage and his intellectual approach to the whole situation. It had a very profound effect on me, as it did a lot of people.

At the time the black church was a rallying ground for voter registrations and community organizing. It was then that Oscar's vision of the church as a socially active institution helping to bring about a better life for black people took shape. Involved in civil rights activities, he found inspiration, as did black people everywhere, in the Christian story of life as struggle and hope for better things to come. At eighteen he joined the military, then later went to college. Unlike many boomers who lost faith during college days, he graduated feeling stronger in his faith. He explored Islam and Roman Catholicism, but never seriously enough to consider switching. The church he had known in his boyhood years was far too powerful and real for him ever to truly abandon it.

In recent years Oscar has come to feel he should put more emphasis on his own personal fulfillment. Passion for social causes, important as they are, can be emotionally draining. Influenced by Dr. Howard Thurmond, a well-known and inspiring preacher, he recognizes that people need to balance their personal and social commitments. He also recognizes the need for a spiritual basis on which to have an identity as a whole person, some inner awareness of who you are and what you stand for; otherwise you are weak and cannot carry out your obligations to others. "It is very important to seek personal fulfillment and growth so that you have the strength to respond and give something to those folks who need your help."

Today, as a single father with three children, Oscar has grown cynical about his church. Aside from feeling burned out and needing his

20

own space, he feels somewhat unaccepted by the church and by his mother for, as he says, "living in a situation in which I am not married." He no longer attends services at the African Methodist Episcopal Church where he grew up; he visits around from church to church and considers himself an "itinerant churchgoer." Many of his friends have turned fundamentalist. He is disappointed that the churches are no longer as concerned with social justice and community problems as they once were. Priorities seem all mixed up:

> They seem to be more concerned now with self than with the betterment of the community. . . . To see who can build the biggest, best building . . . buy bigger and better pews or more fancy windows . . . raise tremendous sums of money to buy the minister a car, clothes, or just give him outright cash.

He would like to see the churches putting their energy into good causes like getting better housing for the elderly, building a community health clinic, and getting funding for programs for unemployed youth and for teenage girls who are pregnant.

Will Oscar return to more active involvement in the church? Quite likely, if he can find a congregation that blends social consciousness with a deep spirituality. But it will have to be a church with a vision. Says Oscar:

> I still find a lot of comfort in the Gospel. I've always looked upon Christianity sort of as a liberation theology. You find a lot of that theme throughout the Old and New Testaments. That is a thing that really turns me on about Christianity, and I guess at some point I will become involved with some other congregation. But right now I don't find any being about the sort of things that I would like to be involved in.

MOLLIE STONE

Life is a journey in which you learn from your experiences and grow as a person. Ever since her teen years, Mollie Stone has known that you have to "go after" life, you can't just sit around and wait for it to come to you. She grew up in a suburban, upper middle-class Jewish family in Westchester, New York, and was deeply exposed to the youth counterculture of the late 1960s. She has lived in many parts of the country, including Oregon, California, and Colorado. Now, at age thirty-eight, she is a school counselor and single mother with two children, living in Massachusetts.

When asked what her high school years were like, she takes pride in how she identifies herself: "[We were] the first generation of kids that became drug-involved and politically involved at the same time." A child of the 1960s, she beams with excitement as she describes her experiences. By age fifteen she was getting involved in "love-ins" and "be-ins" in New York's Central Park. "Marijuana, LSD, opium . . . whole days in Central Park getting stoned . . . sometimes with as many as a thousand people." It was lots of fun as well as a spiritual experience:

> You would lay in the sun and you would feel relaxed and you would talk with people and meet people . . . and there would be flowers and music . . . a very heavenly kind of feeling . . . that's when I started feeling some kind of my own connection with God . . . it definitely wasn't in a temple, because I only went like twice a year.

Mollie was more caught up in the trauma of the late 1960s than most others of her generation, and she was especially touched by the assassinations and deaths. Martin Luther King, Jr., died on her sixteenth birthday, and that hit close to home. "Something about King and his message," she said. "He spoke directly to me . . . about who I was and who I wanted to be." Some other people died too—Janis Joplin and Jimi Hendrix. Drugs were fun, but they could kill. Her parents wouldn't let her go to Woodstock, so she went "in spirit." A year later she could no longer stand living at home with her parents and took off on her own. She had to get away from the upper middle-class Jewish world she had grown up in. Inspired by the Montessori concept of education and its philosophy of bringing out the hidden potential of children, she took off to Boston to be with her sister and to become the person she wanted to be.

Mollie has been on a spiritual quest ever since. She has explored many of the spiritual and human potential alternatives of the post-sixties period: holistic health, macrobiotics, Zen Buddhism, Native American rituals, New Age in its many versions. She's read a lot about reincarnation and world religions. She once lived for a while in a commune. She became heavily involved in *est* in an attempt to "find herself." Wherever she is, she learns from the people around her. When she lived with her sister, she discovered organic foods. Her first husband was Protestant, so, as she says, "We did Christmas." She was heavily "into" Jesus for a while because she found "his teachings and writings very nondenominational, very spiritual." She's an explorer down many religious paths.

At present she is attracted to Native American religious traditions because of the themes of "connectedness" she finds there—to people, to the land, to the sky. "I just love the way they make that sacred," she says, "in a time like this when so much destruction has happened on the land, the pollution in the air and the mountains and strip-mining and all that, I feel like that energy is very healing." She goes to medicine wheel gatherings and has a sweat lodge in her back yard. She also occasionally goes to a Quaker service and likes what she finds in its quiet, unstructured moments of meditation. "I'm into Quakers a lot these days," she says, in her characteristic way of speaking. Keeping the "inner" and "outer" worlds fused together is important to her: The "inner peace" she finds in the Quaker service is intimately related to the "outer peace" that comes with the Native American stress on relations with people and the earth. She's also "turned on" to Alcoholics Anonymous. She attended AA with her first husband and came to appreciate its practical techniques. Such Twelve-Step programs are "not religious," she says, but are "really spiritual . . . with a lot about God and a lot about higher power, surrender, acceptance, and serenity."

Mollie is ambivalent about her Jewish religious heritage. She likes the mystical aspects of Judaism but finds what goes on in most synagogues boring and lifeless. Organized religion is too narrow and limiting. Creeds and doctrines divide people. She dislikes any kind of religion that gets in the way of her more expansive views—of unity with people and with nature and animals. Yet she admits there is a void. She would like a meaningful communal experience, a gathering where she can share her life experiences within the Jewish tradition. She is thinking of organizing a *seder* using new versions of the Haggadah that incorporate more global, feminist themes. Having attended an "alternative Jewish celebration" with a small group of friends and finding it very meaningful, she hopes to become involved in informal celebrations where she explores with others what the rituals and symbols mean and how they relate to life today.

Most important to her now are her children, relationships (she hopes to remarry soon), and her spiritual growth. She spends a lot of time in her spiritual quests. As Mollie says:

> It's very important to have some spiritual connection . . . whether it's meditation, walks in the woods, Alcoholics Anonymous, the Quaker meetings, the Native American sweats, something. . . . the one piece missing is Judaism, the alternative group of Judaism. But I think that's going to come. That's important to me and it's important to me to make this relationship work that I am in, and I think it is going to because of who I am now and because of who he is.

CAROL McLENNON

Mystery, the unexpected happening, death and resurrection—that's what life is all about, according to Carol McLennon. Carol, thirty-nine, grew up in a strict, don't-show-your-feelings Irish family in a Los Angeles suburb, but with all that was happening—next door in Watts and halfway around the world in Vietnam—her eyes were opened to struggle and conflict as part of life. Today Carol lives near San Diego, California, and works part-time in a business office to help out with the family finances; but work takes the back seat to what is really important to her—being a wife and the mother of four children.

Carol has been an active Roman Catholic throughout her adolescent and young adult years and has never dropped out of church; yet she carries on a love-hate relationship with her church. Love, because faith is as real to her as life, and intimately bound up together; and hate, because the church's hierarchy can be so shallow and so out of touch with the people. She never struggled with the church so much as she did about ten years ago. She already had three children and preferred not to have more, so she decided to have a tubal ligation. As a result:

> . . . people will still say to me, how can you do that? You're Catholic and that's against the church. . . . But it gave me on a whole different look on the church. I can't live by what the church says, y'know? I have to check my own self out with God. And yes, I listen and yes, I read. And you go through the Bible and you don't have Jesus saying to people, look what you did! That's wrong!

The denial of ordination for women in the church bothers her a lot today, "as if only men have a hold on spirituality." She attends spiritual seminars and workshops in many churches and believes that what people need today—no matter what their religious tradition—is to recognize their spiritual possibilities. "I think that's why we have so many drugs, alcohol, sex, y'know . . . I think a lot of it is an emptiness and looking for something to fill an empty spot that they haven't recognized as their own spirituality or relationship with God." Church as hierarchy, as rules and regulations, is not where it is; people caring and sharing, giving and receiving, that's religion in action. "That's the real church . . . when people are there for each other."

Carol is a free-thinking, post-Vatican II Catholic, deeply spiritual and deeply concerned about those in need. The two are closely connected: "You have to care about others, you can't keep it just within yourself."

She finds great meaning in the rich sacramental imageries of her Catholic heritage: in the Eucharist especially, with its death and resurrection mysteries that live over and over in everyday life. "We shed old beliefs and gain new insights, and it's usually through times of sorrow and struggle," she says of the ritual in all of its symbolism, "kind of like the ongoing mystery which is so meaningful." In Communion, "when they say it's the body of Christ which was broken and shed, and you say Amen, it means that's my ongoing commitment. . . . I'll be there for that person . . . they don't have to be Catholic, it can be my neighbor, the people I work with."

Carol finds abundant mystery, repeated cycles of death and resurrection, right in her own family. Becoming a mother was one such moment:

> I was just wiped out, floored, scared to death, overwhelmed. Because at that point in time, I knew there was no turning back. I mean, I'm pregnant, there is no way of turning back now. Y'know, you have to go through the delivery and I'd never been through a delivery before and I had to be a parent.

She has had even more wrenching moments. Recently, her son had attempted suicide. The teenage boy had been struggling with his sexual identity, and neither she nor her husband had realized he was homosexual. Once beyond the shock of the discovery, Carol was able to see within it positive opportunities. In fact, it opened up a whole new world of sensitivities and made her realize that she had never talked to any of her children about being anything but heterosexual. "Death and resurrection again," she says. Now she is present for others as never before. Both she and her husband belong to Parents and Friends of Lesbians and Gays, a group that offers support to teenagers whose real parents are not there for them.

Today Carol is looking forward to her forties. "I am becoming more secure with the person I am. . . . I like myself more, I stand and say what I believe." Of course, there will be more struggles, but as always, she'll learn and grow with them. She has confidence in her children and the generation growing up today. She thinks they just might become more sensitive to the nature and beauty of the world around us. She'll continue in her faith, and also in her struggle with the church: "Like I said, I believe and I'll speak out on what I believe, even though it goes against the grain . . . it's just who I am."

THE MANY RELIGIOUS STORIES

Barry, Linda, Sonny, Pam, Oscar, Mollie, and Carol all tell quite differing stories. Their religious biographies are rich and revealing, a microcosm of boomer religious culture. What comes through in all of them is how their experiences growing up in the 1960s and 1970s intersected with their religious and spiritual lives. Some embraced the cultural changes at the time; others did not, either because they were insulated or because they were repelled by the value changes. Enormous chasms separate their religious worlds, yet they also have common experiences and perceptions. We cannot say the seven are typical in any strict sense, because of how diverse boomers are, but they do embody recurring themes that we encountered in our research.

Naturally, their stories are colored by the influences of social class, ethnicity, region, race, and gender—social niches and categories that historically have shaped American religion. Sonny D'Antonio cannot really be understood apart from his working-class Italian Catholic tradition, or Oscar Gantt apart from his African-American heritage, or Linda Kramer apart from her rural background and lower middle-class status. Yet important as these social realities are, they are not the factors that give us the most insight into boomer religion and culture today.

Boomers share experiences that cut across their diverse backgrounds, such as great expectations and disappointments, the Vietnam War, the civil rights movement, the women's movement, and other shifts in cultural values. It is these more psychological and deeply experiential themes rooted in the life stories of boomers, and not just social roles and categories, that are crucially important. Boomers see religion in somewhat different ways than their parents did—with a greater concern for spiritual quest, for connectedness and unity, and for a vision that encompasses body and spirit, the material as well as the immaterial. To understand them, we have to pay attention not just to what they believe and practice, that is, religion in some narrow sense, but to how their lives as a whole take on meaning and direction.

In this book we explore in some depth the lives of these seven boomers. All of them will show up in later chapters because they give expression to themes that help in understanding the generation's religious and spiritual culture. Because life stories allow us to "get into" another person's life, they reveal dimensions of experience that are often overlooked, or which cannot be readily grasped by other research methods. Their stories portray religion in connection with events and experiences, helping us to understand how members of this generation "see," "feel," "believe," and "relate" to the world. If, as noted in the Introduction, religion is at the deepest level a "cultural system" that orders and gives meaning to life, then we would expect their experiences growing up to have directly influenced their search for a holistic view of reality and how they order the categories of experience—of self, of others, of nature, of the sacred. Stories also show religious life to be something far more open and fluid than stable or fixed. Dropping out of church or synagogue, switching faiths, spiritual journeys and quests, deciding to join a Twelve-Step group, returning to a congregation with small children—all point to dynamic religious and spiritual patterns.

INNER LIVES AND OUTER COMMITMENTS

Many of these men and women are undergoing major changes in their lives at this time. How they see themselves in relation to others is undergoing revision, new vistas of self-understanding and of commitment are opening up—in short, it is a time of soul stirrings. Soul refers to the animating essence, or force, of life; and for boomers it is a time of growing and maturing, of refocusing life. The trajectories on which their lives are unfolding sometimes move in opposite directions: Some, who for years were turned inward on themselves, are now reaching out to others for deeper commitments; others, who have long been rooted in webs of relationships and communities, are reaching out to find more fulfilling selves. In either direction there are shifts in what pollster Daniel Yankelovich describes as the "giving/getting compact"—the set of rules defining what people give to others in all their commitments, and what they expect in return for themselves.[1]

These stories all bear on the current debate about how American culture may be changing. A great deal of discussion of late has centered around America's highly individualistic values, and much of it focuses on this generation. Recent terms and phrases to enter into our national discourse place the debate largely in a generational context—the "Me Generation," turning inward, yuppies, narcissism, the "big chill," a "decade of greed." These are more than just catchy words; they express the concern that American individualism may have grown to excessive proportions. With so much stress on such values as freedom, success, and self-fulfillment, critics argue that our capacity for commitment to others suffers.[2] Traditional social institutions and practices are eroded in a culture where individuals are much freer to make choices about how they live and to pursue their own interests. Many fear that belonging and loyalty to religious institutions are undermined, and that a more private and self-absorbed culture is emerging, one that is based on consumer choice.

Much insight has come out of this discussion on what is happening in contemporary culture, yet people's stories reveal much richer nuances in real life than the debate would suggest. Our stories here suggest there is no simple one-to-one relationship between individualism and religious involvement: Many highly individualistic Americans choose to belong to a religious community; others, equally individualistic, opt out of religion altogether. Barry Johnson, the North Carolinian who recently returned to active involvement in a church, is no less individualistic than is Pam Fletcher, the Massachusetts housewife who has nothing to do with organized religion. Individualism is not the antithesis of religion. And spirituality, the world of the interior life and its deepest meanings, is much too difficult to chart or reduce to simple one-to-one relationships. In either instance we have to examine how a person *defines* his or her action as a behavior of choice in order to understand how the inner selves of individuality mesh with religious and spiritual responses. A person's own account of experiences and motivations provides a basis upon which to explore the linkages. Hence people's own stories are the means of exploring these complex, and often subtle worlds of meaning.

Our concern, then, is to listen to the stories of the people we have interviewed, and to try to discern the intricacies of religion and culture. A highly subjective, self-oriented culture encourages people to be different, to rely on themselves, to dream of new ways to make their lives meaningful. We assume that boomer culture is highly individualistic, that levels of personal freedom and autonomy run high; but given all of this, we want to know: How do boomers themselves talk about religion—about meaning, value, their place in the scheme of things, their destiny? How do they view the place of spirituality in life? And if organized religion is important to them, how is it the nexus between their individualism and their broader quests for meaning and belonging?

THE LARGER CULTURAL NARRATIVES

People's life stories are never just *their* stories, or even those of their generation; they are also the stories as told by the larger culture. Our shared stories connect our sense of self with the larger social order and anchor us in a meaningful context, in time and space. A cultural narrative, to quote Clifford Geertz, is a "historically created system of meaning in terms of which we give form, order, point, and direction to our lives."[3] Put differently, a cultural narrative establishes the broad frame of reference in which a person's ordinary story makes sense. Such narratives provide the symbols and themes we draw on in apprehending the world and ordering our own personal experience. Even in a very subjective culture, there are broader, more encompassing stories that locate and give meaning to people's lives.

One such narrative is the biblical story of the covenant. In one sense this is the most fundamental religious story that Americans historically have told. Americans have understood themselves using biblical archetypes, as a chosen people and in accord with the will of God, and have fashioned a civil religion with its own national beliefs, rituals, and symbols. Linda Kramer is the only one of our representative boomers who explicitly connects her story with the covenant interpretation, although some of the others describe themselves and the country in ways that are informed by it. Whatever may have been the significance of a covenant tradition in the past, most boomers seem not to talk in this way, or are unable to articulate it. Oscar Gantt draws from a religious narrative as well: an Exodus story of a people's suffering and bondage, of protest and liberation. African-Americans have not shared in the dominant covenant tradition in the same way as white Americans and have fashioned instead a story of their own struggle for freedom, also closely linked to biblical archetypes and born out of the black experience in America.

Other narratives, although less explicitly religious, have important consequences for the way Americans live and think and believe. When Barry Johnson speaks of becoming disillusioned with his country during the Vietnam years, and says that he is still antiwar, he is saying something about the loss of credibility of the narrative about America's mission to the world; and when he talks about some good things happening in the 1960s, he is saying something about how he welcomed the new values of global consciousness and personal well-being, and of the emptiness of the success ethic and yuppie-style materialistic values. His life is meaningful when patterned after these larger narratives.

Mollie Stone's sense of self is shaped by the story of psychological well-being. In seeking self-fulfillment, she has used the therapeutic language that has as its primary concerns personality, self-worth, and self-esteem. This frame of reference is deeply personal and oriented to feelings. On the surface the language may appear to have little to do with religion, except perhaps to contribute to her disillusionment with

Judaism; but in a more important way, it has helped her to re-vision her life as deeply spiritual and is the basis on which we can begin to understand the inner logic of her quests. We cannot really understand Mollie or appreciate her spiritual journeys without recognizing how this language has opened up new vistas for her.

In all the stories, the personal accounts mesh with the larger narratives. This is important not just in the sense that people's lives reflect these larger narratives, and often a mix of themes from them, but also because it moves us from the level of the individual to the level of society. The language they use is not just their language, but the vehicle through which they more broadly understand themselves and their place in the world. Language is the cultural framework through which they reflect about what it means to be religious and spiritual, and about who they are as Americans.

SPIRIT AND INSTITUTION

The distinction between "spirit" and "institution" is of major importance. *Spirit* is the inner, experiential aspect of religion; *institution* is the outer, established form of religion. This distinction is increasingly pertinent because of the strong emphasis on self in contemporary culture and the related shift from objective to subjective ways of ordering experience. Boomers have grown up in a post-sixties culture that emphasizes choice, knowing and understanding one's self, the importance of personal autonomy, and fulfilling one's potential—all contributing to a highly subjective approach to religion.

A subjective, deeply personal approach to religion permeates the stories: Mollie Stone is "into" Quakers these days; Oscar Gantt is exploring his own inner life; Linda Kramer listens to Dr. James Dobson's radio messages on faith and psychology; Barry Johnson reads popular spirituality books; Carol McLennon occasionally attends spiritual seminars. A psychological language cuts across traditions and socioeconomic strata with its appeal to the common concerns of spiritual growth and experiential faith. For some, spirituality is a personal quest, largely independent of any religious community; for others, spirituality is cultivated and expressed within a faith community. For many, maybe even the majority of boomers today, personal faith and spirituality seem somehow disconnected from many of the older institutional religious forms.

For many, having any kind of relationship with a religious institution is problematic. In the 1960s large numbers of youth dropped out from the churches and synagogues. Some, like Barry Johnson, are now returning to active participation in a congregation; but many others, like Sonny D'Antonio, show little sign of returning. Pam Fletcher never had any meaningful relationship with organized religion and is unlikely to have any in the future. In a deeper sense, there is a question of authority over which boomers are deeply divided. To whom or to what can you turn for reliable answers to religious questions? On what basis are religious beliefs and moral values to be organized? Whose truths are to be accepted? Such questions are vexing in a culture as pluralistic and relativistic as ours, and in an age when traditional authorities have lost influence. The answers to such questions are often divisive and emotion-ridden, and especially so if people try to "impose" their beliefs and moral values on others. Americans hold strongly to the rights of individuals to make their own decisions in moral and religious matters and resist such intrusion in the public arena.

Spiritual styles vary greatly. Some people are self-consciously anchored in a single tradition, and their faiths reflect essentially the teachings of that tradition; others seek to combine religious beliefs and practices drawing from many traditions. Styles vary in both form and content. As has always been the case, the normative faiths of Americans are amazingly fluid and flexible.[4] But especially today a dynamic, democratic religious culture is evolving, its many elements ever recombining, mixing and matching with one another to create new syncretisms. Probably no quality of the contemporary religious and spiritual ferment is of more interest, or of greater significance in the long run for American religion.

Throughout all of this discussion is the central theme of growing up in the sixties, and how the events and experiences of that era influenced the lives of this generation. Even the deeply ingrained cultural narratives on which Americans had for so long relied to make sense of their lives were deeply jarred by the events of those years. As we have seen, the jolts reached to the very foundations of their religious and spiritual understanding. Thus if we are to grasp their stories, and fully appreciate how their lives took on meaning during those years, we must look more closely at that tumultuous time that has come to be called simply "the sixties."

CHAPTER 2

A Time When Mountains Were Moving

During the late 1980s, the popular television program "thirtysomething" featured a generation of upscale young Americans struggling with careers, marriages, children, and incipient middle age. The struggles were hardly peculiar to this generation, yet the characters seemed to face them in their own way. "There's something nostalgic about the attitudes of 'thirtysomething' people," writes one commentator, "they're like World War I veterans, like they've been through a war together." Television programs depict the lives of boomers, the commentator goes on to say, by "refract[ing] elements of optimism and world-weariness through plots that aren't always neatly tied up at the end of each episode and through realistic, complex characters who don't always behave well."[1]

Nostalgia, optimism, world-weariness, complexity—all are elements bound up in the lives of the people we interviewed. The stories they tell of growing up all reveal these nuanced and refracted interpretations of American life. But what was it about those years that produced such experiences and interpretations? What were the shaping influences of the period that so jolted their religious and spiritual lives? The answers lie in the sweeping social and cultural changes that engulfed the boomers and jarred the cultural narratives that had been passed down to them from their parents. History and demography came together at a crucial moment, at just the time when so many were moving out of childhood into adolescence and adulthood. Other generations were affected, too, but none with the lasting impact and shared *zeitgeist* of the boomers. For them, the sixties was more than simply a decade: It had something of a mythic reality with a power and momentum all its own.

THE SIXTIES

As with all myth, "the sixties" has many possible meanings and interpretations. Often the people we talked to described their years growing up and its impact on their lives in metaphorical and semimythical language. Carol McLennon, for example, speaks of her adolescent years as a "really rich era," and Barry Johnson talks about growing up when "things were happening." Perhaps Mollie Stone captured the era best when she spoke of "a time when mountains were moving." Those less articulate stumbled for words to express themselves, but were no less caught up in its mythical realities. Most of our informants looked back on the era as a special time of hope and anticipation, of new horizons. Even those who frowned on some of what happened during those years spoke fondly about many of their memories.

It was a time when many things did change—social and sexual mores especially. Some of the most visible things associated with the sixties' counterculture—drugs, rock-and-roll, casual sex—have taken on legendary character. The 1986 *Rolling Stone* survey reported that 65% of those growing up during the 1960s had engaged in premarital sex; 30% had lived with someone of the opposite sex before marriage; 5% of the females acknowledged having had an abortion. More than one in ten had tried psychedelic drugs like LSD. Fifty-four percent felt that rock-and-roll music was a positive influence on young people in the 1960s. Commenting on these statistics, the magazine's David Sheff says:

> This generation endorsed sexual freedom and altered consciousness. And rock & roll was the pulse, the heartbeat of a new age. Elvis Presley's music said, "Free your body." The Beatles said, "Free your mind." Their lyric "I'd love to turn you on" had a symbolic as well as a literal meaning. Turning on was a metaphor for becoming enlightened, but it also had a straightforward meaning: having sex and taking drugs.[2]

Yet it is easy to exaggerate. Our survey shows a generation more divided by the social mores than does the *Rolling Stone* survey. One-half of our respondents had smoked marijuana in their earlier years; almost two-thirds said they had attended a rock concert; 20% had taken part in a demonstration, march, or rally. We did not ask about sexual practices. Certainly, the involvement in drugs, rock-and-roll music, and political activism point to major changes in keeping with the reputation of the sixties as a period of profound cultural changes. But we should not overlook the one-half of our population who did not try drugs, the one-third who never attended a rock concert, and the overwhelming 80% who were not politically active. Many were far less caught up in the counterculture, its controversies and protests, than we tend to think. Once we get beyond the stereotypes that still linger on from that era, we discover a generation growing up in the 1960s and 1970s that was incredibly diverse.

This is better shown in Figure 2.1, which combines the several items above into an index showing the extent of exposure to the sixties' counterculture.[3] Statistics here are telling: 13% scored "high," indicating a positive response to all three items; but 26% scored "low," with negative responses to all three items. The majority—as we would expect in a normal distribution of responses—scored in the middle two categories. Comparing the upper two categories with the lower two categories, we find a generation deeply divided between traditionalists and counterculturalists, the former outnumbering the latter 54% to 46%.

Age-cohort differences in countercultural experience are important: The first wave of boomers, born between the years 1946 and 1954, experienced more directly the upheavals of the decade than did those of the second wave, born between 1955 and 1962. Caught up in a climate of social and political protest, the former were more involved in demonstrations, marches, and rallies. But more of the younger ones report having smoked marijuana and having attended rock concerts. Militant political activism declined during the 1970s, but the drugs, music, and "new morality" lived on. No longer were drugs and unmarried sex all that surprising for younger boomers growing up in a counterculture that had by then become structured by its traditions and rituals. "The sixties" as a mythic reality lived on even for those who grew up in the 1970s.

The two age groups experienced a different social and political history and so have differing collective memories. Older boomers remember elementary school bomb drills in the 1950s; and later, in the 1960s, John F. Kennedy, freedom-rides, city riots, and Vietnam. They confronted the upheavals of the decade head-on in their late teens and early twenties. Caught at the epicenter of a cultural earthquake, many were traumatized

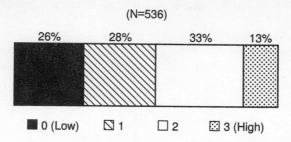

(N=536)

26%   28%   33%   13%

■ 0 (Low)   ◪ 1   ☐ 2   ▨ 3 (High)

Figure 2.1 Exposure to the Sixties

and transformed by what was happening around them. A great many of them became passionate visionaries and dreamed of "building the New Jerusalem." In contrast, younger boomers remember at an early age the deaths of Martin Luther King, Jr., and Bobby Kennedy; and later, in the 1970s, long gas lines, Three Mile Island, and Watergate. They came of age in a quieter time marked less by protest than by scarcity and environmental scares. Economic recession was a reality of the 1970s, setting limits and constraints on life possibilities. If the older boomers were "challengers," ready to take on "the establishment," the younger ones were "calculators," intent upon setting priorities for what to go after in a world where you cannot have it all.[4] Unlike their older siblings, who saw chaotic change as revolution or as revelation, the younger ones saw it more as the world in which they had been born into, and to which they must adapt.

What they all share is "the sixties," even if they didn't live it the same way. The two waves are much more alike than they are different, more unified than separated. They are bound by a shared sense of time, and an optimism tempered by the disillusionment that came with assassinations, Vietnam, and Watergate. What unites the two waves more than anything else was the changing climate of moral values and sensitivities, a shift in cultural values that would have a lasting impact on them. Especially in the realms of sexuality and family life, of personal lifestyles and preferences, the "New Morality" would distinguish the young from their parents and would become a source of division among themselves of lasting consequence. Those most influenced by the counterculture adopted new outlooks that have, by and large, remained with them and that continue to distinguish them from those who were less involved. Figure 2.2 shows, for example, that those who were highly involved in countercultural activities back when they were growing up— for some, as many as twenty-five years ago—are *still* far more liberal in

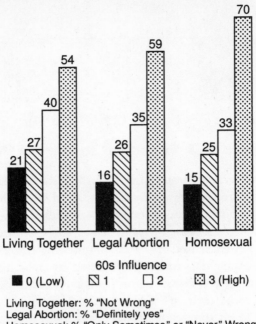

Living Together: % "Not Wrong"
Legal Abortion: % "Definitely yes"
Homosexual: % "Only Sometimes," or "Never" Wrong

Figure 2.2 Moral Values

their views on unmarried couples living together, on whether or not a married woman should be able to obtain a legal abortion, and on homosexual relations. Patterns for the three moral attitude items are remarkably consistent when tabulated with our index of countercultural exposure, suggesting that the sixties had an enormous and apparently lasting impact on members of this generation.

As a cultural or mythic entity, more so than a chronological one, the period had its own *zeitgeist,* or spirit of the times, demarcating it from other times. Annie Gottlieb says the sixties began in 1963 with the death of President Kennedy, and ended in 1973 with the energy crisis and economic recession. That would define the sixties, as she says, "as a decade of *upheaval plus affluence*—the two ingredients that together account for the special character of the time."[5] We would add two other features as well, the *gender revolution* and role of *higher education and television,* that helped define the period and shape the lives of those growing up at the time.

UPHEAVAL

"I can still remember," says Barry Johnson. "I remember sitting in chemistry class in the tenth grade when it came over the loudspeaker. I'll never forget that as long as I live."

November 22, 1963, lives on in the memories of millions of schoolchildren who heard the announcement over the school public address system, went home stunned, and for three long days watched events unfold on television as a nation grieved its loss. President John F. Kennedy's death was a gripping experience, especially for young children, many of whom deeply admired the young president and his family. Schoolchildren at the time knew Kennedy not only as a political leader, but as a father who had young children of his own, and in death he loomed larger than life. Television's role in galvanizing an emotional experience was incalculable: the countless replays of the assassination, Jackie Kennedy's bloodstained suit, the flag-draped coffin, little John, Jr.'s, salute, the murder of Lee Harvey Oswald, the long weekend culminating in a state funeral.

For schoolchildren across the country, the event provoked intense reactions and led to serious questions. As a young boy, Barry wondered: "If there's an active God in this world, what is he doing? . . . The world is out of control. It's just exploding." Many children wondered how the nation would get along without its leader. The feeling of loss seemed to persist longer for children than it did for adults, far longer than in a normal process of grieving. Kennedy had been a symbol of youthful leadership, someone who had a vision of an American future, and who had a caring and personal touch. His death wiped away all of that for children and teenagers who had been hopeful and optimistic about their country. His assassination left a deep emotional scar: Three-quarters of the schoolchildren in a Detroit study at the time said they felt the loss of someone very close and dear, eight in ten felt ashamed that such a tragedy could happen in America.[6] Among our respondents it was the event most frequently cited in shaping their childhood and adolescent years. According to many of them, it marked the time when the mood of the country began to change.

Youth growing up during the 1960s had been born into a world shaped largely by the politics of the cold war and the postwar family life that fit so comfortably with it. The late 1940s and 1950s had a quality all their own: a time of almost uncontested conservatism, as reflected in the emphasis put on family "togetherness" rather than individual needs, conventional gender roles, churchgoing, anticommunism, and free-enterprise capitalism. An expanding economy combined with the GI Bill and VHA loans gave unprecedented numbers of Americans the opportunity to obtain an education, to get a better job, and to buy a home in the newly emerging suburbs. Working-class men and women enjoyed as never before hopes for sharing in the American Dream. With security as the common thread, cold war ideology and domesticity reinforced each other. Young people were expected to follow in their parent's footsteps, embracing the containment ethos that undergirded both foreign policy and family life in the 1950s. Except for a handful of beatniks, youth at the beginning of the decade of the 1960s showed every sign of growing up pretty much as they had the decade before. They reflected their parents' optimism and satisfaction with their lives. In a salute to the new decade, *Look* magazine in January 1960 published a poll saying that all was right with the world: Americans "naturally expect to go on enjoying their peaceable, plentiful existence—right through the 1960s and maybe forever."[7]

But the dream of a peaceable, plentiful existence was short-lived. After Kennedy's death optimism faded, as more and more people became disillusioned with the prospects for both peace and a plentiful life for all Americans. The middle years of the decade were unsettling enough, with civil rights demonstrations, urban riots, and the Vietnam War, but 1968 was staggering. For the first time, a majority of Americans actively turned against a war in progress. Sentiment was slow to crystallize, but once it did it was firm. In that unforgettable year, Americans witnessed the Tet offensive, President Lyndon Johnson decided against a bid for reelection, Martin Luther King, Jr., and Robert Kennedy were murdered, and the Democratic Convention in Chicago was the scene of violent confrontations. These events are all seared in the memories of boomers except for the very youngest—the first generation ever to witness history through the unifying image of television.

By 1968 radical students had galvanized into "the Movement" spearheading cultural and political change. A generation that was to be cool turned out to be explosive: They broke out of old social mores and explored sexual freedom, drug use, and the so-called "new morality"; they expressed their frustration over a stalled civil rights movement; they opposed an escalating war in Vietnam. The rebellion amounted to a repudiation of conventional middle-class life—"Culture War," in Loren Baritz's words[8]—aimed at a reordering of human relations and of the values by which people live. The world had to be remade, for that which their parents had created was no longer viable. Containment at home and abroad no longer made sense. Conditions had changed radically in a generation's time. Rather than a continuation of the easy-going, comfortable times of their childhood, the late 1960s emerged as a reversed mirror image of the late 1940s: The fathers of the baby boomers had come home from a glorious war; their sons refused to go to a not-so-glorious war. The mothers had poured into the homes, proud to be wives and mothers; their daughters poured out of them.

The "war of values" was often fought at home—against parents, against brothers and sisters. Debate centered on America itself, what it stood for. The civil rights movement sharpened for many what Gunnar Myrdal had called the "American Dilemma"—the discrepancy between the egalitarian values as professed and racially discriminatory practices. Militant students sought resolution in protests and demonstrations aimed at exposing these ethical inconsistencies. Less politically active young Americans felt their consciences pricked, especially by the violence, intense expressions of racial hatred, and tragic deaths. For many whites the death of Dr. Martin Luther King, Jr., was the event that shocked them into seeing the severity of this discrepancy. Equality, not just as principle but as practice, would thus emerge as a strong commitment on the part of white boomers. Out of the struggle came greater racial justice, and also greater awareness and appreciation of cultural diversity and a concern for people as people, and not because of their social appearances.

The antiwar protests further exposed discrepancies in American-style democracy: If Americans truly believed in the principle of self-determination, why were we in Southeast Asia trying to shape a people's destiny? Nothing divided the nation more during these years than the Vietnam issue. Time has brought about considerable healing, but if you scratch the surface of a boomer, deep emotions still pour out. All seven of our boomers spoke of the impact of the war on their lives. All of them found themselves, as did the great majority of Americans, pulled into support of the war or its opposition; even Pam Fletcher, probably the most apolitical among them, discovered that as much as she wanted to get away from the news on television night after night, she couldn't shut the war out of her life.

Vietnam split the older boomers right down the middle. They are still split: 51% of this age group now say they opposed the war; 43% supported it; and the remaining 6% are still unsure. Women often experienced it as "struggle" and "heartache," both personally and in their relationships with men. It was all these things and more for men, for those who went to Vietnam and for those who didn't. Of the three men—Sonny D'Antonio, Oscar Gantt, and Barry Johnson—one enlisted in the military rather than wait to be drafted and got as close as the Philippines; the other two escaped the draft through the lottery. Neither of the men who owed his life to the luck of the draw (one spoke of being "saved" by it) felt he could discuss the war with his father. All seemed to have learned something about fragile and wounded relationships, and also, perhaps, that in a highly rational, technological world, there is still an element of chance and maybe even a little of the miraculous.

The country was torn between hawks who wanted to win, and win decisively, and doves who wanted simply to get out, the sooner the better. Levels of frustration and alienation ran high. "The country just sort of got involved," as Barry Johnson put it, "with something that totally polarized it." The division ran deep, forcing strains at the most profound levels of national life. Religious talk undergirding national goals and purposes became deeply polarized: Religious conservatives spoke of God as favoring freedom and competition, of America as having a unique, divine role in world affairs, and above all, the importance of personal moral values and salvation; religious liberals spoke in a different voice, emphasizing the common concerns of humanity for peace, justice, and human rights, and of the responsibility of America to take action to help bring about a better world. The two types of discourse are themselves differing versions of America's "civil religion"—that amorphous set of Judeo-Christian beliefs and symbols by which the nation's traditional principles and goals are given sanction. While never a fully coherent set of beliefs and symbols in its functioning in American life, the languages of civil religion became more pulled apart, and themselves a source of tension and discord during these years. For boomers, talk about God, country, and patriotism could never be quite the same as it had been for their parents' generation.

Whether religious or not, many in the boomer generation grew weary of the war. Over time, growing numbers came, as did Barry, to a "fundamental feeling that it was wrong." Having grown up in the South in a politically conservative home, he did not easily find fault with his country; only gradually did he come to the awareness that the war was symbolic of the country's misdirected goals and values. The war taught him two immensely powerful lessons: that America was not always right, and that political leaders weren't always to be trusted. Many young

Americans lost faith in their country's moral superiority and in a technology that tried to make the nation's military might increasingly invisible and remote. Seeing the napalm-scarred faces of children on television
and hearing day after day about "body counts" and "loss-ratios" eroded
what confidence was left in the nation's war machine. Older boomers
were the most affected: They had grown up with more confidence in
the country than had the younger boomers. They had farther to fall in
their disillusionment. Many have yet to regain confidence in the country and its leadership. Twenty-nine percent of the older boomers said
they had little or no confidence in the country today, compared with
24% of younger boomers. Among the half within the older cohort op-
posing the country's involvement in the war, the lack of confidence in the
country runs considerably higher today—upwards of 40%.

The impact was even more subtle: Boomers still feel some "distance"
from almost every institution, whether the military, banks, public schools,
Congress, or organized religion. A 1985 Gallup Poll found that boomers
were the least trusting of all age groups toward social and political institutions, even less so than for those younger than themselves.[9] Alienation
and estrangement born out of the period continue to express themselves
as generalized distrust of government, of major institutions, and of leaders. As Seymour Martin Lipset and William Schneider point out, baby
boomers are less polarized in their distrust of both big labor and big
business than older generations.[10] Whereas older Americans have tended
to distrust one or the other, boomers generally distrust both. Compared
with other generations, their distrust of institutions simply runs deeper.

Boomers continue in their separation from traditional social and political roles. The separation is expressed is many ways: in lower levels of
political party loyalty, in preferences for talking about who they *are*
rather than what they *do,* in an even greater reluctance to use titles like
"Mr." or "Mrs." Less inclined to be conformists, they favor instead their
own deeply personal and individualistic preferences, which shows up in
consumer choices: less loyal to particular brands, more suspicious of
advertising, more likely than older consumers to prefer a product made
by a new company than by a well-established business, more likely to
vote out political incumbents and take chances on new political faces and
ideas. Thus they tend to reject social labels that lack individual meaning, labels that remain, as social psychologists Joseph Veroff, Elizabeth
Douvan, and Richard Kulka say, "objects of suspicion, as though they
were different from—even contradictory to—the core self, the essential
person."[11]

Boomers today often lack connections in their local communities. They are less likely than their parents to belong to social organizations concerned with community welfare. They tend to be less locally involved in social activities—except in family and neighborhood affairs. According to the *Rolling Stone* survey, members of this generation are less active in their communities now than they expected to be. Asked whether the phrase "being a concerned citizen, involved in helping others in the community" better describes their generation or their parents,' 21% chose their generation, while more than twice that number chose their parents'.[12] The boomers themselves readily admit a difference in generational styles. This appears to be something of a sore spot: Most of the respondents in the survey were not pleased with their record of community participation, and three-quarters of them felt that their reduced involvement was a change for the worse.

AFFLUENCE

Boomers were born in a time of considerable affluence and almost limitless expectations. The 1950s and much of the 1960s were times of economic growth and widespread optimism: The Gross National Product was up, unemployment was down, inflation was low; people were moving out of the cities into the suburbs; more Americans owned their homes than ever before; the country would put a man on the moon within a decade. The American Dream was alive and doing well—at least in the beginning of their lives. Their future was unmatched by that of either their parents' or grandparents' generation. Landon Y. Jones, writing in 1980, summed it all up with the title of his landmark book on the boomers: *Great Expectations*.[13]

Advertising played a big part in shaping their expectations from an early age. Good economic times, a more consumption-oriented society, and the use of television for mass marketing all came together at just the time when the largest cohort of children ever in America was being born. Not surprisingly, the children grew up acutely aware of themselves as consumers. Advertising serves not only to sell products, but to promote consumption as a way of life, and boomers were catered to like no generation before them. Jones writes: "They were the first generation of children to be isolated by Madison Avenue as an identifiable market. That is the appropriate word: isolated. Marketing, and especially television, isolated their needs and wants from those of their parents. From the cradle, the baby boomers had been surrounded by products created especially for them, from Silly Putty to Slinkys to skateboards. New products, new toys, new commercials, new fads—the dictatorship of the new—was integral to the baby boom experience."[14]

Surrounded by so much that was new, middle-class boomers had more than just expectations. They had a sense of entitlement: a right to interesting jobs, livable incomes, good times, rewarding lives. Children were raised to express themselves and to feel good about themselves, believing that somehow sheer abundance would nurture them. In the early years of school, children were taught to enjoy the process of creative learning and not worry so much about the goal: paint and draw what you feel. Liberal child-rearing philosophies on the part of educated, upper middle-class parents encouraged freedom and personal development, the fulfillment of wants and needs. Not all boomers were brought up on the permissive teachings of Dr. Benjamin Spock, however. Many lower middle-class and working-class children, indeed probably a majority of school-age children in the 1960s and 1970s, were brought up in more traditional ways. Thirty percent of our respondents, mostly from upper middle-class backgrounds, described their upbringing as "permissive" or "very permissive," as compared to 52% who described theirs as "somewhat rigid" and 17% as "very rigid."

But the cultural winds were definitely blowing in the direction of heightened expectations. The upheavals of the period had so profound an impact on their lives growing up, in great part because of these hopes and dreams. Rising expectations widened the gap between aspirations and realities, but also, as political scientist Ronald Inglehart argues, contributed to a "silent revolution" in values.[15] Unlike the revolution that took place in the streets, with civil rights marches and antiwar protests, this one was quieter and more subtle, but no less important. Inglehart argues that in times of prosperity—as opposed to economic insecurity—values tend to shift in the direction of greater concern for individual well-being, interesting experiences, quality of life, tolerance of diversity, intellectual and spiritual development. Whereas economic insecurity encourages acquisitive values, economic security fosters greater inwardness and quest for meaning. Building on Abraham Maslow's notion of a "hierarchy of needs," he emphasizes that once economic survival needs are met, then higher-order needs of the self come into play to shape people's values. This latter he describes as "post-materialist," emphasizing the break with more bourgeois, material-oriented values.

These sweeping value changes touched Americans in their inner lives. According to a major study on American culture, a new sense of self was in the making—away from social roles toward a more inner-developed, more psychological view of self. In *The Inner American,* Veroff, Douvan, and Kulka found young Americans more willing in 1976 than in 1957 to mention personality factors in describing how they differed from others. When asked to describe themselves, Americans increasingly focused less on their ascribed characteristics, and more on personal qualities. They observed a sharp decline in social connections and a shift in the "locus of control"—that is, a sense of self more of their own making than created by a conformist culture.[16] An older culture of self-denial that had long guided Americans was giving way to a psychological culture concerned with feelings, with self-expressiveness, with personal adaptation, and therapeutic solutions.

Pollster Daniel Yankelovich saw the changes as a major shift, replacing the old ethic of self-denial with a new ethic of self-fulfillment. He spoke of the "giant plates" of culture moving, of abrupt transformations in orientations to self and to society. Those living closest to society's fault lines—the young—were the first to feel the shifts and the resulting dislocations. He looked to the college educated as the cutting edge, and how the fundamental questions these young Americans were asking had changed:

> Instead of asking, "Will I be able to make a good living?" "Will I be successful?," "Will I raise happy, healthy, successful children?"— the typical questions asked by average Americans in the 1950s and 1960s—Americans in the 1970s came to ponder more introspective matters. We asked "How can I find self-fulfillment?" "What does personal success really mean?" "What kinds of commitments should I be making?" "What is worth sacrificing for?" "How can I grow?"[17]

Others felt the tremors as well. The new values spread into much of middle-class America, and gradually into those sectors of the population ready to express their discontent—housewives, blue-collar workers, high school students. By the mid-1970s, Yankelovich continues:

> Americans from every walk of life were suddenly eager to give more meaning to their lives, to find fuller self-expression and to add a touch of adventure and grace to their lives and those of others. Where strict norms had prevailed in the fifties and sixties, now all was pluralism and freedom of choice: to marry or live together; to have children early or postpone them, perhaps forever; to come out of the closet or stay in; to keep the old job or return to school; to make commitments or hang loose; to change careers, spouses, houses, states of residence, states of mind.[18]

By the early 1980s, the pendulum appeared to be swinging back. Yankelovich observed an easing away from a more radical quest for self, and an emerging "ethic of commitment" with a growing emphasis on concerns for others and relations with the world. Disillusioned with the excesses of personal freedom and self-fulfillment, the winds of change were blowing in the direction of a better balance between obligations to self and to others. He envisioned a new ethic that would shift the axis away from preoccupation with self (either self-denial or self-fulfillment) toward connectedness with the world—to people, institutions, places, nature. Boomers were still skeptical about institutions, political leaders, and social labels, but they were turning toward some types of commitments. The new ethic was gathering force, as Yankelovich saw it, around two kinds of commitments: closer and deeper personal relationships, and the switch from instrumental values to sacred/expressive ones.

This trend toward commitment is apparent in the boomers we interviewed. Mollie Stone, the single mother in Massachusetts who told us about her days as a "flower child" in Central Park, is the most obvious case of someone deeply immersed in her own self, but who is now trying to revise the giving-receiving compact. Today she would like to be married and to have a more stable family life. Partly a reflection of demographics, many boomers—like Mollie—are now in their mid- to late thirties and early forties and are concerned with marriages, families, and parenting. But there appears to be something more—a profound search for ways to reach out and connect with others, and to find a more satisfying balance of concerns for self and for others. Commitment amounts to what Yankelovich describes as a "giving/receiving social compact," and many today are recognizing that such a compact is open to revision as people's lives and circumstances change.

Though much energy is now directed at working out a meaningful and balanced sense of commitment, this does not mean that boomers, by and large, have abandoned their expectations for fulfilling lives. To the contrary, whatever revisions of the giving/receiving compact are occurring, it is in the context of some deeply held values that crystallized during their years growing up and continue to be of great importance to them. One is tolerance. Eighty-seven percent in our survey said there should be more acceptance of different lifestyles. Social background, level of education, and region of country do not matter: Boomers generally hold to the view that lifestyles should be a matter of personal choice. Tolerance was extended in their generation to those not just different racially or socioeconomically, but with differing sexual orientations and lifestyles. Options in virtually all realms of life are taken for granted.

Another value they hold dear is belief in themselves. Eighty-six percent of our respondents say that if you believe in yourself, there is almost no limit to what you can do. Seventy-one percent say a person who is strong and determined can pretty much control what happens in life. Even failure is seen as something to be blamed on the individual, not society. Sixty-six percent agree that if someone does not succeed in life, usually it's his or her own fault. The better educated and those most deeply influenced by the counterculture are somewhat less inclined to agree, and more likely to see society as playing a part affecting people's life chances, but self-reliance is a tenet of faith among boomers. "Brought up in an environment of change," writes Michael Maccoby, "they have learned to adapt to new people and situations, and to trust their own abilities rather than parents or institutions. They value independence, and they accept responsibility for themselves."[19]

Victims of their own great expectations, many in this generation have experienced a disheartening gap between their perceived potential and realized achievements. Economic opportunities failed to keep pace with their aspirations. Many with college degrees were forced to settle for jobs and incomes lower than what they had assumed was befitting of college status. The optimism of the 1960s faded in the 1970s—a decade remembered for gas lines, inflation, and a rising cost of living. The tightening of the economy came at just the time when many of the older boomers were forming families, trying to buy their first homes, and discovering the difficulties of maintaining marriages, raising children, and having satisfying careers, and optimism gave way to the "big chill." One-third of our respondents report having to "scale down their expectations"—true for both the older and younger waves. Expecting so much in life, they have discovered that nothing—homes, family, love, friendship, wealth—comes easily.

A third value is the belief that strength comes from within. When boomers are asked to describe themselves, they focus on personal, individual qualities. Both their successes and failures may contribute to a greater introspectiveness. A focus on self helps to explain, for example, the high priority given to family, friends, and interpersonal relationships. Having been estranged from more organized formal institutions, many still prefer a more personal means of relating to the social world. Much energy is spent in personal relationships, obviously a source of immense satisfaction. It likely accounts for why so many boomers turn to therapy and counseling as a solution to problems and why they like a high degree of personal service in the marketplace. Introspection also bears on openness and sharing of feelings. Asked to evaluate a list of changes from the time of their parents' generation, respondents in the *Rolling Stone* survey chose one change above all others: 83% felt that greater openness and willingness to share personal feelings was a change for the better.[20]

These are hardly new values. The quest for psychological well-being itself has roots reaching deep into the American past. As early as the mid-1800s, Ralph Waldo Emerson, in his essay on "Self-Reliance," had written of his opposition to tradition and conformity and looked to individuals relying on their own inner resources as a means to truth and wisdom. He called upon people to recognize the power within them and to use that power for their own fulfillment. In his writing on "Nature" and "Wealth," he further elaborated on the expansive qualities of the human spirit: "Who can set bounds to the possibilities of man?" he asks, and then implicitly answers his question by reminding his readers that "the world exists for you."[21] Optimism, personal transformation, and the union of mind and matter were all Emersonian themes that later generations of "positive thinkers"—from Mary Baker Eddy to Norman Vincent Peale—would draw on. Members of the boomer generation have felt a special affinity with such thinkers and have been inspired by their teachings.

The rise of psychotherapy further liberated the self from its bondages to external authorities. Freud established a new, idealized image of selfhood: a person who has an analytic attitude and strives for well-being as a way of overcoming the neuroses generated out of social life, a sane self in an insane world. After Freud came the "humanistic psychologists" who popularized notions of human potential and self-actualization, again on the assumption that society was detrimental or restrictive to the emergence of a more vibrant, healthy self. Humanistic psychology spread widely among the college educated in the 1960s and 1970s. Influenced by a faith in the flexibility of human nature, and inspired by the traditional American values of self-improvement and individualism, the boomers were to become the carriers of an ethic of self-realization that had been in the making for a long time and was now a dominant cultural theme in American life. It could hardly be otherwise. In a society that had so many inducements to material advancement and self-interest, it is not surprising that "self-fulfillment" and "self-help" would be seen as healthy correlates. Two hundred years have passed from the time Benjamin Franklin published his autobiography, a self-help book of sorts of a man in quest of virtue, to today's flourishing market of books, videos, and audiocassettes catering to psychological needs—the popular expression, as Philip Rieff says, of "the triumph of the therapeutic."[22]

GENDER REVOLUTION

Of all the sixties' revolutions, none had a greater long-term impact than the gender revolution. The changing sexual rules and relationships of the period mushroomed into a major social movement that has radically altered marriage, family, parenting, and career patterns. By the 1980s there were significant increases in the number of couples cohabiting, single-parent families, blended families, lesbian and gay families, couples without children, couples with children no longer at home, and families consisting of an adult and an aging parent. Family types, lifestyles, and new gender roles proliferated. Freedom of choice had invaded the more private, intimate realms of sexuality and family, producing an immense variety of acceptable alternatives.

The boomer generation came into adulthood just at the time the gender revolution was in the making. Events coalesced early in the 1960s to give shape to a broadly based women's movement. In 1963 Betty Friedan published *The Feminine Mystique,* which spoke directly to women who had lived by old standards.[23] Women had far fewer opportunities to break into the labor force; but even more of an impediment was the mystique surrounding women themselves—as wives and mothers. Speaking of the "problem that has no name," Friedan urged them to break away from their domestic confines, go back to school, and pursue careers. The book became an immediate bestseller, giving voice to discontented women across the country. Much of the discontent came from wives and mothers older than the first wave of boomers who were just beginning to reach adulthood, women who had struggled to conform to the prevailing family norms of their time, but who were increasingly disenchanted. Women who had married and raised families in the late 1940s and the 1950s—the period after World War II leading up to the 1960s—especially felt pressures for change. Their discontent over lack of career opportunities and gender roles defining their meaningful activities largely to the kitchens and bedrooms was a powerful outpouring of support for change, bonding them with their younger "sisters" in the movement.

Simultaneously, the birth control pill, approved for sale in 1960, gained widespread usage the first few years it was on the market. Technology converged with the mounting women's movement, giving it an immediate and far-reaching impact. For the first time, a woman could truly feel she was in charge of her body, that sex was possible without excessive worry about becoming pregnant. By de-coupling sex and pro-creation, the pill gave women a degree of choice and control hitherto un-known. Critics feared it would lead to freer sex and changing moral values, which it did, but its greater impact lay in the power it gave women over their own lives. It freed women to accept and assert their sexuality, to demand recognition as human beings with sexual appetites no less pro-nounced than men's. It freed women for opportunities of their own choos-ing, emancipated them from old bondages, and thereby altered significantly the power relationships between men and women. Women of all social classes were affected, but none more so than middle-class women: "Now, for the first time, millions of middle-class women could rationally and safely plan careers, conceive of marriage as a true partnership, calculate the rational economic future of the family, and think differently about what it meant to be a woman of the middle class."[24]

Catholic women also sought prescriptions. By the mid-1960s about two-thirds as many Catholic women as Protestants and Jews were using the pill. Today, between 80% and 85% of Catholic women approve its use.[25] Its reliability encourages them to ignore the church's centuries-old prohibition against artificial birth control, though not always with-out personal struggle and guilt. Carol McLennon, the post-Vatican II Catholic from Southern California, tells of her own struggle leading up to her decision about birth control:

> So after the third [baby], I decided, Brad and I will work on this real hard and we'll just not get pregnant. No more shlepping around. It really caused a lot of tension. Because it seems like you get into bed at night and you'd hug, and then you'd start thinking what day of the month is this and, y'know, God, we can't do it now. What are we gonna do? Let's go find this, y'know . . . and that's not what God meant either. I mean our relationship as husband and wife was meant to be loving and caring and, y'know, I just couldn't imagine living all the rest of those years with that kind of tension. But, as it ended up, we didn't have to. I ended up pregnant again by the end of the year. And then came the guilt. Tremendous guilt. Why did I have this horrible thick guilt? And it was because I really didn't do what I knew was the right thing to do. So after Carla I had the tubal liga-tion.

Carol's decision to practice some kind of birth control was a significant step to take. For her, as for many Catholic women, the pill or its equivalent was their first significant rebellion against the church, and it meant that their attitude toward the authority of the church on other issues would never be quite the same again.

The pill provoked profound social changes. It helped lower the birth rate and brought an end to the postwar baby boom. It helped raise the age at marriage after decades of decline, as more and more women chose to postpone a committed relationship. That in itself was a major change—creating a "Postponed Generation," or the delaying of the responsibilities of adulthood. It spelled doom to the old containment ethic of the earlier period. Women could now enter the labor force with less fear of losing jobs as a result of unexpected births. Marriage need not stand in the way of pursuing a career. With good "family planning," young working couples could enjoy the early years of their marriage with double incomes. Even to have children at all was now an option. It contributed to a changing, more liberal stance toward divorce: 18% of the boomers we surveyed were themselves currently divorced or separated, and another 13%, now married, reported previous marriages. It also helped indirectly to redefine men's roles in the direction of greater gender equality, both in the workplace and at home.

Thus boomers as a generation would have to deal with an enormous array of gender and lifestyle changes, affecting the lives of both men and women. The technology of birth control combined with the burgeoning sixties' youth culture encouraged the young, as historian Elaine Tyler May points out, to be risk-takers in ways that their security-oriented parents found unthinkable.[26] They embraced new gender role definitions and sexual norms; and while many may be concerned today about promiscuous sex and AIDS, the majority has not turned its back on the gains from the gender revolution. Indeed, 77% agree that *more* needs to be done to advance equal opportunities for women. Eighty-one percent agree that it is good for women to have jobs outside the home, and 71% say it is all right for women to work even if they have preschool children at home. This generation strongly endorses "egalitarian marriages," in which husbands and wives share decision making in family matters: 74% disagree with the statement that "by and large the husband ought to have the main say-so in family matters." Three-quarters of boomers say they would like husbands and wives to share responsibility for work, homemaking, and child-raising; while just one in ten prefers a "traditional marriage," in which the husband works and the wife stays at home. Views on shared work, homemaking, and child-raising is one thing, however, and what actually happens at home is quite another. Indeed, the evidence suggests that although men have started to "help out" more with domestic chores, working women still do double duty and are responsible for the lion's share of child care and housework. In the new world of two-career families, women still bear a greater responsibility for, to cite Arlie Hochschild's phrase, the "second shift."[27]

EDUCATION AND THE MEDIA

Finally, we consider education and the media. The boomer generation is the most educated generation in American history—twice as many baby boomers went to college as their parents, three times as many as their grandparents. Educational institutions expanded at every phase during their childhood and growing-up years—first when they were in kindergarten and elementary school, then in the junior high and high school years, and later still when they went off to colleges and universities. Eighty-five percent of baby boomers in our survey finished high school. Over 60% have attended college, 38% earned college degrees, and 17% have a postgraduate education.

Schools during the 1960s and 1970s exposed students to a wide variety of ideas and influences. The sheer increase in numbers of people living and interacting in one place had an impact: It opened their eyes to diverse ways of living and believing. An expanding curriculum in the humanities and social sciences had an effect as well. New courses in religion and philosophy introduced students to the world religions, to critical thinking about the Bible, and to metaphysical questions never before raised. Oscar Gantt remembers taking such a course in college and his encounter with a Jewish professor with whom he could explore questions and doubts about his own faith. Some of his beliefs arising out of an African-American heritage were challenged, and it helped him, as he says, "to better understand my spiritual self or what I was seeking spiritually." For many like him, college was a time of encountering religious pluralism, of discovering and meeting people who differed in their beliefs about God and the sacred, and of finding out that religious truth is itself something that is deeply personal and deemed by many as more relative than absolute.

On college and university campuses across the country, of course, the counterculture was flourishing. Young people who were in college at the time were almost twice as likely as noncollege students to have attended a rock concert, smoked marijuana, and protested the Vietnam War. The counterculture sensitized the better educated to new values and experiences, encouraging them to be more open and experimental in matters ranging from family and sexual styles to religious views. The so-called "new religions"—Zen Buddhism, Meher Baba, Transcendental Meditation, and many others—also flourished, introducing students to Eastern spirituality. College students were twice as likely as noncollege students to say they practice meditation techniques. Others, however, were not so greatly influenced by the changing cultural and religious climate, especially those attending small colleges or business and technical schools. Linda Kramer, in a business school at the time, knew about the drugs and different lifestyles that university students were into, but she was effectively sheltered from all of that even while living in the same Ohio city.

During these years a new basis of cultural cleavage emerged that fell along educational lines. With the growth of science and technology, the boomers—more so than any other generation—came to be deeply divided by level of education. Education is probably the best single predictor for a range of attitudes and values, such as racial tolerance, anti-Semitism, egalitarian gender roles, alternative lifestyles, and tolerance of nonconformity of various kinds. And the same holds for traditional religious beliefs and practices. During the 1960s and 1970s, levels of religious belief, of worship attendance, and of participation in organized religion declined considerably among the better educated, and more so than in previous decades. On matters as varied as belief in God, interpretations of the Bible, Sabbath observance, prayer, and church and Sunday school attendance, there were precipitous declines.[28] More than anything else, education contributed to the deepening division between liberals and conservatives within religious communities, and to a growing split between the more conventionally religious and the more secular sectors of the population.

So great and widespread were the differences in attitudes, values, and beliefs that some have argued that a "new class" emerged during this time. In an "information-oriented" society, a class that valued knowledge and its uses and interpretations, and was more liberal in its outlook and more supportive of government spending in the areas of education, welfare, and environmental protection especially, seemed increasingly set off from the more traditional classes.[29] Whatever the changing ideological configurations, one thing was certain: The relation of religion and education was undergoing a major shift in society. Whereas for a long time the better educated held to about the same levels of conventional religious belief as the less educated and were more involved in religious activities, in the 1960s these patterns began to reverse with the declines among the better educated.

Higher education generated new and more secular meaning systems competing with theistic interpretations of the nature of reality. Social scientific modes of explanation, for example, have gained ascendancy, emphasizing the role of social forces in shaping people's lives. This is more true for the better educated than the general population. Forty-six percent of postgraduates in our survey, compared with 29% of high school graduates, agree with the statement: "If someone does not succeed in life, often it is because society has not given the person a chance." Postgraduates are less likely to regard God, or supernatural forces, as having a strong influence on them, and more likely to attribute influence to how they were brought up or to those in power in society. Social scientific thinking has become widely diffused in contemporary society, and among boomers especially, who as a generation have been the most exposed to this mode of constructing reality.

American-style individualism, shorn of its religious underpinnings, is a type of meaning system as well. This particular type of thinking elevates the person—rather than God or social forces—as responsible for his or her own destiny. Willpower and determination are the critical factors shaping a person's life and success. Individuals have within them the power to make life as they want it. Pam Fletcher, the Massachusetts housewife, is an example of one who thinks largely in these terms. She holds to a utilitarian philosophy emphasizing her own choices and actions as what are important in life. Decisions influence outcomes: You put your effort into being a good person, or working hard, and hope you succeed. She is hardly alone in her views—well over half of our respondents agree that "hard work always pays off." Even more agree that "a person who is strong and determined can pretty much control what happens in life," and that "if one believes in oneself, there is almost no limit to what one can do." These latter constructions of reality are particularly pronounced among the less well educated.

If education helped to create a variety of meaning systems, the media had an impact as well. The boomers were, as already noted, the first generation to grow up with television: They watched the assassination of a president and other national leaders, civil rights demonstrations, the Vietnam War, nuclear test explosions. Television brought the violence and destructiveness of our national life right into the living room for all to see. More than any other medium, television shaped consumer tastes and raised their levels of expectations for the future. It was also a consuming medium. By the time the average boomer had reached sixteen years of age, television had captured an estimated 12,000 to 15,000 hours of his or her time.[30] Although they watched children's programs, much of that time was spent watching adult programs. In effect, television introduced the generation to a very adult world at a very early age.

Unquestionably, television limited the amount of time boomers had with their peers and parents. It became the major source of information shaping their definitions of reality, exceeding that of books, newspapers, teachers, religious leaders, perhaps supplanting the family itself. Researchers at the University of Michigan, interviewing the high school class of 1965 along with their parents, found considerable evidence that the family socialization process had weakened: There were few agreements between the two generations on racial equality, drug use, gender views, political attitudes, and religion.[31] Although the investigators did not examine the role of television, there can be little doubt that it contributed to the diminished importance of the family in the transmission of cultural values and beliefs.

Perhaps the most important impact of television was that it replaced the *word* with the *image:* Henceforth the dominant medium would be the fleeting, discontinuous flow of electromagnetic pictures. Instancy and intimacy would be the distinguishing features of this new medium; seeing, not reading, would become the basis for believing. The implications were staggering, far beyond anything we have yet grasped. And once again boomers could claim a first: the first generation to experience what amounts to a major transformation in mode of communication. Music sensitized them to the auditory dimensions of experience, and television opened up realms of visual experience, both of which have had a powerful effect on how Americans ever since have defined truth and knowledge, and even reality itself.

RELIGIOUS PROTESTS AND SPIRITUAL EXPLORATIONS

Upheaval, affluence, gender revolution, education, and the media all shaped boomer experiences. Disruptive events and rapid social changes jolted their lives, distancing them from the major institutions and challenging core values and the cultural narratives by which generations of Americans have understood themselves. They shared the great economic expectations of the 1950s and early 1960s, but they also shared the disillusionments of the 1970s, forcing many to scale down their material dreams. Not surprisingly, as the commentator quoted at the beginning of this chapter suggests, boomers look like veterans, having been through a war together.

Nowhere were the jolts felt more than within institutional religion, in the churches and synagogues across the country. Most dropped out in their late teenage years or early twenties. Those who were involved in the civil rights movement and antiwar protests left in disillusionment with a church that seemed so feeble, so impotent to bring about changes in a world where so much had gone wrong. Many Catholics left in frustration and anger over the church's positions on issues like abortion and divorce. In all the religious traditions, many simply dropped out. Some felt that the mainline churches were spiritually and theologically impoverished; but most, it seems, just quit going, not out of any strong doctrinal or moral objection, but because church or synagogue seemed irrelevant to them.

The youthful protest against organized religion appears to have been far more broadly based than is often thought. Over 60% of the young adults in our survey dropped out of active involvement for a period of two years or more—somewhat higher for Jews and mainline Protestants, but not less than one-half for Catholics and conservative Protestants. Levels of dropping out were about the same for boomers born before 1955 as for those born afterwards and are only slightly higher for men than for women. Perhaps most surprising of all, education appears to have had little influence on this—those without a college education dropped out about equally with those who had a college degree. In fact, those with a high school education or less dropped out more so than did college graduates, but postgraduates abandoned the churches and synagogues more so than any of the others.

Clearly, something happened to alter fundamentally the generation's ties with religious institutions. The fact is that the religious involvement of boomers changed drastically, and in a relatively short period of time—from when they were children until their early adult years. Nine out of ten people in our survey reported attending religious services weekly or more when they were children eight to ten years old. Many of them were baptized. As children they were as religious as any generation before them in this century—at least in terms of their exposure to and early involvement within religious institutions.[32] But by their early twenties, slightly more than one-fourth were involved to the same extent; the great majority had dropped out altogether or, if still attending, they did so irregularly. Those who had been baptized as children did not join churches through profession of faith, or confirmation, at levels that might have been expected on the basis of their numbers—becoming instead the church's "missing generation."[33] They dropped out of the mainline churches and synagogues in unprecedented numbers, resulting in a substantial loss of members.[34]

Dropping out of organized religion during the young adult years, at least for a transitory period in a person's life, is a deeply embedded cultural pattern in America. Previous generations have drifted away from religious institutions in which they were brought up during their young adult years, when they must decide for themselves what they believe or whether to get involved in a congregation. What is really significant religiously is not that they drift away, but whether or not they return to these institutions later on in their lives—which many are now doing, as we shall see in later chapters. Still, it would appear that for the post-World War II generation, the extent of dropping out was greater than for their parents' generation, and that educated, middle-class young Americans abandoned the religious institutions in proportionally greater numbers in the 1960s and 1970s than in earlier times.[35]

More important than anything else in shaping a religious response were the experiences growing up in the 1960s and 1970s. As Figure 2.3 shows, there is a relationship between exposure to the cultural upheavals and religious involvement. Among those who were the least touched by the music, the drug culture, and the social and political unrest that ripped the country at the seams, well over one-half dropped out. But for those who were more exposed, levels of dropping out rose considerably higher—from 56% up to 84%. The cultural reverberations of this tumultuous period clearly had an enormous impact on the youth's estrangement from organized religion. The patterns hold for men and women, for the younger and the older groups, for those who went to college and those who did not, and in all parts of the country.

The extent of the estrangement and value shift is evident by looking at the changes in generational attitudes. Figure 2.4 shows a discernible break on some key attitudes between pre-boomers and boomers. On measures of strength of religious identity, the importance of arriving at one's own beliefs, whether religious attendance is necessary to being a "good" Christian or Jew, and in views about the rules of morality within churches and synagogues, there is a 5- to 15-point spread between the cohorts born before 1946 and those born after that time. The end of World War II is like a cultural fault line—the differences greater on either side than between those born in cohort 1 (1926–1935) and cohort 2

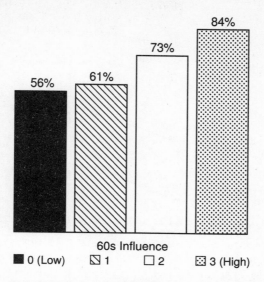

60s Influence

■ 0 (Low)   ◨ 1   ☐ 2   ⊞ 3 (High)

Figure 2.3 Religious Dropouts

(1936–1945), or between those born in cohort 3 (1946–1954) and co-hort 4 (1955–1962). "In an epoch of change, each person is dominated by his birth date," wrote sociologist Norman Ryder in an essay on gen-erations and social change published in 1965, words that aptly described the boomers.[36]

What happened religiously is much the same as what happened po-litically. Boomers in the late 1950s and early 1960s were a generation well on their way to a normal respect for the political process: They had high levels of trust in government and felt that political leaders cared about what people thought. But within a span of ten years—from 1963 to 1973—they abandoned their once hopeful outlook for a new course of political independence and institutional separation. By their late teens and early twenties, trust in government plummeted, party loyalty de-clined, and the number of political party "independents" shot up.[37] The analogy to organized religion seems indisputable: greater separation from institutions and a corresponding increase in emphasis on individual choice.

While religious responses were shaped by the cultural ferment of the 1960s, the roots of the protest reach further back into the child-hood years of the boomers. The years in which many of the older boomers grew up—the 1950s—were an aberration in many ways. In

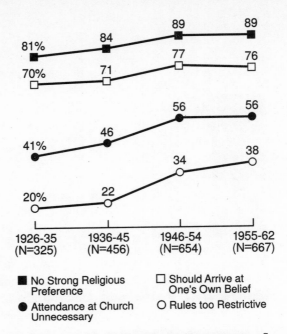

81% 84 89 89
70% 71 77 76
41% 46 56 56
34 38
20% 22

1926-35 (N=325)   1936-45 (N=456)   1946-54 (N=654)   1955-62 (N=667)

■ No Strong Religious Preference   □ Should Arrive at One's Own Belief
● Attendance at Church Unnecessary   ○ Rules too Restrictive

Figure 2.4 Birth Cohorts and Attitudes toward Organized Religion

some respects it was a very religious era, still looked back on with nostalgia; yet in other ways it was very secular and riddled with paradoxes. The close intertwining of domestic ideology and cold war militance may have produced a powerful countercultural response. A stable family life seemed necessary for national security and for maintaining supremacy over the Soviet Union. Cold war tensions may have encouraged a retreat into the home in search of security but may also have sown the seeds for a strong institutional backlash, beginning with the "soft" institutions of the family and religion. The 1950s, as one commentator observes, was "an era of suppressed individuality, of national paranoia, and of largely unrecognized discrimination against minorities, women, the poor, foreigners, homosexuals, and indeed most of those who dared to be different—the era that came to an end with the onset of the '60s was a time bomb waiting to explode."[38] Heightened expectations, too, especially as translated into new, more permissive child-rearing philosophies, had an impact: Dropouts in our survey were twice as likely as those who did not drop out to describe their upbringing as "permissive" or "very permissive."

But there were other, more positive repercussions from the turbulent 1960s. Jolted out of the established faiths, many turned inward in search of basic answers to life. The so-called "new religions" flourished in the latter years of the decade. Fueled partly by the drug culture, insights from the Eastern mystical religions, and the music of protest, the religious consciousness of college-educated, middle-class youth especially was transformed, paralleling changing notions in the realms of family and sex, in politics and economics, in lifestyles. There was a blossoming of the spirit in a thousand forms—everything from astrology to Zen—known simply as "alternative religions." Later, in the 1970s, there was an evangelical and fundamentalist Christian resurgence. Youth turned to "born again" faiths in surprisingly large numbers. No longer defining themselves through the conventional religious labels they had inherited, they turned inward to their own spiritual explorations.

This turning inward would have a lasting spiritual impact. The impact would last because theirs was a generation whose foundations had been shaken and for whom there was no returning to the old ways of believing. Commenting on the existential depths of the generational experiences, Craig Dykstra recently wrote:

> The suspiciousness of the '60s has not gone away, and no escape from it is sought by the new religious seekers. Rather the search is for a truer, healthier suspiciousness, one that really can smoke out deceit, oppression, violence, and evil—even in its loveliest and most attractive forms—and tell it for what it is. To support the suspiciousness there must be something that is not suspiciousness itself, something that is not so ultimately suspicious it must finally suspect everything. What we have here, I think, is a search for God.[39]

This search, in an increasingly pluralistic moral and religious setting, produced a new salvational dilemma, namely, that of finding one's own spiritual path in the midst of so many alternatives. Fundamental questions, such as "Who am I?" and "What am I doing with my life?" took on fresh meaning. Religion—like life—was something to be explored. Old cultural and religious scripts had lost power over them, forcing them to think through anew their religious and spiritual options. As a generation they were predisposed to post-material values, to pursuing greater equality, peace, environmental protection, and quality-of-life, far more so than the generation before them. They reasserted values of self-fulfillment and human potential, far more so than did their parents. They led the way in exploring lifestyle choices and extending tolerance to people of all preferences and persuasions, far more so than did their parents. A generation with high expectations for themselves and for others, they came to know what it is like, in poet Emily Dickinson's words, "to dwell in possibility."

Ironically, despite a great deal of alienation from traditional religion, the circumstances of their lives led to a great deal of potential interest in spiritual matters. The period left not just a lasting mark on their lives, it left many marks. Members of the boomer generation were touched in ways that have led to many differing, and even alternative, spiritual and religious trajectories. It is to this array of possibilities that we turn as we take a closer look at our representative boomers.

PART TWO

Spirit

CHAPTER 3

Mollie's Quest

Among the people we interviewed, no one remembered the sixties more fondly than did Mollie Stone. "That era changed my entire life," says the single mother from Massachusetts, her face beaming as she recalls her years growing up. Those years came right at the peak of the youth counterculture: drugs, sex, rock-and-roll music, civil rights demonstrations, antiwar protests, all were familiar to her. Living in Westchester near the love-ins and be-ins of New York's Central Park, she had a head-on confrontation with all that was going on, and she loved it: "It was the culture that I liked . . . the sixties' culture and everything that it represented."

What was it about those years that she liked so much? Was it the political activism? Yes, partly. The demonstrations and protests all created a sense that she was involved in something exciting and was helping to build a new heaven and earth. Was it psychedelics? Yes, that was part of it, too, even though she was not as heavily into drugs as were many others at the time. Hallucinogenic drugs opened up ways to expand consciousness, which for disaffected youth at the time was a means of escape. Getting high led to psychic adventure. But there was more to the sixties than politics or drugs, there was also freedom. Freedom from the old conformity. Freedom to break out of social structures that impoverish and exploit. Freedom to be yourself. In Mollie's words: "It was get[ting] out of what was oppressive and rigid and limiting, and you know, death-like to the spirit." Her choice of words reflects a deep concern for the inner life—that the spiritual not be smothered by a harsh social order. Several times during the interview the word "spiritual" came up: She was a free-spirit, a spiritual person, someone concerned about her children's spiritual values. Whatever the 1960s was all about, it had to do with something deeply spiritual.

The term *spiritual* often summons up vague and outdated imageries. In the minds of many, spiritual implies otherworldliness, or some notion of disembodied powers moving freely in mysterious ways. Western culture is riddled with dualisms, a good example being the way in which spirit is thought of as the opposite of the body, or as distinct from that which is worldly. A spiritual person, it is said, is someone who has escaped the concerns of this life, choosing instead otherworldly or ascetic ideals. But for Mollie, this is not true. For her, spiritual means just the opposite: something very worldly, having to do with relating to the earth and sky and animals and people; and something very bodily, having to do with health, happiness, and feeling good about herself. Mollie's spirituality arises out of her own experience. In its truest sense, spirituality gives expression to the being that is in us; it has to do with feelings, with the power that comes from within, with knowing our deepest selves and what is sacred to us, with, as Matthew Fox says, "heart-knowledge."[1]

Knowledge like this does not come easily. For Mollie, it took the stormy experiences of the 1960s, which transformed her consciousness and gave her a new awareness of who she was as a person. This came about while she was still in her teens, and not without a great deal of pain. She had a strained adolescence, left home estranged from her parents, and she still doesn't have a very close relationship with them. But out of that cauldron of intense experiences her horizons were greatly expanded—beyond her conventional, upper middle-class upbringing, and beyond her family's rather casual religious practices. Like many in her generation, she found middle-class, materialistic values and ideologies oppressive and stifling; in a capitalist society, profits are always a central incentive, and often at odds with the goals of racial equality and justice that were so important to her. Traditional religious observance as she knew it in her Jewish family seemed distant from, and irrelevant to, what was happening around her. Synagogue ritual was impersonal and empty. Magic and mystery appeared to have been lost in a culture that had become excessively rational, objective, scientific, or as she says, "death-like to the spirit."

Mollie's disillusionment reached far deeper than was the case for most young people. She was skeptical of religion that seemed to make no difference in people's lives and very critical of a class structure that allowed whites to benefit from the labors of impoverished blacks. For her, the two were inseparable. Something was wrong with religious ritual removed from everyday life and with religious practices that were indifferent to how people are treated. Religion seemed so captive to the status quo, so supportive of a particular group's interests. Middle-class piety struck her as hollow, with its concern with proper belief and behavior, with faith that was more comforting than challenging, and with moral respectability. She was not alone in her feelings: As many commentators writing on American religion at the time observed, the churches and synagogues gave expression and legitimacy to a set of commonly held cultural values such as progress, security, conformity, and confident living—all wrapped up and called "the American Way of Life."[2] And, of course, there was racism and the legacy of racial discrimination institutionalized within religion.[3] For Mollie, the sixties shattered the easy blend of bourgeois values and traditional religion, provoking serious questions about the very foundations of life itself. Philosophy and politics, faith and ethics, the worlds around her and within her—all were bound up together. In this sense the 1960s was more than just a social protest or getting high, it was a spiritual crisis.

INNER WORLD AND OUTER WORLD

Molly still remembers, and articulates very clearly, what happened during those eventful years growing up and how her world took on new meaning:

> The world outside of upper middle-class suburban Westchester opened up for me as it hadn't before. And that included the inner world, which I think was partly due to drugs and the kind of spiritual emphasis that began to appear around that time. And also the outer world of going to marches, going to rallies, and seeing all those hundreds of people that were united on a single topic, of like-mind, or had a strong feeling about something.

Mollie, like many in her generation, no longer believes that turning to drugs offers much help. She is among the many of her age group who have changed their mind and no longer endorse the legalization of marijuana. Almost three-fourths of the boomers we interviewed, in fact, now oppose its legalization. As a counselor in the public schools, she deals with children every day whose lives are messed up because of drugs and alcohol. She has left behind much of the celebrated freedom of the era and is now more concerned with getting on with her life, raising her children, and beginning a new marriage. She seldom thinks about marching or demonstrating anymore: The old era of social protest and dreams of building a better society have long since passed. Just two things are important for her now, her family and her own spiritual growth.

Her expanded horizons are still with her, and doubtless will continue to be. She continues on the journey on which she set out in the late 1960s, exploring one after another of the great world religions, macrobiotics, Native American and eco-feminist spiritualities. When she speaks of life—spirituality in the broadest sense—it has to do with interconnections: the self in relation to others, to nature, to the world. Hers is a holistic vision that places emphasis on integrating of body and spirit and balancing the cognitive and expressive aspects of life. Life is a whole, in both a metaphysical and mystical sense. All creation is united, the individual into the community and the community into nature. Hers is a coherent vision that moves away from the Cartesian split of subject and object so typical of much of Western thinking. To Mollie, such distinctions must be abandoned, for they are antithetical to spiritual well-being. Unity, peace, and harmony are her ideals, both personal and planetary.

The sixties gave her a vision of the "inner world" and "outer world" coming together in some meaningful whole. She had discovered the two could not easily be split apart: Marches and demonstrations on behalf of a better society had helped to clarify her own values and principles; and acting with integrity on the basis of those values and principles, she found she had to reject much of middle-class life, or as she put it, "get out of what was oppressive and rigid and limiting." She expresses the same holistic view toward the environment today: You can't feel good about yourself and about what you are doing if you are exploiting Mother Earth when you ought to be paying homage to her for food and the sun and the warmth and the rain. One must live in relation to the elements and must feel the harmony, the peace, and the power that come from being at one with the universe. Then, and only then, can the spirit survive.

Mollie Stone is exceptional. Her confrontation with the turbulent era in which she grew up was far more direct and intense than was true for most members of her generation. Her lifestyle today continues to bear evidence of its great impact on her—in her dress, her choice of music, the furnishings of her house. Spiritually, she is in a league to which few others we talked to would belong. But it would be a mistake to dismiss her as an aging flower child dabbling in esoteric and fringe spiritualities. Mollie wrestles with some fundamental problems now confronting

Western religious consciousness. Her spiritual quest touches on concerns that are widely shared in her generation, though not always articulated as well or felt so deeply by many of her spiritual brothers and sisters. The truth is she embodies qualities of the spirit that, in milder form, are quite common in the boomer population.

THE REDISCOVERY OF THE SPIRITUAL

William James long ago distinguished between tradition and experience, between secondhand and firsthand religion. Tradition has to do with what is socially inherited as distinct from experience, or that which is authentically the individual's own.[4] For many boomers, this dichotomy is very real. Because they felt some distance from religious institutions when they were growing up in the 1960s and 1970s, it has not been easy for them to fit in as adults. The connection between one's deepest personal feelings and the institutional frameworks of society remains fragile. The world inside the churches and synagogues often seems far removed, if not downright alien, to life as experienced outside; the institutional languages of creed and doctrine often come across as stale and timeworn—hardly conducive to "firsthand religion." Yet as a generation many yearn deeply for a religious experience they can claim as "their own." The yearning for some kind of immediacy is expressed in many ways, in both traditional and nontraditional languages: centering one's life, focusing within, knowing God, getting in touch with yourself, the higher self, finding "it."

The concern is to experience life directly, to have an encounter with God or the divine, or simply with nature and other people, without the intervention of inherited beliefs, ideas, and concepts. Such striving is understandable, not simply because secondhand religion can be empty of meaning, but because only personal experience is in some sense authentic and empowering. Individuals are inclined to regard their own experiences as superior to the accounts of others, and the truths found through self-discovery as having greater relevance to them than those handed down by way of creed or custom. Direct experience is always more trustworthy, if for no other reason than because of its "inwardness" and "within-ness"—two qualities that have come to be much appreciated in a highly expressive, narcissistic culture.

As Mollie so aptly illustrates, inner experience is the wellspring of authentic spiritual and religious life. For out of this inner realm of the self—of feeling and subjectivity far removed from the outer realm of roles and relationships—arises a sense of what is true and right to that person's experience. This amounts to the realization of a vital truth: The spiritual and religious, to be meaningful, must relate to people's everyday experiences and give expression to their deepest feelings and concerns. A person must find his or her true self, and allow that self to assert itself, in order to be genuinely spiritual. Young Americans have come to these truths, in part, because of the inner-directedness of the 1960s and 1970s and its great emphasis on the pursuit of the self as an ideal: through values such as self-fulfillment, self-acceptance, and the intrinsic benefits of experience itself. All are values deeply rooted in the optimism, questfulness, and flexible conceptions of human nature characterizing American culture.

It has been said that Americans practice a "supply-side spirituality"—believing profoundly that abundance rather than scarcity, plenty rather than poverty, is our true spiritual condition.[5] If this is the case, then abundance is to be regarded as natural, and anything less is deemed not in keeping with human potential. Building on themes articulated by Ralph Waldo Emerson, the notion that humanity was entitled to an inexhaustible supply of possibilities and satisfactions—including the potential for divinity within every individual—forged a strong positive conception of the spiritual self, as a humanly constructed entity, always in process of becoming.[6] The notion of entitlement also shaped a distinct religious ideal and aesthetic. If Americans could dream about unlimited material achievement, they could also explore a thousand spiritual ideals: images of themselves as healthy, energetic, and powerful; visions of America as a special place, where new things were done in new ways; voyages in time along a path of spiritual development toward higher spiritual ground; and a way of life that was affirmative, optimistic, confident, self-assuring, and prosperous. In this matrix of thought and expression, the well-being of spirit and of body, of inner happiness and material accomplishment, are intimately related and of a single order of reality. Life is a whole, and that wholeness itself is something always in the making.

In yet another sense, the pursuit of self has led to a "rediscovery": that psychology and spirituality are not exclusive domains but are themselves integrally related. Though in modern times religious questions have often been taboo in psychotherapists' offices, the division between the spiritual and the psychological is actually a relatively new phenomenon. For millennia, shamans, witch doctors, and priests made no hard distinction between emotional, physical, and spiritual healing. All were aspects of an individual's fundamental relationship with a larger universe of spirits and powers. A sense of wholeness was essential to a person's well-being. Today this essential oneness of life is being reclaimed, or envisioned as something that ought to be reclaimed. The rediscovery of inner experience puts young Americans, often armed with the post-Freudian theories of Carl Jung and Abraham Maslow, more in touch with themselves: asking questions about meaning in life; peak experiences; searching to find ways of feeling, and not just thinking about, their relationship to the surrounding universe; and exploring the authority and healing power of the nonrational, the mythic, and the dreamlike. The result is that psychology has become the vehicle for an emerging form of religiousness—what Lucy Bregman describes as "psychological religiousness," which she says is a new way of encountering sacrality and ultimacy.[7]

One factor in the rise of this form of religious expression is the enormous growth in recent years of the informal spirituality promulgated by Alcoholics Anonymous, Alanon, and other Twelve-Step programs. Offering resources and guidance for recovery from various addictive dependencies, these programs portray individuals in a one-to-one relationship with God, or a higher power, before whom the person admits powerlessness (over alcohol, drugs, or whatever the addiction). The addict then takes an inventory of inner strengths as well as weaknesses; and through vigilance, prayer, and meditation, the person seeks to make amends in his or her life and to find the power and support necessary for recovery. Individuals see themselves in a spiritual journey, "letting go" of addictive behaviors and feelings and cultivating a sense of themselves as healthy and responsible people. This involves breaking out of the addict psychology and rediscovering the true self through honesty, surrender, acceptance, discipline, sharing, and serenity.

This bridging of the psychological and spiritual realms is given a huge boost in the flourishing self-help movement. More than two hundred different Twelve-Step groups now hold meetings across the country.[8] Twelve-Step-based books are available not just for alcoholism and drugs, but for everything from overeating to "shopaholism," from sexual compulsions to religious addictions. Other manuals on spiritual growth readily extend the self-help principles for individuals dealing on their own with emotional scars resulting from abuse, incest, and rape, and for overcoming guilt, shame, anxieties, and fears of all kinds. Joy, harmony, growth, peace, love, enhanced creativity, and visions of a higher purpose are all held up as rewards to those who can find healing and turn their lives around. Religious and spiritual terminology is cast in general, inclusive terms, as found in the following description of spirituality: "Growing through connecting with your Higher Self and to a Higher Power—the God/Goddess within and without, Christ, Allah, Buddha, the All-That-Is."[9] Popular books like M. Scott Peck's *The Road Less Traveled: A New Psychology of Love, Traditional Values, and Spiritual Growth* reflect a blending of the religious and the psychological.[10] Spiritual growth and mental growth are considered one and the same. Such notions as sacrifice, discipline, and sin, from a religious vocabulary, are recast in psychological terms. Grace and love are shown to be the means by which a person recovers and grows. For many in the boomer generation who did not have a religious upbringing, or who have been cut off from organized religion, books like this one can introduce them to religious teachings and convince them that religion—defined broadly—is not so alien after all.

This turning inward is not limited to a handful of people on a spiritual quest, like Mollie. As shown in Figure 3.1, a majority of the respondents in our survey indicated a preference "to be alone and to meditate." One question we asked was: "For you, which is most important: to be alone and to meditate, or to worship with others?" The purpose of the question was to distinguish between a spirituality associated with aloneness versus that arising out of worship in a group. Fifty-three percent said it was more important to be alone and to meditate, 29% indicated worship with others, and 18% said either both were important or they were unable to choose between them. Fourteen percent indicated that they actually practiced some type of meditation. These practices are more common among the better educated: among high school graduates, 9%; among the college educated, 16%; among those having done professional or graduate work, 29%.

A common theme in this turning inward is the emphasis on exploring religious and spiritual traditions. Exploration gets elevated to the level of a spiritual exercise in an age that is aware of the great diversity of religions. After the Beatles journeyed to India in the 1960s, many youth became excited about yoga and the mystical wisdom of gurus. Americans were exposed to Eastern movements such as Zen Buddhism, Hare Krishna, Divine Light Mission, and Transcendental Meditation, and to indigenous traditions such as Native American religions. While the so-called "new religions" are far less visible now than two decades ago, the spiritual teachings of these and other religious traditions are well known today—probably more so now than then.

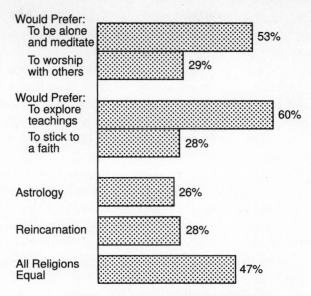

Would Prefer:
To be alone and meditate — 53%
To worship with others — 29%

Would Prefer:
To explore teachings — 60%
To stick to a faith — 28%

Astrology — 26%

Reincarnation — 28%

All Religions Equal — 47%

Figure 3.1 Spirituality

Interest in the paranormal and psychic experiences is widespread and appears to have increased during the 1980s: Clairvoyance, ESP, precognition, déjà vu, and related experiences of the "supernatural" are more commonly reported now than a decade or two ago, and more so among the college educated than among those with less education.[11] Mythical and psychical themes find popular expression on the screen in such films as *Star Wars, E.T., Close Encounters of the Third Kind,* and more recently, *Ghost.* Bookstores across the country today carry paperback editions of the *I Ching,* the works of Krishnamurti, the writings of Joseph Campbell on mythology, the teachings of Starhawk, and scores of publications on Theosophy, witchcraft, the occult, faith healing, *tai ch'i,* nature cults, spiritualism, yoga, astrology, herbal medicines, crystals, channeling, neo-Paganism, and on other related topics. Exploration opens up new vistas, making possible a synthesis of ideas, beliefs, and practices, including the New Age possibility of "creating your own reality," as one of its slogans promises.

How widespread is this open, exploring approach to religion? Do many favor it over commitment to a single faith? Our survey suggests it is fairly common. We asked the following question: "Is it good to explore many differing religious teachings and learn from them, or should one stick to a particular faith?" Sixty percent of the respondents said they preferred to explore, 28% said stick to a faith, 11% could not choose or said do both. Like practicing spiritual disciplines, faith exploration is related to level of education: 52% of the high school educated endorse it, as compared to 66% of the college educated, and 69% of the postgraduates. Age, gender, and the other standard demographics seem not to matter very much. The fact that education correlates so well underscores the important role of higher learning in exposing members of this generation to alternative religions and of fostering an exploratory, more relativistic stance toward religion. For boomers, education and exposure to religions have been experienced together.

Figure 3.1 also shows three items that shed some light on the open attitude toward exploration as well as extent of exploration currently. Forty-seven percent agreed (and the same percentage disagreed), with the statement "All the great religions of the world are equally true and good." Overlooking the 6% without an opinion, this would indicate that about one-half of all boomers hold to a nonparticularistic view of religion. Older boomers are somewhat more inclined to this type of religious universalism. As to extent of exploration, 28% of all boomers say they "believe" in reincarnation, and 26% "believe" in astrology. Again, age and gender seem not to matter very much; neither is level of education very important, with the lesser educated perhaps slightly more inclined to these beliefs. While the appeal of both astrology and reincarnation seem to be growing among the better educated, there has long been an attraction to them, and to astrology especially, in the more traditional, marginal sectors of society. Now, it appears, their appeal is becoming more broadly based across society.

GOD, HIGHER POWER, AND HIGHER SELF

Spirituality and notions of deity are closely linked, and thus it is not surprising that many in this generation are asking fundamental questions about the meaning and existence of God. To explore the inner self and its relations to the larger world is to open up possibilities of new symbolic constructions, or "pictures," by which humans imagine the ultimate forces shaping life.

Most boomers, like most Americans, believe in God. The polls repeatedly show that Americans overwhelmingly affirm such a belief: When asked, "Do you believe in God?," 94% to 95% respond, "Yes." Asking the question this way, however, tends to gloss over subtle differences both in conceptions of God and in conviction. Recent studies indicate, for example, that levels of doubt and disbelief are often greater

(N=536)

Don't believe in God	1%
Don't think it is possible to know if there is a God	3
Uncertain but lean toward believing	16
Definitely believe in a personal God	72
Definitely believe in a Higher Power	8
TOTAL	100

Table 3.1 Belief in God

than the polls would suggest.[12] Among the better educated especially, doubt is fairly common. There is widespread variation as well in the images of deity that believers hold. Even among mainline churchgoers, imageries differ along lines of gender, anthropomorphic versus more abstract qualities, "soft" versus "hard" attributes.[13] The religious imagination, it would seem, knows few limits. Much depends on how the questions are worded when people are interviewed: If respondents are given a chance to express doubt, often they will do so; and if allowed to draw distinctions in belief, they are likely to do so. Certainly this is true for the young adult generation, whose levels of doubt and uncertainty as well as alternative ways of believing are higher than for the population as a whole.

Almost one-half of the boomers we interviewed say they "never" doubt the existence of God; doubt increases with level of education, from 50% among high school graduates up to 65% among the postgraduates. The beliefs themselves are shown in Table 3.1. For boomers, as for Americans generally, there are very few atheists—only 1%. Agnostics, or those who say it is impossible to know if there is a God, are found in greater numbers—but still only 3%. Neither atheism nor agnosticism is as common as secular portrayals of the generation might suggest. Uncertainty is much more likely. Sixteen percent say they are uncertain but lean toward believing. Doubt, or lack of firm conviction, is thus far more common than hardened disbelief or skepticism about the unknowable. Another 8% affirm belief in a higher power. Both uncertainty and belief in a higher power are more common among the better educated. This leaves the vast majority, or 72%, who say they definitely believe in a personal God. Among boomers, this traditional image of God is held somewhat less so than for Americans as a whole, primarily because of the large numbers in this generation—almost one-fourth—who are either uncertain about their belief or who hold to a more abstract, nonpersonal conception.

The whole question of religious imagination, or how the divine gets pictured symbolically, is enormously important, and touches upon the more subtle spiritual changes now underway among boomers. Most young Americans are quite traditional in their views: They think of God as a personal, supernatural being who hears prayers, watches over them, and often responds to their supplications. God is close and approachable, typically thought of as a loving Father, yet reigning over the world as an omnipotent and righteous being active in human affairs. This combination of attributes, both personal and powerful, has led to what might be called, in the words of philosopher and theologian David R. Griffin, the *generic idea of God.* To quote Griffin:

> According to this generic idea or definition, the word God refers to a personal, purposive being, perfect in goodness and supreme in power, who created the world, acts providentially in it, is sometimes experienced by human beings, especially as the source of moral norms and religious experiences, is the ultimate ground of meaning and hope, and is thereby alone worthy of worship.[14]

Protestants, Catholics, Jews, Muslims, and others all have their slightly differing "versions," but most Americans—young and old—can agree on this rather general view of God. Contemporary religious pluralism and trends in science, rationality, and secularity have helped to shape, often out of a defensive posture, a generic theism.

In the modern era, however, growing numbers have come to find this generic view of God rather bland and uninspiring. With so much death and destruction, tragedy, and evil in the world, some find it difficult to maintain a notion of an all-good, omnipotent deity. Although hardly the first to press this question, the boomers have grown up hearing about the Holocaust and have experienced so much in their time—assassinations of national leaders, the threat of nuclear warfare, environmental destruction, AIDS—that the question is given a new and pointed significance. The older patriarchal conception of deity appears for many in contradiction with the liberating forces bringing new life to minorities, women, and the Third World—sectors that have long been denied freedom and justice enmeshed in structures often legitimated by religious leaders in the name of God. Moreover, many of the older notions about God seem out of sync with the modern world, where reason and experience are privileged over revelation and authority, where so much of what happens in life can be explained naturally, without recourse to divine intervention. In popular conception theism involves the notion of a God up there or out there somewhere, and thus distant and removed from life in this world. One problem with this image of humanity's relationship with the divine, as Matthew Fox points out, is that it stifles the soul. He notes, as Jung warned, that one way to kill the soul is to "worship a God outside you."[15]

This situation has led to a variety of responses—some a return to more orthodox religious views, others a more radical departure from them. The evangelical and charismatic revivals of the 1970s and 1980s served to infuse new experiential meanings into old images. For example, many young Americans affirm traditional belief in God by holding to highly personal images, as in the case of "born again" evangelicals, fundamentalists, and charismatics. God is pictured in warm, familial images as one with whom you can have a direct, personal relationship, even daily conversations. This God is thought of in very human terms: God, as it were, is created in one's own image. Such imagery often coincides with a dualistic conception of an ongoing warfare between the forces of "good" and the forces of "evil"—that is, a conflict between a personal God and a personal Devil.[16]

Others have abandoned the older cosmologies and views about God, turning inward in their quests. This has led to an awakening of new and living—although often quite ancient—images of the divine. One is a view of God as creative power. When human beings are creative, they experience oneness with that power. Creativity is, in one sense, the ultimate experience. It characterizes all that is good—truth, beauty, love, hope, life itself. To be creative is to be godlike. Divine reality is thus not something removed from life, but creative energy flowing in all things. When we asked our respondents who did not believe in a personal God how they would describe what they believed, the two most frequently cited images were life force and cosmic energy.

If the divine is found in creative energies, the divine "no" must extend to that which is destructive or demeaning of human potential. That which cripples the capacities of people—injustice, exploitation, the various "isms"—runs counter to human freedom and self-expression. Hence there is a close affinity between creativity and the post-sixties cultural emphasis on self-actualization: In fulfilling one's potentialities, one lives up to and embodies creative possibility. The kind of person one becomes depends on the capacity for creativity, or of grasping the growth possibilities. As John Denver once put it:

Love is everywhere, I see it.
You are all that you can be, go on and be it.
Life is perfect, I believe it.
Come and play the game with me.

Another image that has been rediscovered is God as Mother, which bears a close affinity with creativity. "What does God do all day long?" asked Meister Eckhart, the thirteenth-century mystic, only to answer his own question: "God gives birth. From all eternity God lies on a maternity bed giving birth."[17] An extraordinary image, yet history is replete with maternal imageries in many eras. The Virgin, the Madonna, the Goddess, and Sophia are among the images that express a feminine archetype. In reaction to the traditional, patriarchal conceptions of God, many Americans today hold to feminine images: One-fourth of the boomers say they can imagine God as Mother.

Yet another attractive image is that of Unifying Presence. Over against the dualisms of God/nature, God/us, and body/spirit that have so long engulfed Western thinking, holism offers a balanced and integrated vision of reality. The self is the indwelling of God. The world is the abode of God. All is one, and one is all. In the tradition of the ancient Upanishads, we find the oneness of our Atman with the all. Or put differently, we discover the higher self, the transpersonal self that unites us at a mystical level with other selves—something akin to Ralph Waldo Emerson's notion of the "oversoul." And it unites us not just with others, but with nature and creation. This type of imagery is grounded in the earth and is deeply relational. Connectedness and the sacred web of life is the theme linking the self, the larger community, and the whole of creation—"all things in God and God in all things."[18] Imageries giving expression to God as unifying presence would include: higher self, Cosmic Christ, Earth Mother, the world as the Body of God.

THE "RELIGIOUS" AND THE "SPIRITUAL"

Along with the rising concern for spirituality and new imageries of the divine are shifts in religious vocabularies. Almost all of the people we talked to had an opinion about the differences between being "religious" and being "spiritual." While they did not always agree as to what the difference was, they were sure there was one. The two realms have become disjointed, according to the majority of our respondents. To be religious conveys an institutional connotation: to attend worship services, to say Mass, to light Hanukkah candles. To be spiritual, in contrast, is more personal and empowering and has to do with the deepest motivations of life. A practicing Roman Catholic in our study put it this way:

> People can be spiritual and not religious. . . . To me religious is practicing . . . going to church . . . receiving Communion. Spiritual to me is just being in touch with your higher power, I guess.

It is interesting to see how this woman combines a Catholic conception of the religious with a nontraditional view of God and spirituality defined as being in touch with a higher power. Her response makes clear not only the mix of the traditional and the nontraditional, but the differing vocabularies for the religious and the spiritual. In a similar fashion, a thirty-year-old medical student, and loyal Presbyterian, told us that being religious is "to be in church and sing hymns and say prayers with people and go home and have it be Sunday." She identifies the religious with institutional activities and in a temporal dimension—Sunday as a special day. This is not unlike the views of most churchgoing boomers, who regard Sunday as special even though its religious meaning as sacred time has changed greatly. She describes "spiritual" simply as "thinking about things and contemplating." She mentioned, as did others, that reading is important in the pursuit of spirituality. As books, audiocassettes, and video resources have become more available, spiritual growth is viewed as something you can cultivate on your own.

A forty-year-old neurologist and Jewish agnostic married to a Seventh Day Adventist looks at the religious and the spiritual in the following way:

> I'm certainly not religious, in the sense that I don't believe in God and I don't subscribe to standard religious doctrine; but I think I'm spiritual, in the sense that I have a very deep sense of world realities. I don't know where they come from . . . [My wife] says they come from God, of course, from Judeo-Christian tradition, which may be true, but I don't know . . . but I feel extremely strong about the importance of right action for others, being fair to others. A lot of these things came out of the civil rights movement. I have very strong feelings about that. I get extremely upset or angry when I see evidence of injustice or prejudice. And that to me, that's part of being spiritual. Another part of being spiritual to me is sort of this sense of reverence about the world, which I think religious people attribute to God or their relationship to God; for me, it's much more abstract. And again I'm not sure where it comes from, I think

I'm probably more sensitive than most people, at least most people I'm in contact with, to reap the beauty of the world and history and life and how moving it is to wake up in the morning and see the flowers coming up and the clouds in the sky . . .

Religion for this man is doctrine and tradition, and spirituality is more immediate and experiential. He puts the emphasis on what arises out of an individual's own realm of experience, what comes through reading and meditation. Social justice and reverence for nature—two themes dear to the hearts of many reaching adulthood in these years—give shape to the meaning of spiritual for him as well. Interestingly, he credits his spirituality in large part to the civil rights movement and how it shaped his sensitivities to people; but his wife attributes it to God. A religiously mixed marriage and a spiritually mixed metaphysics!

Yet another respondent—a thirty-two-year-old Asian-American, reared Methodist but currently not active in any congregation—picked up on some of the same themes but also underscored a critical point about the relation of the religious and the spiritual. He observed:

You can be spiritual without being religious. I think religious . . . would be more specific. The faith is more specific, certain doctrines. Spiritual would be really general, wider. I think that's how you can be spiritual without being religious. Maybe even be religious without being spiritual. Show up for church and go through the motions.

Just showing up and going through the motions is what many boomers abhor about churchgoing. This generation cannot be understood apart from the disjunction between inner feelings and the broader institutional expressions. It is a huge gap, and one that is keenly felt by many persons. If the religious institutions—that is, worship services and religious activities—lack vitality and seem removed from their everyday lives, boomers are inclined to judge them to be empty and irrelevant. Worse still, just going through the motions of religious involvement can easily smack of hypocrisy to a generation that has felt estranged from social institutions and insists upon authenticity and credibility as prerequisites for commitment.

A related problem for contemporary religious consciousness is the reification of the religious. When the institutional forms of religion become fixed, objective entities—that is, abstracted as a belief system or somehow set apart from the everyday world, as has happened in Western tradition—there is real danger that they will get cut off from the inner meanings and feelings that gave them life to begin with. Religion risks losing its subjective and experiential qualities, thus becoming ritually dry and unmoving. The word "religion" derives from the Latin *religio,* which historically was used in a variety of ways: to designate a greater-than-human *power,* to refer to the *feelings* that people have in responding to such power, and to the *ritual acts* by which people expressed their awe and respect in relation to such power. In every instance, as Wilfred Cantwell Smith points out, *religio* embraced the human capacity to perceive meaning and design in life, "to see, to feel, to act in terms of, a transcendent dimension."[19]

It is this latter quality—of seeing, of feeling, of acting, in a unified manner—that many boomers find missing in organized religion. Whatever *religio* might once have expressed, it does not always do it very well in a world that is very pluralistic, highly compartmentalized, and secular. Hence some of them do more than just drop out of the churches and synagogues; they turn to serious metaphysical quests on their own in hopes of finding a more fulfilling way of believing and living.

HIGHLY ACTIVE SEEKERS

Mollie is one such person. She numbers among a small but a very significant portion of the population: highly active seekers, or people for whom spiritual and metaphysical concerns are a driving force. These are people who are more than just interested in spirituality, or who might occasionally pick up a book on the subject: They are *deeply involved in their own personal quests.* For them, life is a journey, an adventure that leads to new discoveries, and to insights that can flow only from experience and autobiography. Journey implies a hope for the unity of things, for combining thought and feeling, doing and being, the inner and outer worlds. Journey conveys the notion of ongoing movement, or as Tex Sample says, "a living, moving, experiencing, feeling, deepening, growing search."[20]

A distinguishing feature is that these intense seekers prefer to think of themselves as "spiritual" rather than as "religious." They feel most acutely the tension that exists between spiritual experience and its expression in conventional religious forms. For such people organized religion can become, as the humanistic psychologist Abraham Maslow once said, "the major enemy of the religious experience and the religious experiencer." This happens, Maslow asserts, when "people lose or forget the subjectively religious experience, and redefine religion as a set of habits, behaviors, dogmas, forms, which at the extreme becomes entirely legalistic and bureaucratic, conventional, empty, and in the truest meaning of the word, antireligious."[21] Put simply, for such seekers deeply concerned with the experiential and the mystical, religious institutions can be stifling.

Mollie feels stifled by the religious. This comes through in a question asking about the meaning of the terms "religious" and "spiritual." Her responses reveal that the two have to do with quite differing identities:

INTERVIEWER: Religious and spiritual are two different things?

MOLLIE: Yes, they are. With religion you have to choose one, you have to be locked in, which I don't want to be.

INTERVIEWER: Is spiritual more open?

MOLLIE: Uh huh. It's like an individual definition of your relationship to God and nature and religion and family and humanity.

INTERVIEWER: And this allows you to draw from various sources and traditions, if it helps you in your relationship to God and the rest of humanity?

MOLLIE: Absolutely. In fact, there's so many great teachings in all the religions, how could you ever choose one or the other? I can't.

Following Mollie's lead, we have defined these highly active spiritual seekers on the basis of how they view themselves. In the survey we asked respondents, first, if they considered themselves in any way to be religious. We chose to keep the question open-ended, letting the respondents decide for themselves what the word "religious" might mean and if it appropriately described them. Eighty-six percent answered yes, 14% no. Of those who said no, we then asked the follow-up question: "Do you consider yourself to be a spiritual person?" Sixty-five percent of those who had rejected a religious identification said yes, they considered themselves "spiritual."

As shown in Figure 3.2, this group of intensely spiritual-minded people constitutes about 9% of the boomer population. Compared with others of their generation, they are older, more of them are white collar and professionals, and they are better educated. However, they earn less in their jobs and careers. More are female. Fewer are married. They are more liberal in political views. As we would expect, these seekers have low levels of institutional religious involvement.

Several features of this sociodemographic profile are worth noting. In some respects the seekers resemble those Yankelovich identified a decade ago who were greatly concerned about their personal self-fulfillment: the

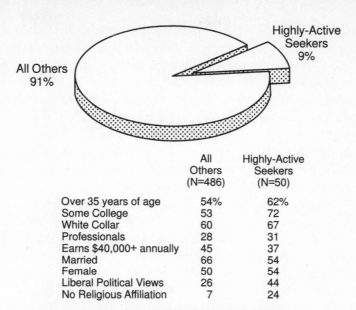

	All Others (N=486)	Highly-Active Seekers (N=50)
Over 35 years of age	54%	62%
Some College	53	72
White Collar	60	67
Professionals	28	31
Earns $40,000+ annually	45	37
Married	66	54
Female	50	54
Liberal Political Views	26	44
No Religious Affiliation	7	24

Figure 3.2 Spiritual Seekers

well-educated, upscale, liberal-minded professionals.[22] They are the spiritual counterparts to his more secular searchers. Preoccupation with self-fulfillment appears to have declined since then, but our seekers still express such concerns more so than others. For example, 32% of seekers as compared to 28% among all others, agreed with the statement, "I feel the need to find more excitement and sensation in my life," one of the items used in Yankelovich's research. Yet in other respects they differ. The seekers are now older, and somewhat different in lifestyle and outlook than the younger boomers who are more conservative politically and more traditionally religious. That they earn less than average income is telling: they are well-educated and liberal-minded, but not so upscale. They share an idealism and dreams of a more just and compassionate world but have not benefited economically as have many others of their generation. Many have scaled down their expectations and work in the lower-paying service professions such as teaching, nursing, social work, and counseling; some operate small businesses as artists or sell their crafts. Switching jobs and careers is fairly common. Some are like Alex, the suicide in *The Big Chill*, who "chose to experience life through a seemingly random series of occupations."

Beyond this basic profile, we inquired into their family and religious backgrounds and current social networks. Some have argued that a liberal family background was conducive to religious experimentation for those who grew up in the 1960s.[23] Nonreligious and very tolerant religious parents, the argument goes, generate a more open, exploratory approach to religion than conservatively religious parents. Permissive child-rearing patterns are said to encourage a more flexible, less traditional style of religious commitment. Dr. Benjamin Spock's influence especially has been singled out as contributing to more permissive child-rearing patterns for the baby-boom generation.

Our survey found support for the argument about liberal family backgrounds: Highly active seekers are more likely to come from homes where the parents attended religious services less frequently. Fifty-eight percent of seekers had mothers who attended religious services weekly, as compared with 67% of all others. Thirty-eight percent had fathers who attended weekly services, as compared with 50% of all others. Mollie Stone's own religious background is a case in point: Her parents were not very active in their local synagogue. These seekers come from all the major religious traditions. As to the child-rearing argument, there is even more convincing support. A majority (53%) of seekers described their upbringing as permissive, but only 29% of all others did so. They were less likely to have had close relationships with parents. One-half of them report a close relationship growing up with their mothers, and 19% with their fathers, as compared with 58% and 43% for all others, respectively.

As to social networks, seekers are more likely to be social isolates, or to have fewer strong social relationships. They have broken away from the churches and synagogues, an indication that they are not perhaps as socially anchored in their communities as are most other Americans. Conventional believers have their faiths reinforced through association with others of a similar outlook; but because seekers are more individualistic and eccentric in their beliefs, there is less reason for them to rely on the support of social networks. The lack of strong social ties is functional for them, freeing them to pursue their own personal spiritual journeys uninhibited by conventional sanctions. Again, Mollie Stone's experience is not that uncommon: She does not have many close friends or relatives who share her mystical views.

They also tend to have fewer friends who know one another, who live in the same area, who are from the same national or ethnic background, or who attend a church or synagogue regularly. Insofar as these are dimensions of social networks, such seekers consistently have fewer contacts. Perhaps the most telling question is the one that asks, "How many of your friends know each other?" Having friends who know one another implies greater density of relationships, that is, social interaction among them, and presumably greater reinforcement of worldview. On this crucial indicator, most Americans are four times as likely than the highly active seekers to say that "nearly all" or "most" their friends know each other (42% as compared to 10%). These people are, in fact, among the least socially embedded of any of the many constituencies—both religious and secular—that we looked at.

MYSTICAL RELIGION

What about the religious and spiritual characteristics of seekers? Do they fit the descriptions others have found? Years ago, Ernst Troeltsch spoke of "mystical religion," by which he referred to a type of religion with an emphasis on "direct, inward and present religious experience."[24] Troeltsch had in mind more than just the experiential aspect of religion, but rather a new, emerging form of religion with its own system of beliefs that was quite different from either the sectarian or churchly varieties of religion. In fact, Troeltsch envisioned this "third type" of religion as becoming increasingly common in the modern world because of its affinity with the trends toward greater individualism and personal autonomy.

Mysticism has several major characteristics. One is that union with God is possible through spiritual growth. This implies progression of the soul's relationship with the divine, or spiritual evolution, which is taken to be the proper goal of all such striving. A second characteristic is that religious experience is seen as an expression of a universal religious consciousness. Such experience leads to an acceptance of religious relativity and to the doctrine of polymorphism, or belief in the truth of all religions. Finally, religious and metaphysical ideas blend together in mysticism to form a monistic, or unified, worldview. Monistic orientations emphasize that there is one and only one ultimate absolute essence, which is the true nature of all apparently separate beings and things. Because of the rejection of dualism and of literal, cognitive truth in favor of experiential truth, syncretism of seemingly disparate religious and secular ideas is common. Grasping the meaning of life in intense "peak" or ecstatic experiences, mystics down through the centuries have appreciated symbol, myth, and fantasy because of their power of metaphoric interpretation.

Troeltsch argued that mystical religion is most likely to be found among the educated middle classes—those most likely to appreciate the freedom to interpret religious beliefs and symbols as they please. Individualism, personal development and self-fulfillment, and the pursuit of truth are all values of greater importance to the educated classes; they are also highly compatible with mystical religion. In comparison with either sectarian or church religion, mystical religion has to do with inner freedom and the experience and potential of the self rather than living by social convention or shared religious norms. The personal religious journey in pursuit of truth is seen as a worthy goal in itself, as more important than either affirming a particular creed or living by communal values. Hence mysticism is much more of a free-floating style of spirituality on the part of individuals and tends to lack strong communal or organizational expression.

Mystical religion does not easily lend itself to survey research, but we did ask one question we thought might be insightful to this type of consciousness. Respondents were asked if they agreed or disagreed with the statement, "People have God within them, so churches aren't really necessary." Right to the point, the question taps two views common to spiritual seekers: one, an immanent as opposed to a transcendent view of God; and two, an anti-institutional stance toward religion. As we expected to find, intense seekers are more likely than the rest of the population to believe that God is "within" us: Figure 3.3 shows that 60% of seekers view God in this mystical sense, whereas only 27% of the others do so. As expressed in its most radically individualistic form, God and self become one.

These mystics draw from a variety of religious traditions and are disproportionately inclined to believe in ghosts, in reincarnation, and in psychic powers. All of these phenomena appeal to experience and intuition—the bedrock upon which mystical New Age religion rests.[25] As Figure 3.3 shows, they are also more than twice as likely to practice meditation. A direct, intense personal experience is the common, underlying theme of these beliefs and practices. Unity arises not from the beliefs and practices themselves but out of the *experience* of them. As Robert Wuthnow has observed, the mystical experience takes on authority as the only "real" or reliable way to make sense out of one's world.[26] Like the visionary and the poet, the mystic does not discover the world, she *creates* it. For the mystic, Wuthnow goes on to point out, the very definition of reality itself is under human control: Through the mystical experience, order gets projected onto an otherwise incoherent reality. The emphasis is on transcending ordinary life and experiencing deeper, more meaningful levels of reality. Mystics live in this world of projected order and meaning, in which visions are not uncommon and voices are sometimes heard, a world that is as "real" to them as it is strange and alien to many others, to religionists and secularists alike.

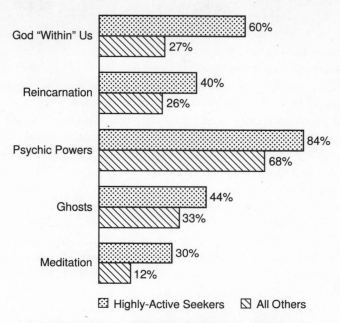

God "Within" Us — Highly-Active Seekers: 60%, All Others: 27%
Reincarnation — Highly-Active Seekers: 40%, All Others: 26%
Psychic Powers — Highly-Active Seekers: 84%, All Others: 68%
Ghosts — Highly-Active Seekers: 44%, All Others: 33%
Meditation — Highly-Active Seekers: 30%, All Others: 12%

⊞ Highly-Active Seekers   ◌ All Others

Figure 3.3 Highly Active Seekers: Beliefs and Practices

In keeping with their intensely personal approach to religion, mystics are prone to critical views about organized religion. In the survey seekers emphasized the importance of arriving at personal beliefs independently of churches and synagogues. They tend to view such institutions as having lost the real spiritual part of religion and to look on their rules of morality as too restrictive. Having a direct and inward experience of God, it follows that seekers would have deep existential concerns: They think more about questions of meaning and purpose in life and about why there is suffering in the world. They tend not to accept necessarily the answers as provided them by a particular faith or tradition. They dwell on fate and the dilemmas of life simply because their understandings of why life is as it is are rooted more in their own biographies and experiences than in any grand religious narrative that purports to provide answers for all times and in all places.

One feature that makes mystical religion attractive is its adaptability. It encourages not just religious syncretism, but also blends easily with secular systems of thought, including the arts, philosophy, and science. The mystical types in our survey are more likely than those who identify themselves as religious to endorse the view that "science may someday find answers that religion has long been concerned with" and to disagree with the statement, "Science and religion will always be in conflict." They are more inclined to hold to a scientific rather than a biblical view of creation. They are also more monistic, holding to a unified conception of reality. They are inclined toward a oneness with nature and the material world and to feel a sense of kinship with other species.

Today's seekers understand the forces governing their lives and shaping the world along the same lines as mystics always have. According to Troeltsch, Wuthnow, and others, they should be less likely to hold to a traditional theistic view of God, or supernatural forces, as influencing their lives, and more likely to advance social scientific or psychological explanations. For many college-educated men and women who grew up during the 1960s and 1970s, the languages of social forces and of self-exploration are very attractive and meaningful. These are modes of reality construction, or ways of understanding themselves in relation to the world around them, appropriate to contemporary life. And for such seekers this is quite common: They are much less likely to believe that a transcendent God shapes their lives, and more likely to point to people in power and new insights they have learned about themselves as influences. Mysticism finds easy compromise with contemporary culture, especially the scientific and therapeutic cultures, which adds to its appeal for many boomers alienated from the religious establishment.

THE WEAKNESSES OF MYSTICISM

Yet for all its positive affinities with contemporary life, mysticism has some weaknesses. One is its difficulty to sustain. A mystical meaning system requires one after another confirming experience, since it derives not from historical traditions so much as from a mental or spiritual conception of life. Mollie knows fully well this problem: She works hard at creating new experiences that build on what she already believes. Power lies in the visual image of how her inner and outer worlds connect; visualizing how they connect is the way to her felt realization of the higher self. In keeping with the shamans of earlier times, hers is a pilgrimage of the visual—a "homestead of the mind"[27]—that draws from the resources of her mental and emotional faculties. Mystical visions help to sustain a particular metaphysics, and thus have the power to transform life; but because of their fleeting and transitory character, the realities, and any transformations that flow from them, suffer from the lack of a strong social base.

Mysticism naturally resists an institutional structure, and so is not easily passed on from one generation to the next. It lacks shared rituals, an affirming community, a sense of belonging. Mollie knows this problem, too: She worries that her children may suffer from a lack of commitment, that they will not fully understand the teachings she would like them to know about. She works at finding ways for her children to participate in the ritual sweat lodges. She wants them to know about Jewish and Native American beliefs. But this is not easily accomplished outside of formal structures. There are limits to what she knows and can teach her children; and despite her genuine enthusiasm, she can never fully convey her experiences, feelings, and excitement to her children. Without ongoing rituals and a strong communal base, she is always "working at" how to make it all real within the family. Many boomers outside of organized religion expressed similar frustrations about how to bring up their children with moral and religious values, a frustration often intensified by their own lack of understanding of religious teachings.

Yet another weakness of mysticism is its incoherence. Mollie knows of the unity she wants in her life, but it does not come easily; indeed, much of her frustration lies in her inability to arrive at a sustained and coherent worldview. Getting the inner and outer worlds together poses problems, especially when she tries to integrate so many differing religious and spiritual teachings. She holds out strong hope for a holistic vision and experience she feels is possible, and that she feels she once had in her earlier years. This concern for balance is reflected in the direction her spiritual quests are taking at present—in her conscious and deliberate effort at combining Native American meditations and rituals with occasional visits to Quaker gatherings. The two groups are not all that different from one another in some respects. What fascinates Mollie about them and about some other groups, including Orthodox Jews, is that they have rituals that, as she says, establish "clear connections" and "create a kind of feeling around commitment to that belief system." It is how people *practice* a faith, or the links between beliefs and all of life, giving religion the force of a commitment, that most interests her.

Like many boomers, she would like a more stable set of family religious rituals, yet hasn't found the connections, the feelings, the commitment she is looking for. How can she commit herself if she doesn't feel that a particular religion pulls it all together as she would like? She has grown in her journey, but her quest is still incomplete. She wants very much to reclaim her Jewish heritage and bring it into her spiritual orbit. If only she could find a satisfactory alternative Jewish celebration, maybe her spiritual quest might be finally resolved. But try as she may, Mollie seems unable to get it together; her expectations of an alternative Jewish group and its accommodation to her highly syncretistic spiritualities are not easily met. Her dream of an encompassing vision giving her life a sense of unity has not been fulfilled; when she speaks of what gives her life the greatest meaning, she resorts to the language of "spiritual connections" and of "pieces" that fit into a larger puzzle. She's a *bricoleur*,[28] one who tries to piece together a religious outlook and set of practices, yet with only limited success. Life for her remains a quandary, her quest unfulfilled.

To be sure, Mollie would not trade her quest for easy answers. Like many others of her generation, she is too much caught up in her ambivalence and alienation to ever find a comfortable home within organized religion. But she longs for more of a religious home than she has. For all the celebration of freedom and journey, she would like something more in the way of a group experience and affirmation of spiritual roots than she now has. So let us turn next to the opposite end of the religious continuum—to a "homestead of traditional faith"—to see what that experience is like for many boomers today. For only by exploring this other homestead can we begin to understand how the 1960s and 1970s have given us spiritual journeys for boomers that are so different from one another, and yet so similar.

CHAPTER 4

Walking with the Lord

If the 1960s had produced a spiritu-
ality only of the sort Mollie Stone represents, our task of describing it
would be fairly simple. Mystical expansiveness and journey theology
would be the themes to explore; the flight into self would make for the
dominant motif. But religious countermovements and a resurgence of
traditional faith and lifestyles were as much a part of that era as were the
mystical quests. Indeed, the hold of traditional religious culture on the
boomer population should not be underestimated. As we have already
seen in chapter 2, a majority of the men and women who grew up during
that period were *not* that heavily involved in the youth counterculture.
These more traditional youth did not embrace values and lifestyles in the
way that the popular imagery of a generation enveloped by "sex, drugs,
and rock-and-roll" might lead us to expect; instead, their lives reveal a
much richer diversity of moral values and cultural experience. And the
same holds with their spiritual styles.

Consider Linda Kramer, the born-again Christian living in Ohio. Her
firm faith and solid midwestern moral values are a stark contrast to
Mollie's eclecticism. Linda grew up in a Christian home, in a family
that "loved the Lord and worshiped regularly." She did not rebel against
her parents. She did not drop out of church as a teenager. She has been
a committed church member throughout her life—so committed that she

would find it hard to imagine being anything other than a Bible-believing Christian. Growing up in a small town in Ohio, she wasn't exposed in so direct a way to the youth values as was Mollie, despite the fact she was a member of the "class of '65"—the celebrated high school class that was supposedly the embodiment of the trends of that era.

But Linda, too, is a product of the sixties: Her view of the world, her worries about moral decline in the country, her concerns for family life, even her sense of self, all bear the marks of her years growing up. She defines herself and her world largely in opposition to the moral and cultural changes of that era. She was a young adult when the so-called New Christian Right burst onto the scene with its attack on secular humanism and liberal Christianity. The moral relativism and permissiveness arising out of that era in great part inspired the conservative religious response. It was an era of too much choice in morals and lifestyles, as many came to think. To evangelicals and fundamentalists at the time, the great social ills—easy abortions, pornography, homosexuality, a rising divorce rate, the seeming collapse of the traditional family, godlessness in the schools—were all signs of moral decay, and reason enough to mobilize a campaign to return America to its Protestant religious roots. They were determined to tell another "story" of America from that being told by liberals, radicals, and secularists.

Linda's conservative religious views mark her as someone who still understands herself as set apart—from both the secular world and other, more liberal Christian believers. She makes no apology for her faith, even though, as she says, "It's not a nice name any more, being a fundamental evangelical Christian, because of the televangelist scandals." A religious conservative she is, yet she is also an interesting mix of old and new religious themes. There is enough of the old to anchor her solidly in a religious past, and just enough of the sixties' experience to distinguish her from a previous generation of religious conservatives.

In this chapter we explore Linda's world and its meanings as another version of the sixties' experience, one quite different from Mollie Stone's. What is the attraction of evangelical and fundamentalist faiths to many boomers today? How is this generation's experience reshaping these faiths? These questions will take us into more familiar terrains of American religion than did Mollie's quests. As popular religious types, fundamentalists, evangelicals, and charismatics are better known than spiritual seekers. Yet we must be careful with old typecasts and stereotypes, for, as we shall see, Linda's religious world is in some ways not quite what we might expect.

FINDING SHELTER

Linda's own self-descriptions tell us a lot about her. She speaks of being "sheltered" from the 1960s—by which she means she wasn't into drugs and sex or experimenting with the new lifestyles of the period. She attended a two-year business college after high school and was never greatly exposed to the student subculture. More than simply a way of describing her upbringing, "shelter" takes on metaphorical significance in how she sees herself and her life unfolding as an adult. It is a crucial theme for many rightward-leaning evangelical boomers whose faith took shape during these crucial years: in its emphasis on human nature as sinful, in a strong faith in a personal, transcendent God as radically "other" from society, and in a view of the church as a warm, supportive place over against a world that is very dangerous and corrupt. Shelter conveys notions of escape, retreat, sanctuary, withdrawal—as a character type, Linda is psychologist Carol S. Pearson's archetype of the "orphan" in a fallen world.[1]

Leaving the small town for the city was for her a big move. It was something like her own personal Exodus—out of a land of innocence and into a sinful world. If, as has been argued, conservative faiths thrive at the intersections where tradition and modernity meet rather than in intact stable settings, then Linda's is a case in point.[2] For when she moved to the city, she became aware of just how much she needed a strong personal faith. It was then that she realized that religion ought to be more than a "rote thing," more than just a habit of going to church or casually saying you believe in God. She wanted a church that is alive and people who are deeply committed to God. As she came to believe, a Christian is caught up in a battle with Satan on one side and God on the other; a person cannot simply stand on the sidelines, but must join God's team and stand up for what is right. Heaven awaits those who do, and damnation those who don't. Her views were forged out of the chaos and confrontation of the times: of political assassinations, riots, hippies, cults, Vietnam, Watergate, the women's movement, the gay rights movement. These events and developments pushed her to look for continuity amidst all the change, for a faith shaped in opposition to so much that was happening around her.

Today Linda's life is anchored in a huge suburban megachurch. She finds comfort in this large faith community and its encompassing canopy of supportive beliefs and moral values, all enmeshed in an extended web of social relationships. To the extent possible, contemporary religious conservatism creates it own insulated world in which believers can live. Social networks invested with a great deal of religious meaning fan out from the local congregation—including family and kin, schools, friendships, and special interest groups. Consequently, Linda puts much of her energy into her marriage and raising her children in a Christian home; she prefers friends who are committed Christians; she finds much personal support in small-group activities at her church; she relies upon and benefits from the larger network of fundamentalist and evangelical teachings as found in Christian books, recordings, videos, and popular radio and television programs.

Like Pilgrim in John Bunyan's narrative, she sees herself on a path that calls for steadfast devotion amidst many twists and turns along the way. Life is a journey in which one must constantly work at strengthening faith through prayer and Bible study, or as born-again Christians say, "walking with the Lord," or "walking the Christian walk." This walk involves submitting one's life to Christ and cultivating Christ-like virtues, such as love, humility, patience, and forgiveness. In addition, there are the biblical injunctions to refrain from the works of the flesh, such as uncleanness, adultery, idolatry, drunkenness, and the like. At the center of this worldview is an unfaltering belief that Jesus Christ was sent by God to save the world and that salvation is possible only through him. Linda is not all that unusual in the belief: 60% of all boomers in our survey speak of Jesus not just as a great teacher or spiritual example, but as the Savior who brings salvation and makes possible a right relationship with God.

MAINTAINING BOUNDARIES

Having a "right relationship" with God is a phrase that is used a lot among conservative boomers. We heard it from evangelicals, fundamentalists, charismatics, and especially from those in the holiness tradition. The assumption is that if a person has a right relationship with God, then all else falls into place. This is a crucial aspect of the conservative Christian worldview, a foundation on which a total vision of reality becomes possible. Life is viewed as a series of concentric circles, with a person's own relationship with God at the center and expanding outward—to family, to church, to others. "Everything else I do is based on that," commented an electrical engineer who is a Nazarene.

To have a right relationship, the self must be disciplined and controlled. Without some strictures on the will and the self, a person is prone to obey his or her own interests and desires and to disobey God's rules.

Among the many brands of evangelicals, fundamentalists, and charismatics, one hears many expressions such as "dying to self," "knowing the Lord," and "following the Holy Spirit." They focus much energy on keeping relationships with God alive and on restoring them if threatened, and on helping people to grow in their understanding of themselves and of faith. Small groups that constitute a "meta-church" are thriving in Linda's church as they are in conservative churches across the country. Not just for Bible study and prayer, but new types of groups—often based on Twelve-Step recovery models—have mushroomed in the churches, in response to the growing self-help movement and its emphasis on helping people to deal with their feelings, fears, and frustrations. The video revolution has played a big part as well, providing cassettes on cultivating the Christian life and on how to "recover" from and deal with a variety of pains, losses, sufferings, and addictions.

The language about "dying to self" and "knowing the Lord" does more than nurture a religious identity, it helps to define and maintain cultural boundaries. In a world where there are so many choices, clear-cut boundaries are essential to the everyday practice of faith. Linda, for example, relies on a widely used aphorism for describing her relationship with God. "The basis of sin in our world is really the self," she says. "I learned an acronym quite a few years ago—JOY, which means Jesus, Others, You. And if you put them in that order, your life will work out." Making use of the JOY formula, she draws a distinction between believers and those who "just live for self, whatever will gratify them, whatever material possessions will make them feel good and not concerned about others." She is quick to make judgments about the self-indulging, materialistic trends of contemporary culture. She speaks very passionately about how self-centered and status-conscious people have become, yet ironically, she too is caught up in the same culture. She drives a new station wagon and looks forward to the time when the family can move into a nicer home. She worries about whether her children will "make it" in school. Despite the rhetoric of separation, she and other conservative boomers make accommodations to the larger culture all the time, though they do not think of them in this way.

KNOWING WHAT IS RIGHT

Setting boundaries, even if they are arbitrary, can have powerful psychological effects. Life in a large city exposed Linda to a world of religious and cultural pluralism on a scale she had not known before and brought home to her how people must be self-consciously committed to their beliefs. In a world threatened by disbelief, strange new cults, and lifestyles that were at odds with her morals, there seemed to be only one proper response on her part—to affirm all the more her Christian faith. Unlike those who found the questioning of old faiths and ideologies appealing and who welcomed the rise of new religions, her reaction was to guard against any watering-down of her faith. This was her response back in the early 1970s, when she saw how college students in those days lived, and it has been her stance ever since.

For Linda, and for many rightward-leaning evangelical Christians, it is a tenet of faith that by reading the Bible, you will be led to "know" what is morally right. Right and wrong are established in God's Word, and through the Holy Spirit's dealings with individuals, people can "know" what is right. Even on an issue like abortion, she is confident that the scripture makes clear its support for a right-to-life position. This type of knowing is far different from the moral relativism of contemporary America, which encourages individuals to base their actions on utilitarian motives and personal preferences. For a woman "just to think that she is in control of her own body and not to consider the life within her" is, in Linda's judgment, a wrong decision. What is wrong is that a woman is making a decision on the basis of her own individual interests, and not out of concern for life, which ought to be recognized as wrong according to God's truth. Nor are a person's own preferences or wishes sufficient. There must be some external authority in moral matters, otherwise people will act in accordance simply with their feelings— especially in a highly individualistic and subjectivist culture. The excesses of the sixties serve in this respect as a backdrop, reminding Linda and others like her how easy it would be, and how potentially dangerous, to fall back on the maxim right out of the hippie culture: "If it feels good, do it."

Yet there is tension arising out of this basis of morality, felt especially among religious boomers. Officially, religious truth is for conservatives Bible-based, Christ-centered, and Spirit-controlled, which amounts to a trinity of checks over against the current emphasis on the individual's freedom in making moral decisions; but the culture of choice and expressive individualism is deeply ingrained in all realms of contemporary life and affects how people think about moral and religious matters, even the discerning of divine will. The sixties forced the question of making moral decisions. Many in Linda's generation have come away firmly committed to believing that there are absolute standards that can be known; yet others, including some born-again Christians, perhaps wish there were such standards but are unsure or not fully convinced that they exist. This erosion of moral absolutism resting on a literal rendering of the Bible comes through in the ponderings of a Southern Baptist woman from North Carolina:

> I think if you study the Bible and you pray and you are in tune, you instinctively know what's right for you. I am not the kind of person that can excuse everything that everybody says was right for them. I don't believe that. I think a lot of people are just using that for an excuse, but I don't know.

Knowing and feeling that you are right provide justifications for withdrawing from the world. Some of the conservative Christians we talked to voiced a connection between knowing what is right and avoiding temptations. Linda's feeling "lucky not to have been involved in drugs" is perhaps her way of giving God the credit. Others we talked to were more direct in attributing to God the fact that they got through the sixties unscathed. A Lutheran woman in Ohio put it this way:

> Oh I was exposed to everything . . . We had the Moonies and the Hare Krishnas. I mean I was around everything. . . . I think God had his hand on me, because I could have very easily got involved in all this other stuff and I didn't. It's like I knew that I had to stay away from it. That it wasn't right.

"THERE NEVER WILL BE ANOTHER EDEN"

Linda, and many others who share her religious views, have a strong sense that many things in the country are not right these days. America was once strong and inherently good, and now they are not so sure. Some express fear that the nation is, as Linda says, in a "downward spiral," which conjures up apocalyptic imagery; but most simply voice great concern about what they see happening around them. The fundamental problem, as Linda sees it, is that the country has abandoned its covenant with God. To live for self is to abandon responsibility for others and to forget our relationship as a people with God. We cannot be a good and strong country, she insists, unless as a people we get back to the fundamentals of faith. Few of the people we talked to actually mentioned the covenant narrative—some possibly because they could not articulate it very well, but most probably because they do not think in such terms. When we probed to learn more about people's fears and concerns, we found that usually they had in mind declining moral values: easily obtainable abortions, the threat of drugs, secularism in the schools, pornography, the breakdown of the family. While born-again evangelicals, fundamentalists, and people in the holiness tradition are the most upset, the uneasiness about the nation's moral fiber is felt much more broadly: 70% of all the boomers we surveyed said they favor a "return to stricter moral standards."

What it means to "return to stricter moral standards" is not always clear, but it is often a way to express alarm about two basic institutions in society: the family and the school. Divorce, infidelity, casual sexual relationships, women pursuing careers that take them away from husbands and young children—the stuff of television soap operas—are regarded as symptoms of a decadent moral order. They are signs, as many born-again Christians see it, not just of a society in trouble, but of the more basic problem that homes are not structured around Christian principles. The family is the fundamental unit of society. If religious teachings fail to take root there, they cannot extend to the larger society; and then there will be no way to demonstrate to the world that God's way is best. Families are the arenas where rules of biblical authority are instituted and the Christian life lived out—a model of society itself. Hence the great concerns about the breakup of families and of what is happening to children.

Many feel that television is a major culprit. To conservatives, television threatens the family in its portrayal of casual sex and unmarried couples living together. Because of its massive influence on our lives, it is seen as the source of much that is unwholesome and degrading. In the eyes of some, it is Satan's way of leading people astray. As a woman in a holiness church in Denver said about television commercials:

> It's not ever selling what it is supposed to be selling. If it's a car, there's a beautiful girl by the car, in a bikini . . . that's right, on top of it, lying all over it. And they show her more than they show the car. So every sixteen-year-old kid thinks that if you buy a Camaro, there will be a beautiful girl lying on top of the car! . . . I think all of us would agree that it is just Satan's way of getting into the core of the family. He's pulling it down, eating away, just like those commercials with sexual innuendoes, it's just sex, sex, sex . . .

In her religious tradition, many believers—even boomers—still do not go to movies because of their secular influence. When VCRs first became available, they had welcomed getting rental movies, since they could monitor what movies were brought into their homes. But now that has become, as she says, "a little bit muddier" because one cannot be sure about the ratings—"What used to be R-rated is now PG, and what used to be PG is now G"—and even if parents object to showing them, children can always find a friend who will.

At the core of the problem, as many believers see it, is a crisis of commitment: People do not take seriously their vows, their duties and obligations—to others and to God. Commitment involves more than simply love, and certainly more than romantic feelings, a sense of happiness, or personal preference. For religious conservatives, commitment arises ultimately out of obedience to God's authority; in our highly individualistic, self-obsessed culture, anything less is to run the risk that the emotional elements in marriage and family relationships will predominate. Linda herself makes this point in a comment about a television game show she had recently watched. A seventeen-year-old whose grandparents had just had their fiftieth wedding anniversary was asked if she thought when she got married that she might be married for that long. "Well, I doubt it," she said, "but maybe as long as I love him." Recognizing that a relationship based on commitment is not the same as one based simply on the drift of a person's feelings, Linda paused for a moment, shaking her head. Then, speaking from her conviction and experience, she said: "Love might not last very long."

The crisis of commitment has to do not just with the family, but also with the changing environment of the public schools. Many boomer parents remember that when they were in school, often there had been school prayers and religious observances—activities that became less common in the 1970s and 1980s. During these same years, science education, evolution, and sex education all received greater attention. To many this shift, combined with a growing emphasis on human reason and value neutrality in the classroom, appeared to be a sell-out to "secular humanism" and an abandonment of a historic religious heritage; the only solution was to take charge of education, and to put God back in the schools. Hence the phenomenal growth in the past two decades of both Christian schools and the home schooling movement.[3] Both developments point to the immense dissatisfaction many parents feel about what they see as the overtly antireligious ethos in the public schools, and the great lengths to which they are willing to go to give their children what they feel they should have: a religious environment and a return to the basics.

Linda's two children are in the Christian school at her church. Here, as in many such schools, the emphasis is undeniably spiritual and the parent-student handbook makes clear its mission: to put "God and His Holy Word at the center of the educational program." Along with reading and math skills, the program stresses discipline, hard work, and character-building virtues; students will be penalized for "disrespect to teacher, unclean life, disrespect to others, and fighting." Students are taught their academic subjects, but they also get what many evangelicals and fundamentalists are most concerned about: an understanding of American life and history in keeping with their beliefs, and appreciation for traditional values in the realms of gender and sexuality. Another born-again Christian from the Buckeye State, who has put her daughter into a Christian school, puts it this way:

> . . . it bothers me what they are teaching the kids in school. . . . They are changing history around. This country was founded on God. The people that came and founded this country were Godly people, and they have totally taken that out of history. They are trying to get rid of everything that even says anything about God to please someone who is offended by it. That bothers me. They are teaching the kids sex education at too early an age. They know too much. If they have all that on their minds all the time, they are going to get into trouble.

Many of the people we interviewed expressed, both in their comments and the tone of voice, a great longing to return to an American past—real or imagined—when life seemed to hang together better. They too are seekers, hoping for a world founded on common convictions. Yet a huge psychic gap exists between the realities of life in today's world and the idealized, nostalgic Norman Rockwell image of America—of small-town life and Sunday schools, of children sitting attentively in school, of families holding hands around the dinner table saying grace. There are many social-psychological mechanisms for dealing with the disparities between illusion and reality, one of which is to exalt the inner religious life as a means of justifying the rejection of the outer world as it is.[4] Psychological feelings of salvation and the satisfaction of knowing that one is following the Lord get raised to an even higher level of salience. This is the case with Linda, who takes a great deal of refuge in her feelings, and who is easily overtaken by her emotions. She becomes very nostalgic even thinking about growing up in her little town, of having attended a high school with only forty members in her senior class, and of her close relations with parents and sisters. Looking back on that setting, she sees it almost as a model of how God would want us to live. She wishes so much that she could hold on to that world today, and better still, recreate it for her children; but reality breaks through on occasion, as, for example, when she acknowledges, with a touch of sadness, "There never will be another Eden."

EVANGELICALS AND FUNDAMENTALISTS

Like one-third of the people in our survey, Linda identifies herself as a "born-again" Christian. She speaks of herself as "evangelical" and "fundamental," quite comfortable with both terms. Most fundamentalists are evangelicals, but there are differences. Fundamentalists are less accommodating in their stance toward the world, more rigid in their views on scripture, and often hold to a dispensational premillennialism, or the belief that Christ will soon return to "rapture" those who are saved before the world undergoes a great "tribulation."[5] Evangelicals come in many stripes; most are on the cultural right or centrist in beliefs and values, but a few are on the ideological left.[6] They are united in their conviction that they have something to proclaim that the world needs. Linda's emphasis on the literal meaning of the scriptures and her separatist posture toward the world are distinctly fundamentalist, yet in other ways she is more accommodating in her stance. All things considered, she might be thought of as a moderately conservative evangelical.

To get an estimate of how many of the born-again boomers lean toward fundamentalist beliefs, we created an index using items from the survey: the question about being "born-again"; whether the Bible is "to be taken literally, word for word"; acceptance of the biblical view of creation as opposed to an evolutionist conception; a strong theistic conception of the world; and agreement that "temptations are the work of the devil."[7] Only those of Christian background were scored on the index. Roughly one-third (38%) agreed with all the items, and therefore fit our definition of a religious conservative. Others who reported being "born again" or having had a "born-again" experience, but who rejected either one or more of the other items, are referred to as moderates (see Figure 4.1). By these definitions, the boomer population generally breaks down as follows: 13% fundamentalist-leaning, 21% evangelical moderates, and all others 66%. This breakdown is not all that different than for the population in the country as a whole today.[8]

Socially and demographically, there are some striking differences—both between the conservatives and moderates, and between "born-again Christians" and the rest of the boomer population. Figure 4.1 shows that the conservatives are slightly older than either the moderates

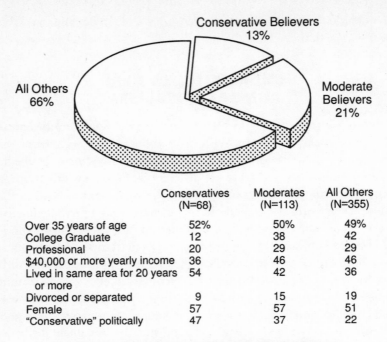

	Conservatives (N=68)	Moderates (N=113)	All Others (N=355)
Over 35 years of age	52%	50%	49%
College Graduate	12	38	42
Professional	20	29	29
$40,000 or more yearly income	36	46	46
Lived in same area for 20 years or more	54	42	36
Divorced or separated	9	15	19
Female	57	57	51
"Conservative" politically	47	37	22

Figure 4.1 Born-Again Christians

or others of their generation. They are far less likely to have a college education and to be employed as professionals. They earn less income on the average. They are geographically less mobile, more deeply rooted in the communities where they live. Far fewer are divorced or separated than for moderates or others. Well over half are women, which is the same as for moderates, and more so than for the rest of the boomer population. Considerably more report themselves as politically "conservative" or "extremely conservative." Evangelical moderates, in contrast, are much more similar to the nonevangelical population on many profile characteristics: in the proportion who are college graduates, professionals, mobile, who come from broken families and are single parents, and in income levels. On several characteristics they are more similar to the more conservative fundamentalists: in the numbers of women who are participants and of those identifying as politically conservative.

The profile for boomer religious conservatives, then, is decidedly middle American. Despite low levels of education and occupational standing among fundamentalists, great numbers of them are concentrated in the managerial and small business sectors and are by no means economically marginal or disprivileged. Evangelical moderates enjoy considerable status and earning power, now matching if not exceeding nonevangelicals in gaining managerial, administrative, and professional occupations. This upward shift in education and socioeconomic standing for religious conservatives is a post-World War II phenomenon, and largely a generational change. Young Protestant conservatives, even more so than Roman Catholics, have experienced a remarkably high level of social mobility during this period, moving from rural areas and small towns to cities and into middle- and lower-middle occupations that would have been undreamed of by their parents. Many grew up in what were called the "churches of the disinherited," located on the fringes of middle-class society, but have now moved into churches that are up-town or in the suburbs.

Thus during the years in which the boomers grew up, a major shift in the social basis of religious conservatism occurred—away from a marginal to a more mainstream position. The claims on status and lifestyle of this younger, more affluent generation are buttressed by symbols of community and family, symbols that have taken on increased significance as its members have grown older, settled into married life, and are raising children, and as their own faiths have come to enjoy more influence and respectability. Much has happened in just about every way conceivable—socially, culturally, politically—since the days when H. L. Mencken portrayed them as "yokels" and "halfwits."

THE NEW EVANGELICALISM

A shift in social location has brought about more accommodating religious beliefs and cultural attitudes. Rapid social change forces new alignments of religion and culture, and for individuals often generates ambiguities and inconsistencies in their beliefs. Linda Kramer's own religious views point to ambiguities, some deeply rooted in the conservative Protestant heritage, and others, as we shall soon see, of more recent vintage. To grasp more fully the attraction of religious conservatism to the boomer generation, we ought not assume too great an internal consistency in people's meaning systems. Evangelical and especially fundamentalist worldviews are anything but tightly integrated dogmatic systems; in fact, as one writer recently put it, they are a "hodge-podge of rather loosely coupled, and even discrete, statements or tenets."[9]

Protestant conservatism, as a worldview and in its relations with modern culture, has historically been riddled with inconsistencies; as George M. Marsden puts it, it is a religious heritage "fraught with paradoxes that have made it sociologically mystifying."[10] Whether to be politically and culturally active or not, to be intellectually oriented or anti-intellectual, to appeal to the subjective feelings or to the rational mind, to stress individualism or community—all are ambiguities that have long characterized religious conservatism, as Marsden describes. With its roots both within Calvinism and in the Enlightenment, the conservative religious heritage is really more an amalgamation of ideas and notions than a coherent set of religious doctrines. The Puritan heritage itself left a dual legacy of a theocratic tradition concerned with upholding culture-dominating ideals as well as a concern for personal salvation. Conservative religious thought rests on the philosophical assumptions of the early modern era, with an emphasis on sure foundations and the certainty of truth, giving it something of a modernist style; yet when combined with biblicism, such a worldview has easily taken on a defensive pre-Darwinian posture over against modern scientific thought. Pulled in many directions, conservative faith has proven to be enormously adaptable, which perhaps accounts for its staying power on the American scene.

As early as the 1940s, a "new evangelical" movement emerged that sought to reform fundamentalist thought, to move away from separatist and dispensationalist thinking, and to modify its anticultural stance. But it was not really until the late 1960s and 1970s that this new movement—evangelicalism in a broader sense—really took off. One reason was the social and cultural shift already discussed. Upward social mobility brought with it a greater accommodation. Religion, if it was to be meaningful, had to appeal to popular culture. An "otherworldly" and pessimistic stance had to give way to a faith concerned with the day-to-day living; literalism was but one of several possible ways to interpret the Bible. Far better than dogmatic exclusivism was an expressive faith and an encompassing, therapeutic approach to the needs of a more educated, upwardly mobile, and career-oriented constituency. Expressive faith was not to be limited to minorities and working-class whites; speaking in tongues, healing, and prophecy could—and did—find their way, in new forms, into the Protestant mainstream and even into Catholicism. "So, in the matter of a few decades," as Richard Quebedeaux writes, "the 'holy rollers' on the margins of society had become the 'new charismatics' at top, people like Ruth Carter Stapleton, Bob Dylan [briefly], and Efrem Zimbalist, Jr."[11]

A second reason had to do more directly with the climate of the times. The new evangelicalism actually benefited from the upheavals of the sixties in paradoxical ways.[12] On the one hand, the new evangelicalism profited from the decline of the liberal-scientific-secular establishment. Questions raised about old values and beliefs encouraged personal quests for solid foundations of belief and action, a basis on which to build a life. With rational and technological values under attack, many youth on college campuses turned to evangelical faiths. Organizations like Campus Crusade for Christ and Inter-Varsity Christian Fellowship (IVCF) capitalized on the mood of the times, making use of sixties' music and art, organizing Bible study and explorer groups, and by casting the faith in terms that students could relate to. As one young woman said of the IVCF during her college days at the University of Virginia: "They really answered, or tried to answer, a lot of intellectual questions and spoke to the place where most college students were." In so doing such organizations contributed significantly to evangelical growth among college-educated youth during the 1970s.

The impact of evangelical organizations on college youth during these years was greater than often realized. Many students from mainline Protestant, Catholic, and even Jewish backgrounds were confronted with evangelical teachings. Though a good number rejected the teachings, they had an influence on many. It was the first time they had heard evangelical faith presented to them in an articulate manner by college-educated religious leaders. One person we talked to, who had been raised Catholic, told about how during her college years her religious life was divided three ways: at the Newman Center (Catholic) for Sunday Mass, at Young Life (evangelical) on Sunday nights, and at the Presbyterian University Ministry on Tuesday nights. Presbyterianism finally won out after graduation, but she credits the evangelical ministry with forcing her to think through what she believed and to arrive at her own faith perspective. Probably more college-educated boomers had experiences similar to this than is generally recognized—which amounts to a subtle impact of evangelicalism even on those who reject its tenets.

On the other hand, the conservative faiths benefited from the attacks on the youth counterculture. An increase in the numbers of unmarried people living together and outspokenness about gay and lesbian lifestyles, combined with record levels of divorce and changing gender roles, all prompted reactions calling for a return to traditional values.[13] For working-class and lower middle-class Americans especially, the "new morality" was an outrage and a rejection of a way of life that many were prepared to fight for in the name of God. During the Vietnam era, protests against the war and attacks on the nation produced still another response—an outpouring of patriotic sentiment, often in the form of highly charged, flag-waving evangelical rallies. These years were, as one writer put it, a battle waged between people committed to freedom and those committed to virtue.[14]

But there was no full consensus on virtue, even among born-again Christians. The Jesus Movement of young, college-educated believers accommodated revivalistic Christianity even further by redefining "sin"—by playing down the importance of old taboos against drinking alcohol, dancing, card-playing, and the like, and by calling attention to injustice, militarism, racism, sexism, and the abuses of capitalism and multinational corporations. Though it was only a small segment of the "new evangelicalism," this movement, along with secular trends, helped shape a changing generational ethos, or new normative standards of what is acceptable behavior. Even for born-again Christians, the shift in moral values was in some ways very dramatic. Sanctions against playing cards, social dancing, going to movies, and drinking alcohol all greatly declined for boomers among born-again Christians as well as others. Even in the realm of sexuality, a stronghold of Protestant moral purism, there were some significant generational changes despite much rhetoric otherwise.[15] But in no realm have the changes been greater than in Sabbath observance. Sunday sports on television, the rise of shopping malls with stores open and movies shown on Sundays, and a growing sense among Americans of the weekend as private time for family and leisure activities all contributed to a reorienting of Sunday activities. In our own survey, only 6% of born-again Christians, and 2% of the remainder of the boomer population generally felt that "going to the movies on the Sabbath" was wrong.

THE CONCEPTION OF SELF

Perhaps the greatest, and also the most subtle, change of all for born-again Christians of this generation lies in the realm of the self—in the way individuals view themselves. As we have seen earlier, there is a fundamental conflict between the God-centered conception of self that many religious conservatives hold on to, and the American-style individualism that fosters greater choice and subjectivity. Conservative Christians, of course, claim to abhor the kind of individualism that presumes free choice and freedom from obligation, and which is so widespread in American culture. To their way of thinking, it represents a serious distortion of God's laws and shows just how far secular humanism has taken us. As one evangelical Christian said: "Right and wrong is right out the window. Everything is a choice."

Linda Kramer speaks out of a similar framework when she says a "moral basis" in life is essential, or else people will simply "live for self" and "not be concerned about others." Enough of the residues of the old Protestant ethic of self-denial still exist to make evangelicals cringe at how self-preoccupied and self-interested the world has become. And yet, often without realizing it, religious conservatives accommodate in countless ways to the cultural individualism they so fervently abhor. The God-centered individualism they endorse and the American-style individualism they reject easily mesh to such a degree that the two strands often become unrecognizable. Even the JOY formula (Jesus, Others, You) that Linda and other evangelicals hold to so dearly is itself geared toward self-fulfillment: By keeping one's priorities properly ordered, one will have a better life. Materialism, competition, achievement, and success—to cite the dominant secular, individualistic values of America—create the context in which evangelicals, like all others, form their beliefs, attitudes, and overarching definitions of reality. Evangelicals, of course, often oppose these values as secular and corrupting influences, yet one of the marks of the "new evangelism" is its accommodation to secular individualistic values.

This mix of religious and secular themes comes through in several ways with Linda, one being the way in which she sees her church. Clearly, she is very committed to her church and deeply anchored in a community of faith—more so that most of the people we interviewed. Yet despite all the talk about a covenental relationship between God and the faithful, and its stress upon duty and obligation, she does not use this biblical language in talking about church. When asked about why she goes to church, or if one should go in order to be religious, she replies:

> You don't have to go to church. I think the reason I do is because it helps me to grow. It's especially good for my family, to teach them the good and moral things. To see that families can operate as a unit.

At one level, Linda's response is quite predictable. Americans tend to see religion as something deeply personal, as prior to and over against any kind of organizational involvement. The self is real in a way that social institutions are not, the latter viewed simply as nominalistic gatherings of individuals. The emphasis on personal faith, salvation, and walking with the Lord virtually assures this kind of ontological individualism. Her way of speaking reveals more than this, however, in its distinctly utilitarian and psychological tones. Church is good because it *does* something: It helps the family by teaching moral values and by binding them together. This view is not too surprising, given her great concern about family life and her fears about her son getting involved in drugs, but it does signal a strong instrumental approach to thinking about religion in people's lives. The comments about herself are even more revealing. She goes to church because it *helps* her to grow: It assists her in becoming a better person and in realizing her potential as a person. This suggests a more subjective self, one concerned with fulfillment and improvement, though she herself does not use those particular words. But clearly, it is a self that is more flexible and manipulatable, open to deliberate attempts at molding it in keeping with the individual's own wishes. Growth is an underlying theme in her accounts of why she has switched churches several times and in her interpretation of life experiences. "Denominations were not important," she says, in keeping with how many boomers see religion: "I would visit churches, some several times, trying to find the place where I felt comfortable." Walking with the Lord has led her to new growth in the faith. As she looks back on her life, these growth-moments have come at critical junctures—when she left home and moved to the city, both times she was divorced, when she adopted her two children. The story of her life is not just that she has survived, but that she has grown at each of these junctures. In keeping with the tenets of "recovery theology" and other inspirational writings combining religious psychology and crisis experiences, she looks upon these as major events in her spiritual walk. Her sense of self has changed as she has come to think of herself as on a spiritual walk, or in a state of "becoming," open to new possibilities of self-understanding. With the psychologizing of faith, more emphasis is given to its results, and to obtaining immediate results if possible—all enhancing the role of calculation and choice in faith.

Fascinating, too, are Linda's views on the family, particularly her opinion about married women with young children working outside the home. Given the symbolic significance of "family values" for evangelicals, we expected a prescribed response. Hence her answer to our question about women working under these circumstances came as a surprise:

A lot of women find that necessary to do for economic reasons. I am of the opinion that if there is any way possible for a mother to remain home with her preschool children, even at a sacrifice of their lifestyle, that she should try to do that or *if the father would choose to do that.* I think that one parent should be at home for preschool children if it's at all feasible to do that economically.

"If the father would choose to do that"—whence that idea? Far from the predictable stance that mothers should be in the home, or that there are intangibles only mothers can give their children, her response signals a far more reasoned position based on notions of an egalitarian marriage and shared parenting responsibilities. These are not notions for which religious conservatives are popularly known; yet a close accounting of evangelical culture, even working-class evangelical culture, reveals a surprising mix of seemingly conflicting feminist and traditionalist values.[16] Later in the interview, she told us that she listened to the radio programs of Dr. James Dobson, the popular Christian family counselor, which helps explain the source of her views. Dobson's appeal lies in his ability to address questions of faith to inner doubts and searchings as well as to family concerns. As a psychologist he stresses finding spiritual resources within traditional authorities such as the Bible, and applying these to everyday life and strengthening the family. What Linda has picked up from him, among other things, is a pragmatic, psycho-religious approach to reconciling changing family and gender norms with biblical teachings.

All of this suggests a major reorientation of conservative Christian thinking. Sociologist James Davison Hunter goes so far as to suggest that a "total reversal" has occurred since the mid-1960s for a young generation of evangelicals in the conception of the nature and value of the self.[17] Traditional assumptions about the self weakened during this period, as the old Puritan culture gave way to a consumer society, especially for younger, college-educated religious conservatives. In Hunter's study evangelical students even exceeded the subgroup in Yankelovich's survey that was most committed to this new cultural orientation in their endorsement of an ethic of self-improvement and self-fulfillment. The endorsement was not, as Hunter makes clear, a case of unbridled narcissism, but rather an interpretation of life's possibilities as viewed through the lens of evangelical faith. What had started out earlier as a quest for a more satisfying life among elite college students had become widely diffused across America, in the evangelical as well as the nonevangelical sectors. As writer Peter Clecak put it, the metaphor of quest so thoroughly permeated the culture that by the end of the 1970s it could be found in groups as diverse as "born-again Christians and atheistic feminists, gay-rights activists and red-neck males, mainline Protestants and hard-line conservatives."[18] Thus even Linda is a seeker, too, an explorer on a psychological journey that is leading her to break out of old strictures and to embrace a new sense of self.

In our survey we included questions similar to those used by Yankelovich and Hunter. We sorted out the hard-core religious

	Conservatives (N=58)	Moderates (N=113)	All others (N=355)
"I feel the need to find more excitement and sensation in my life"	28%	29%	28%
"New insights" learned about the self are said to have a strong influence	60	58	57
"Having a job outside the home is good for a married woman because it gives her more of a chance to develop as a person"	76	76	83
"If one believes in oneself, there is almost no limit to what one can do"	86	86	87

Table 4.1 Views of the Self

conservatives from the moderates, on the assumption that this makes for a fairer test of the changing conceptions of self. Evangelical moderates would be expected to be more receptive to the cultural changes than fundamentalist hardliners; thus, if we can show that the latter have also been affected by the cultural changes, we have better grounds for inferring a change among born-again boomers as a whole. As Table 4.1 illustrates, this is indeed the case: The differences between the two subgroups are virtually nil. Twenty-eight percent of conservatives agree with the statement, "I feel the need to find more excitement and sensation in my life," as compared with 29% of moderates. Likewise, 60% of the former and 58% of the latter say that "new insights" they learned about themselves were a strong influence on them. Even with the other questions, which we thought were more controversial, there are no significant differences. Equal proportions of both agree that "having a job outside the home is good for a married woman because it gives her more of a chance to develop as a person." The same holds with the question, "If one believes in oneself, there is almost no limit to what one can do." Based on these comparisons, it is clear that the values of self-improvement and self-fulfillment have deeply influenced the conservative Christian community.

The extent of this influence is evident in comparisons with the remainder of the boomer population. Values of self-improvement and self-fulfillment are diffused about equally across evangelical and nonevangelical lines. So stated, the question about a married woman working outside the home was deliberately intended to tap sentiment of a double-edged sort: about working outside the home, as well as the chance to develop as a person. That this item evoked responses with differences no greater among the subgroups shows just how widely the new values have spread. Linda Kramer is hardly atypical in her views, since she falls squarely in the three-quarters of the born-again population who endorse these more progressive values. With the fourth item, we see that eight out of ten religious conservatives accept a version of "possibility thinking," or the belief that one can do just about anything if one believes enough in oneself. Obviously, many of the older, more rigid religious notions about the self have been set aside to make room for more adaptable psychological conceptions.

The impact of a more adaptable self among born-again Christians shows up in a variety of ways. Evangelical boomers concerned with the self, for example, are less likely to pray, to read the Bible, to say grace at the table, and to attend Bible study groups. These are all traditional practices expected of committed Christians—crucial to the normative model of a "good Christian"—but are of lesser significance to growing numbers of evangelical boomers today. Those who hold a more modern as opposed to a traditional conception of self also tend to think of Jesus more as a liberator and challenger, rather than in the conventional way as a shepherd; they are more impressed with Jesus' compassion and forgiveness than with the healings and miracles that he performed. A more expansive conception of self appears to find compatibility with liberationist theology and accommodation to modern culture. For evangelical boomers such differences in imagery are closely linked to theological and ideological views.

EVANGELICALS AND THEIR CHANGING CULTURAL STYLES

How do "born-again" Christians differ in their outlook from other boomers? How do the conservative hardliners and the moderates themselves differ? We would expect substantial differences on a wide array of issues. Obviously, the conservatives are more resistant to the cultural values of self-fulfillment and self-improvement, yet as we shall see, these values are more broadly based among born-again boomers generally than is often realized. What follows is a brief profile.

Churchgoing

Some of the most striking shifts in American religious life in recent decades have to do with norms of churchgoing, and especially among

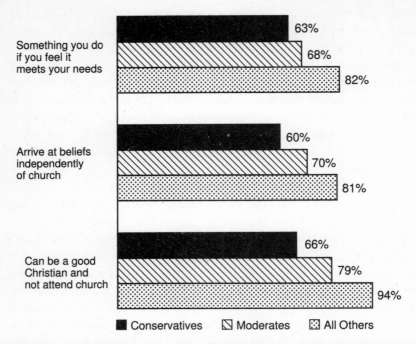

Figure 4.2 Views toward Religious Participation

young adults. Greater numbers of young Americans adhere to what is described as the "new voluntarism": Church is a matter of choice, less a socially ascribed or cultural expectation.[19] A highly subjectivist, psychologically oriented culture encourages a view toward religious participation based less on duty or obligation, and more on whether it "meets your needs." Even the very notion of what is a good Christian is undergoing revision in keeping with the widespread view among contemporary Americans that church involvement is not essential to being a Christian. Following the sixties and the rise of post-materialist values—which placed a high priority on personal well-being and quality of life—many boomers find the teachings and attitudes of the churches out of touch with their own lives, or feel that because of their lifestyles they would not be welcome.

Figure 4.2 shows just how widespread these views are in the boomer generation. When asked about going to church—whether it is a "duty and obligation" or "something you do if you feel it meets your needs"—the vast majority agreed with the latter. Sixty-three percent of the conservatives and 68% of the moderates give the currently popular psychological explanations for why they attend religious services. A similar breakdown is observed in responses to the statement, "An individual should arrive at his or her own religious beliefs independent of any church or synagogue." Two-thirds of conservatives and 79% of moderates say "a person can be a good Christian or Jew if he or she doesn't attend church or synagogue." Not shown here are the attitudes toward what is preached on morality in religious institutions: 13% of conservatives and 23% of moderates find the teachings "too restrictive," to a lesser extent than the others. Unquestionably, there have been major shifts within the boomer culture in its norms of churchgoing.

Moral and Lifestyle Values

Although the so-called "new morality" spread far and wide in this generation, boomers are deeply divided over issues of personal morality and choice of lifestyles. Public opinion polls continue to show that young adults are split in their views on abortion and homosexuality particularly.[20] The splits continue along religious lines. The strongest opposition to abortion comes from born-again Protestants, while the strongest support comes from mainline Protestants, Jews, and those with no religious affiliation. Catholics are more evenly divided on the abortion issue.[21] Boomers are divided somewhat less along religious lines than are older Americans, but even so, the cleavages remain quite strong.

This survey finds boomers to be deeply divided religiously on these issues. Figure 4.3 shows there are strong differences between conservatives and moderates, and between born-again Christians and the rest of the population. Ninety-five percent of the conservatives say homosexual relations are always wrong; 73% say the same for sexual relations before marriage; and 56% say the same for abortion. Responses are significantly lower for the moderates, and much lower still for nonevangelicals. Not too surprising is the finding that conservative sentiment is strongest on homosexuality. Rightward-leaning opinion on premarital sex is strong, even more so than on abortion, which suggests that resistance to the new moral values remains quite solid in the realm of sexuality outside of marriage. A better measure of opinion on abortion is the related item that specifies a married woman getting an abortion because she "doesn't want any more children." So stated, 93% of conservatives and 68% of moderates disapprove, as compared to 42% of the rest of the boomers. Opinion is split on these matters more than on any others that we explored.

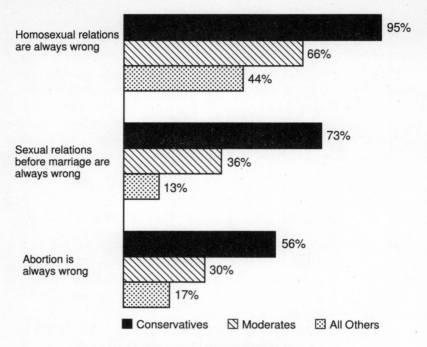

Figure 4.3 Moral Values

Roles of Women

Along with abortion and sex-related issues, the blurring of role distinctions between men and women is one of the major cultural shifts of the times. The new values of gender equality permeate the boomer culture. At the same time, these changes have generated considerable controversy along religious lines. To the fundamentalist hardliners, gender equality poses a severe threat to the traditional submissive roles that women have played. If distinctions between men and women are wiped away, then the biblical model of the family is itself in danger. Evangelical moderates, however, have questioned biblical norms about the submissiveness of women and have shown considerable accommodation to the normative shifts of contemporary American society.

Once again, we observe deep divisions. Figure 4.4 shows that the religious conservatives are equally divided on the item "some equality in marriage is a good thing, but by and large the husband ought to have the main say-so in family matters." That one-half of them reject the husband's authority in the family is an indication of just how far the new

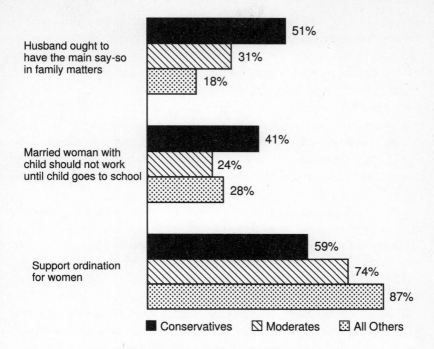

Figure 4.4 Roles of Women

values have spread. It also suggests that there is considerable disagreement within this religious community among young adults over gender issues. Thirty-one percent of the moderates agree with the statement, thus indicating that more than two-thirds reject a patriarchal conception of authority. A similar split characterizes boomer views on women and their work roles. Forty-one percent of the conservatives say that "a married women with a young child should not work until the child goes to school," as compared to 24% of the moderates. In this instance evangelical attitudes are less resistant to women leaving their preschool children for work than are those of the larger boomer population. On the very timely question about the ordination of women, the overwhelming majority of all boomers today—born-again or not—endorse this possibility. Even a majority of religious conservatives support ordination for women.

The impact of the new values, then, touches on a wide spectrum of concerns within the born-again community. With shifts in notions of the self come shifts in institutional norms of belonging, as well as changes in moral orientations and gender sensibilities. Even in that greatest bastion of evangelical traditionalism—moral attitudes and gender roles—the new values have made their invasion. On such questions as unmarried couples living together and a pregnant woman wishing to obtain a legal abortion, there is a greater mix of opinions than often realized. Among women especially, feelings are much more nuanced, evidence of a great deal of frustration awaiting expression. To the extent that such feelings and subtle shades of opinion are recognized in the evangelical community, they undermine the infrastructure of that community; hence little is said about them. But silence here does not mitigate the feelings of many young Americans touched by post-materialist values and psychological constructions of the self.

The more educated, more middle-class evangelical boomers are the carriers of these new values. For this sector the boundaries of evangelical faith and modern culture have been substantially altered in the direction of greater accommodation. More than just a change of boundaries, the meaning of self becomes, as Hunter argues, more ambiguous.[22] Is the self inherently sinful? Or is it essentially noble? The long-term consequences of such ambiguity remain to be seen; but it is reasonable to assume that many born-again boomers have questions that touch on the deepest levels of self-reflection and self-esteem.

It could be that the erosion of traditional views of human nature has reached a plateau, or possibly even that views will harden and shift again in a more orthodox direction. Life-cycle theories, for example, suggest that as boomers age they are likely to become more orthodox in their beliefs. Should this happen there may be limits on the impact of these new values.[23] Yet our observations suggest otherwise. Older boomers, now in their late thirties and early forties, are as open to the values of self-fulfillment as the younger boomers. On some religious items, such as the importance of "following one's conscience" and "agreement that all religions are equally good and true," older boomers are actually more liberal than younger ones. Moreover, it is unlikely that the evangelical boomer population will abandon these new values. Evangelical faith has moved too far in the direction of greater choice and accommodation—toward meaningful and sustained life in today's world—to be able to turn back easily.

ON SURFING AND BREAKING OUT OF LITTLE CUBBYHOLES

Certainly, Linda Kramer does not exhibit all these new, emerging trends. Quite traditional on some issues and deeply embedded in her religious community, she is far from being an embodiment of the underlying shift in values and psychological constructions of the self. Her strong ties with her church and the broader conservative religious community provide a stabilizing anchor in her life. Much of the attraction of evangelical and fundamentalist faiths, in fact, lies in the more clearly drawn Christ-versus-culture boundaries that they offer. Great numbers of boomers, along with Americans of all ages, seek the security and support found within such religious communities.

Yet Linda Kramer permits us to see the breakup of older religious and cultural styles and the emergence of new ones. She is a good example because she shows that the new values emphasizing the self are reaching beyond the middle class, and into the lower middle-class and working class. The changing values transcend social class lines and touch on virtually all aspects of people's lives—their worldviews, their orientations to themselves and to others, even their deepest sense of who they are as men and women. For Linda, as for the more educated and professional members of her generation, the values are rooted in the expansion of choices and awareness that the self is flexible and capable of enrichment.

The possibilities of a more satisfying sense of self are increasingly taken for granted by white middle-class Americans. But even among the many evangelical subgroups—African-Americans, Hispanics, working-class whites, the handicapped, housewives, Southerners—the values placed on the self are widely diffused. Exploring one's own inner life and taking responsibility for one's self empower on their own terms—across lines of race, social class, and lifestyle. The "new evangelicalism" in its many forms has proven to be very adaptable—and especially so for the boomer generation. The attraction lies in part in its theology, which simultaneously sets *limits* on choice while *accommodating* it—or put differently, because evangelical faith contains choices within a fairly narrow moral and belief framework.

Here are two final illustrations:

A college-educated woman, and a recent recruit to the Vineyard Christian Fellowship in southern California, told us that she "surfs for the Lord." Working as a sales agent for a distributing firm, mother of two young children, and recently married for the second time, she says that for her surfing is a spiritual experience.

"Can you really surf for the Lord?" the interviewer asks.

"Absolutely. He's the one who makes the waves," she replies.

After her first marriage broke up, she took up surfing and found it a means of coping with her feelings and of cultivating her inner strength. But more than just that, there was something deeply spiritual and settling about it. "You're alone, and participating in what he gave us to enjoy. It's when I feel I'm closest to God." Rebuilding her life, enjoying the waves, and dwelling on God in her leisure moments were all bound up together. "New evangelical" boomers have not only discovered the self, they have discovered pleasure as a means of enhancing the self!

Another woman, without a high school diploma and in a much different life situation, expressed with great feeling what it is like to find her own space. A member of a holiness church in North Carolina, married to an alcoholic, mother of seven children, and suffering from years of abuse and low self-esteem, she had this to say when asked about how she deals with her life:

> I'm becoming more aware of my options, I guess you call them. [The marriage is] something I got into, and I got into with my eyes open. But I've also learned that it's not me. But just because I'm married to him, he may believe this way, y'know, [but] I can believe my way and I can do my thing. . . . I'm becoming more aware about my values, they're mine. . . . So I'm becoming, uh, how do you put it? I'm opening up to the world more now. I still got my values, I still got my ways but I'm reaching out more, I'm not in my little cubbyhole anymore.

Few stories we heard were as moving or as powerful as this one—career women with graduate degrees in psychology could not have described a woman's experience of breaking our of her "little cubbyhole" any better.

These two women are discovering aspects of their inner lives they were not in touch with before. Their lives are opening up to new challenges and are empowered by an emancipated sense of self; the religious and the spiritual are breaking out of old molds, never to be quite the same again. All are subtle shifts in the alignments of faith and culture for born-again boomers in the 1990s, which raises an interesting question: Are Linda Kramer and Mollie Stone becoming more alike, and if so, just how big is the great divide between them? This is the question to which we turn next.

CHAPTER 5

Across a Great Spiritual Divide

Every spring on the outskirts of Los
Angeles, thousands of people show up for a huge, month-long Renaissance
fair. On weekends people from surrounding states and from as far away
as northern California descend on a large field nestled between the mountains, packed with tents, exhibits, and performing stages. On first impres-
sion we conclude the obvious: Here is a huge gathering of people that
have come together to celebrate the art, food, language, crafts, and cos-
tumes of the sixteenth and seventeenth centuries. Like a Renaissance fair
held anywhere else in the country, it's an exciting and festive occasion.

Looking more closely, however, we get a clearer understanding of
what is going on. Many people are in their thirties and forties. Children
tag along with their parents. As judged by cars in the parking lot, it is
largely a middle-class gathering. Bumper stickers such as "Save the
Whales" and "Visualize World Peace" are seen everywhere. As they get
out of their cars, some people take off trendy outer garments and shoes
and don strange garb and sandals. They all walk hurriedly toward the entrance gate: We sense a collective euphoria, as if we are about to enter a
new world. Near the entrance a small group of evangelical Christians,
similar in age, hands out tracts to those who slow down long enough to
grab them and occasionally engages someone in conversation. One member sits behind a table, selling Christian bumper stickers that read,
"Honk If You Love Jesus" and "Salvation: Don't Leave Earth without

It." They try to make an evangelical witness to those passing by in a friendly and upbeat way.

Inside the fairgrounds excitement fills the air. Men and women stroll down the exhibit lanes, the women wearing garlands of ribbons and flowers, the men wearing open, flowing shirts and often sporting bandannas. Faces beam with childlike innocence. Friends meet and hug one another. Parents explain to children what is going on. All seem drawn into a mystical sense of community. Here and there, small groups break into song and dance, and everywhere pungent smells and smoke dazzle the nostrils. Music of the New Age streams from flutes and recorders; astrologers and psychics pore over tarot cards and charts; peddlers hawk their candles, crystals, beads, potions, incense, and herbs. Occasionally, a monk in medieval gown, wearing a cross and carrying a shepherd's staff, stalks the grounds.

A Renaissance fair, yes, but something more: a "happening"—a reunion of the sixties' generation! It's a palatable mix of the old and the new, of the frivolous and the serious; a time when individuals take leave of their present lives, and at least for a brief moment, delve back into a common past. It has been said that the sixties generation is like a tribe with its roots in a time, rather than a place. Like many human tribes, this one was founded on a vision of what life might be and a sense of solidarity forged out of group experience. At the fair they celebrate and share this culture, this memory, some deeply spiritual views that they hold about life, and also, perhaps, a fascination with their own origin myth: the experience of the sixties, which to a great extent made them who they are even today.

Not all members of the boomer generation, of course, care to celebrate a reunion of the sixties. And certainly, they have not all turned to New Age spirituality or evangelical Christianity. Many who showed up at the fair were obviously there just for fun—neither religious nor spiritual in any deeply committed way. The distinctly Californian flavor of the fair is apparent in the way in which West Coast people of diverse backgrounds easily mingle in an atmosphere of tolerance and acceptance. But it is a significant event because—like the tip of an iceberg—the fair is a visible, exaggerated expression of religious and spiritual themes that, in milder and more subtle form, have touched the lives of boomers everywhere. Mollie Stone would feel at home at the Renaissance fair; Linda Kramer probably would not, but some of her more upscale, middle-class evangelical and charismatic kin might.

THE GREAT SPIRITUAL DIVIDE

As this illustration makes clear, boomers are deeply divided in religious and spiritual styles, yet there are underlying experiences and values that draw them together. Mollie and Linda are examples—of both the differences and the commonalities. At one level it is quite clear that these two stand on opposite sides of an enormous religious gulf. It is more than just one standing "inside" the Renaissance fair and the other standing "outside"; the two women give voice to living in two vastly different symbolic worlds. So different are the worlds that we can think of them as representing the polar extremes around which much of boomer religious and spiritual life is organized today. This great spiritual divide is expressed in four very fundamental ways: in boomers' views of the self, of religious authority, in their meaning systems, and in their spiritual styles.

Conception of Self

First, the two women have differing conceptions of the self. Mollie Stone is the embodiment of the self-fulfillment quest. She is an autonomous, highly independent person seeking to become fully actualized. So concerned with her own pursuits, she is not sure what to make of a question that asks about obligations to others. Self takes priority over role: "Just spending your life working at a job, being married, and having kids has never really quite set well with me." To a considerable extent, others must fit around her. Linda Kramer, on the other hand, is far more traditional and holds to a view of the self that is constrained and subject directly to God; she sees fulfillment arising largely out of submission to divine will. When asked about obligations, she gives the conservative religious response: Putting self ahead of others is sin. The self must be held in check, never given too much freedom. Role has priority over self: A woman should find fulfillment at home, as wife and mother. As such, the two women represent the endpoints of a broad spectrum— the extremes as most people would see them.

Authority

No religious issue separates boomers more than the question of religious authority. Is the locus of authority within the self or outside the self? Mollie, of course, searches within for truth and meaning. Authority rests in a self that seeks to be free of all external constraint and able to develop into its full potential. Inner authority liberates and empowers, external authority interferes with one's capacity to truly love and relate to one another. The language she uses in talking about spirituality—centeredness, connectedness, harmony, journey, quests—all arise out of personal experience. She draws on religious traditions, but in the context of the self and its search for meaningful experience.

For Linda, authority rests in an external source: a transcendent God who has saved her through the death and resurrection of Jesus Christ, all of which is revealed in the Bible. We must rely on something more than the fleeting self. People live and die, but the Word of God is forever. What the Bible teaches is "timeless" and "objective," part of a larger plan of salvation offered to those who believe. She uses a language of faith, informed by biblical and church tradition, to describe her relation to God, to a religious community, and to the world.

Meaning Systems

Corresponding to these two extremes on authority are two differing religious constructions: "mystical" versus "theistic" meaning systems. A mystical meaning system is one, like Mollie's, that seeks wholeness and overcoming of the barriers separating people from one another and from God and nature. Emphasis is on feelings and experiences in life more so than cognitive understandings. Hence "explorations" and "journeys" are the means through which Mollie discovers who she really is. In Peter Berger's scheme, hers is an inductive religious approach: She begins with human experience and reaches out to the many religious traditions for whatever insights she can find.[1] One picks and chooses. One absorbs all that contributes to self-understanding. God is immanent, to be found "within" her own life experiences. In its most radical form, hers is a vision of God and self and world that is one. Like all mystics, Mollie believes that the force responsible for shaping reality is her own frame of mind. Morality stems from this encompassing vision. Virtue lies in being sensitive to her own needs and being open and honest. Feelings and authenticity give shape to her moral outlook.

A theistic meaning system like Linda's has at its center a belief in God as the force governing life. God not only influences her daily life, but also shapes all of reality and makes life meaningful in some ultimate sense. There is no substitute for a strong personal faith—a direct, experiential relationship with a transcendent God who is above and beyond the world. This is the one true faith that saves and leads to eternal life. Hers is a deductive religious response: She reasserts the authority of a religious tradition in the face of modern secularity. The world may be collapsing around us, but one can still believe in God. Religion means being loyal to this true faith and is something deeply moral. Foremost is the covenant between God and his people. Morality is rooted in obedience and carrying out God's will. Moral and religious discourse centers around "rules" and "commandments."[2]

The sixties resulted in a fragmentation of meaning systems and moral orders. In a major study of youth and their beliefs during that decade, Robert Wuthnow observed that two types of meaning systems—the mystical and the theistic—emerged as more separate and competing symbolic worlds.[3] Steven M. Tipton speaks of an "expressive" style of ethical evaluation oriented to self arising out of the sixties counterculture and its romantic tradition, as opposed to an "authoritative" style based on faith in an absolute objective God who reveals himself in scripture.[4] As he describes, the conflict of values between mainstream American culture and the counterculture during that time helped to frame moral alternatives and set the terms for their mediation. Mollie and Linda thus exemplify two major differing epistemologies, or approaches to constructing reality out of symbols and experience of that era and of making moral decisions.

Spiritual Styles

The two women also have contrasting spiritual styles. Mollie's is best characterized as "letting go," and Linda's as "mastery and control." Both are distinctly American in their simplicity and pragmatism, yet the two are very different in orientation.[5] Letting go amounts to freeing oneself from all that is beyond one's personal powers to control: guilt, shame, abuse, and belief that one can solve one's own compulsions and addictions. More than just letting go, it involves conforming one's mind and heart to the larger flow of powers in the universe. Openness and receptivity to these powers are to be spiritually cultivated, and lives transformed. In so doing one affirms an overriding harmony between the sacred reality and one's own reality, which is what Mollie's spiritual quest is all about.

Taking hold, or being firmly in control of what one does and having mastery over life, is a much different spiritual style. The very opposite of letting go, it rests on a view of the self in opposition to or setting limits to the world around one. Personal discipline and steadfastness, regular Bible reading and prayer, witnessing for Christ, avoiding temptations—in effect, "walking the Christian walk"—largely define for Linda the parameters of Christian spirituality. Whereas "letting go" encourages acceptance and finding harmony in the way things are, "mastery and control" presumes that the individual believer must stick to the narrow path and honor the moral and religious teachings as revealed through the scriptures.

THE PLURALIZATION OF MEANING SYSTEMS

This great divide between mystics and theists increased with the experimentation with new spiritualities during the 1960s, and also as a result of the revived religious dogma it provoked. It was a time, sociologist David Martin says, of "firming up of the religious frame and a sharpening of the edge which faith presents to the world."[6] The cognitive boundaries between evangelicalism and fundamentalism, on the one hand, and a growing New Age spiritual consciousness, on the other, hardened as time passed—leading to a crystallization of people's self-definitions, whether traditionally religious or spiritual, in response to the cultural unrest of the period.

Figure 5.1 shows that those most exposed to the counterculture during their years growing up are far less likely to be conventionally religious even today: They are less inclined to regard themselves as religious, and much more likely to think of themselves as spiritual. At the lowest level of exposure to the sixties' values, only 33% say they are spiritual people; then at the next level, 52%; then 78%; and finally, at the highest level, 81%. These are all substantial increases in spiritual sensitivities. The two—the religious and the spiritual—appear to represent differing modes of consciousness, one negatively and the other positively related to the cultural experiences of that era. There is, of course, some overlap of the two, in the lives of those for whom the distinction is not very real or is irrelevant.

A similar pattern shows up in another question that we looked at in a previous chapter: "Is it good to explore the many differing religious teachings, or should one stick to a particular faith?" This question gets at a fundamental difference in outlook for Mollie and Linda. As Figure 5.2 makes clear, exposure to the sixties' counterculture is related to exploring religious teachings and inversely related to sticking to a faith.

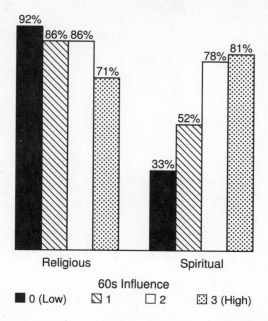

Figure 5.1 Consider Yourself Religious or Spiritual?

Striking here, as with the other figure, is the consistency of the patterns. For those most caught up in the cultural climate of that era, the quest for meaning broke loose from narrow religious pathways; they had a vision of the new heaven and the new earth that went far beyond that of any single religious tradition. Those less exposed and less involved, and for whom the sixties was a storm from which to take refuge, were strengthened in their conviction that one should remain loyal to one's own faith. The sixties had an impact both ways: in broadening horizons, and in reinforcing the importance of holding fast to traditional faith. Using Carol Pearson's Jungian-like archetypes, it might be said that the era produced both "wanderers" and "orphans," those who embrace the world as well as take refuge from it.[7]

Mysticism and theism as meaning systems encompass very differing beliefs, symbols, and "pictures"—about God, about human nature, about the forces that shape life. More than just differing orientations toward religion and spirituality, these broader universes of meanings—or ways of organizing and conceptualizing life—came to be restructured during the 1960s and 1970s. Table 5.1 shows, for example, that a large set of indicators of traditional theistic belief varies with exposure to the

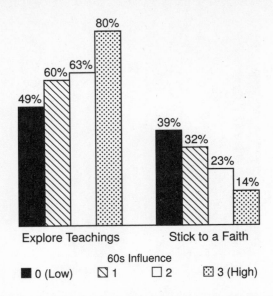

Figure 5.2 Explore Teachings or Stick to Faith?

counterculture. An image of God as a father, viewing life as influenced by God, beliefs in eternal life and in the devil, having a born-again experience, and a pessimistic conception of human nature—all are held more strongly by those who did not embrace the 1960s. This constellation of beliefs and symbols hangs together and is meaningful over against the disruptive experiences of the sixties. Likewise, a set of items tapping mystical consciousness varies in the opposite direction. Having God "within" us, being influenced by new insights learned from ourselves, being alone and meditating, belief in reincarnation, and regarding all religions as equally true and good—all are endorsed more strongly by those who *did* embrace the sixties. This constellation as a whole is predictable on the part of those drawn toward an alternative meaning system. Clearly, along a theistic-to-mystical axis, there was and still is a deep polarization of symbols, meanings, and assumptions about human nature.

Two other meaning systems, more secular in character, are also shown—"individualistic" and "social scientific" outlooks. These constructions of reality, in a hybrid if not always in a pure version, find frequent expression among boomers. The individualistic outlook is more commonly found among people with traditional values of hard work, achievement, and diligence, who typically speak the language of laissez-faire economics; and the social scientific outlook is found among

	EXPOSURE TO THE 60s			
	0 (N=145)	1 (N=142)	2 (N=178)	3 (N=71)
THEISM				
Picture God as Father	81%	74%	64%	54%
Life influenced by God	67	53	44	41
Believe in Eternal Life	95	77	77	70
Believe in Devil	79	65	61	37
"A child is born already guilty of sin"	39	29	22	7
MYSTICISM				
God is "within" us	22	27	34	54
Life influenced by new insights	51	51	57	63
Prefer to be alone and meditate	6	13	14	34
Believe in Reincarnation	25	29	30	39
"All the great religions of the world are equally true and good"	43	45	53	56
INDIVIDUALISM				
Not succeeding is a person's own fault	67	70	66	55
Person can control what happens in life	75	72	67	69
Hard work always pays off	75	63	58	48
SOCIAL SCIENCE				
Life influenced by people in power	70	78	80	84
Scientific view of creation	15	15	20	41
"Science may someday find answers to the questions that religion has long been concerned with"	55	62	64	69

Table 5.1 Meaning Systems

the better-educated, professional, "new class" constituencies. To return to our example of the Renaissance fair: No doubt many who are in attendance there speak these more secular languages. We cannot really grasp the boomer culture today without an understanding of these languages.

Social scientific constructions of reality—like mystical meanings—are positively related to exposure to the sixties. The confrontations with the establishment appear to have provoked an awareness of how social, political, and economic factors shape people's life chances. No doubt the expansion of higher education and a greater public knowledge generally of how society and power structures influence the lives of individuals have also contributed to a more informed sociological imagination. In contrast, individualism as a meaning system is patterned like theism in relation to the sixties: the higher the exposure to the new values, the less the emphasis on individual will-power, self-determination, and self-control. This mode of constructing reality is deeply rooted in the American experience and touches on some of the core values of the culture; it is expressed boldly in the statement, "I am the master of my fate." Both social scientific and individualistic meaning systems may be thought of as deeply entrenched in secular society.

PAM FLETCHER'S SECULAR STYLE

Pam Fletcher gives voice to the individualistic mode of thinking. She was not greatly influenced by the changing values when she was growing up. She does not think of herself in traditional religious terms. She is not sure what to believe about God. In her way of thinking, the individual, not God or mystical consciousness, shapes life; she creates her own world in relation to family and very close friends. Her philosophy that people's own choices determine the meaning and purpose they find in life comes not out of any traumatic experience of the sixties, but from having grown up in a secular family where belief in God was not an issue. Religious belief was not rejected on serious philosophical grounds; rather, it simply was not discussed. In this respect she is fairly typical of a growing secular constituency of boomers who are more a-religious than antireligious.

Individualism might be thought of as a derivative of theism, as a secularized belief system that empowers the individual, not God, as the locus of authority and action. Though this is a voice increasingly heard among boomers, it is a minority voice: Only 4% of our respondents were avowedly atheistic or agnostic. Far more common are those with individualistic meaning systems, highly secularized in their conceptions of the forces governing life, but who affirm in one way or another a divine power or presence, even if they admit to uncertainty in their belief. Indeed, many boomers would fit into such a category—upwards, perhaps, of a third who admit they have doubts about God and have minimal or no contact with religious institutions.

Pam Fletcher's secular views are important in two respects. One is that she illustrates the lack of a meaningful language growing numbers of Americans face when, for whatever reason, they must face life's hard knocks. She does not draw from traditional religious and spiritual resources in trying to make sense of her life, and thus turns to the secular language of fate ("If your number is up, your number is up"). The language she uses may be thought of as a functional equivalent to religion, since it "works" for her and operates as an organizing principle that gives some meaning to her life; yet it leaves her without a fully satisfactory explanation of why things happen, or could happen, in life. She despairs when she thinks that fate might overwhelm choice ultimately, in part because her metaphysics fails to provide much of a final explanation of how these two principles come together in her own life. The lack of a transcendent symbol in secular language limits its capacity to create an overarching "sacred canopy" that is meaningful, locating her life in a broader symbolic world. Pam is not all that unusual in this respect; secularists we talked to often expressed the lack of a broad encompassing framework for interpreting their lives and a yearning to be able to express their deepest feelings about life.

Her views are also important because they point to a distinction that seems to be taking on greater significance in contemporary America—between theistic and secular meaning systems. Both individualistic and social scientific meaning systems have emerged as competing worldviews over against a more codified, more traditional theistic framework of interpretation. The expansion of higher education, the spread of scientific and technological styles of discourse, and the rise of differing languages of morality have all helped to accentuate the boundaries among these meaning systems. There has been a virtual explosion of secular-humanist modes of explanation in recent decades—the vocabulary of psychological expressive needs, the vocabulary of individual success and achievement, the vocabulary of individual rights, the vocabulary of social scientific understanding. All of these vocabularies have more in common with one another than with the language of theism. Not only have these modes of explanation spread and become more common, so too has the awareness among Americans that alternatives to traditional theism are more available today.

The extent to which people adhere to alternative meaning systems, or some blend of ideas from differing sources, is blurred by the fact that among Americans, and certainly among boomers, such matters are regarded as private, and within very broad limits, to be generally respected. Pam Fletcher espouses such respect when she speaks of honoring her husband's wishes about the children being baptized or of the children themselves deciding about religion once they are older. These are deeply ingrained patterns held by Americans, whether religious or not. Privacy is encouraged by the separation of "public" from "private" realms of life in a highly role-segmented society. Even with close friends or coworkers, we often do not know what they really believe, or where they find support for their innermost concerns, or if they belong to any kind of religious or spiritual group. As a Manhattan corporate executive from Greenwich, Connecticut, told us: "I sincerely do not know what the involvement is of the people I associate with 90% of my day. I don't know what their spiritual nourishing is."

Of interest are how the meaning systems relate to the sixties' experiences. Similar patterns for theism and individualism, and for mysticism and science, were observed in previous research on youth in the San Francisco Bay Area in the mid-1970s.[8] These patterns still exist in all parts of the country—evidence that something happened during the years when boomers were growing up that had a lasting impact on how they conceptualize the dominant forces governing life. More than anything else, it was the conflict of cultural values in the sixties that so divided the boomer population and restructured the meaning systems by which they live.The emergence of distinct religious, mystical, and secular languages is not explained by education, social class, age, region, or childhood religious background, which are all factors that presumably have something to do with moral and religious values. Though they did have some bearing on people's lives when they were growing up, none of them really compare in influence with the ferment of ideas, visions, and dreams of that era.

The power of new ideas, visions, and dreams ought not to be underestimated. Theodore Roszak, in *The Making of a Counter Culture*, invokes the image of an "invasion of centaurs" to describe the radical cultural disjunction and clash of conceptions of life.[9] A potent image recorded on the pediment of the Temple of Zeus at Olympia, it signifies what has to be a fearful experience in any time: the experience of disjointedness and schizophrenic responses, the lurkings of hybrid creatures. For the boomer generation, it was an encounter that jolted the very foundations on which cultural meanings rest and gave rise to new religious and spiritual impulses that continue to be played out.

SOME UNIFYING THEMES

Yet, as the example of the Renaissance fair illustrates, there are some unifying trends that cut across boomer culture today. And as we have seen, Mollie and Linda have a good deal in common. Though they are on quite differing religious paths, they have moved in some ways toward one another: Mollie is now past her radical stage of self-preoccupation and is reaching out in her commitment to others; and Linda is trying to give more attention to her own needs as a person and would like not to be stifled by her religious community. Linda would like some of Mollie's self-assurance and growth as a person; Mollie wishes she had some of the anchors that Linda's religious tradition gives her. Each has moved in her own way toward a new stability and equilibrium, despite great differences in beliefs and outlook.

They would probably get along with one another as friends better than we might first imagine. Certainly, Linda would worry about Mollie's prospects for salvation and eternal life, but in public demeanor she is fairly open and accepting toward those with whom she disagrees on theological grounds. In this respect she typifies the new evangelicalism and its greater accommodation to the pluralism of modern society. Inwardly, she may have considerable confidence that she is right and others wrong in matters of faith and morality, but outwardly this is not expressed so boldly. A person's religious preference, at least within a fairly wide range of conventionality, is viewed as just that—as preference—in keeping with American norms of civility, sociability, and good taste. Boomers especially, having grown up with so much cultural diversity, are united except on the very fundamentalist extreme in a posture of "no offense" in matters of personal faith.[10]

The cultural trends of the post-World War II period are imprinted on each of them. Mollie talks much more openly about this ("I was probably too self-centered") than Linda, who feels she must always put Jesus and others ahead of self. They differ in that Mollie's preoccupation with self, at least up until fairly recently, was largely unhampered by commitments to others, whereas Linda's emerging new interest in self is still contained by her religious belief. But in the way each interprets her religious involvement, the outcome is the same: One goes to Quaker meetings and alternative Jewish celebrations and the other to church, but both do so in order to "grow." Certainly, the two have different things in mind when they speak of "growing"; yet the fact that they employ a common metaphor to describe the religious life and draw upon the language of self (whether it be greater understanding, improvement, or fulfillment) points to an underlying unity. Both interpret faith, or quest for faith, with a discourse that has been greatly shaped by the emotional and psychological dimensions of human experience.

They agree as well about the importance of the spiritual over the religious. Neither has any difficulty in pointing to a difference between "being religious" and "being spiritual." Even Linda is quick to distinguish them: Being religious is like going through the motions, trying, as she says, to earn your way to heaven; but being spiritual has to do with loving God, it comes from the heart, a person must feel it. Again the strong emphasis on the inner life, on a mature faith, on feelings comes through. At the same time, because evangelicals put emphasis on a direct, personal relationship with Christ, they tend to view the church as a collection of individuals and are sometimes suspicious of religious institutions. The convergence of themes here is best thought of, then, as a shift every bit as much on the part of Mollie as for Linda: Both want a *genuine* spiritual experience that transcends the dry, external set of behaviors, dogmas, and forms associated with organized religion.

Given the focus on the psychological, much energy is then given to dealing with guilt, shame, depression, anxiety, tension, stress, and the like. New Agers and evangelicals alike focus on these concerns, but in different ways. For mystics, these psychological problems are seen as stemming from metaphysical states analogous to sickness, to be resolved through healing and living according to the law of harmony. If the primary reality is mind, then disease comes from wrong thinking and can be corrected only through "right thinking" combined with "right action." Evangelicals see the same problems as rooted in sin and separation from God; the only lasting cure is to turn to Christ and walk daily with him. Christianity provides a means of coping with these, for through rebirth in Christ comes renewed potential for self-confidence and self-esteem, two attributes that the "new evangelicals" have come to tout a lot.

Both mystics and evangelicals seek to endow all of life with religious and spiritual meaning—including the addictive self in need of transformation. Spirituality is often conjoined with and framed in the language of personal needs, compulsions, or problems. "Addiction" and "dysfunctional families" are not just experiences, they are categories of reflection with an affinity to members of a generation having had so much experience with drugs, alcohol, and sexual experimentation. Hence many see themselves as "victims" and are looking for healing and recovery in a spiritual language that brings about results, wherever they can find it. Not surprisingly, victimization as a theme and its related aspects of spiritual healing, recovery, and growth are the latest, and currently the most debated, topics of metaphysical and theological reflection. Every bookstore today has shelves of inspirational books addressing these themes from many theological points of view—Christian, Catholic, Jewish, evangelical, charismatic, Sufi, and many varieties of New Age.

A closely related theme is the adaptation of spirituality to modern rationality and a resulting standardization of approaches and styles. For

New Agers, there are workbooks such as Louise L. Hay's *You Can Heal Your Life,* with advice, exercises, and affirmations to be repeated for a range of problems.[11] She is concerned with physical illness, but also with failure, poverty, and helplessness, to which she offers guidelines, and specific suggestions for dealing with "relationships," "work," and "the body." For evangelicals, there is a comparable thematic rationalization and codification of the faith in simple formulas. To quote sociologist James Davison Hunter:

> . . . one may note the increasing tendency to translate the specifically religious components of the world view, previously understood to be plain, self-evident, and without need of elaboration, into rigorously standardized prescriptions. The spiritual aspects of Evangelical life are increasingly approached by means of and interpreted in terms of "principles," "rules," "steps," "laws," "codes," "guidelines," and the like.[12]

Experiential religion, healing, harmony, renewal, personal and social transformation, quests for wholeness—indeed, all are themes, as Catherine L. Albanese argues, around which evangelicals and New Agers converge.[13] Both ends of the religious spectrum appeal to a popular, do-it-yourself mentality, reflecting a voluntaristic religious climate where people of almost all persuasions increasingly choose their own private forms of religion rather than rely on the authority of a tradition or a religious community. Both give expression to a turning inward, an introspection that empowers individuals to take responsibility for their own spiritual lives. Both see physical health and material prosperity as signs of blessings. Both express great confidence in a "supply-side" spirituality, or faith in an abundance of spiritual power available to human beings, if only they make right use of it. For both, a key assumption is, in Albanese's words, that "God, or the universe, is the ever-constant source of Supply, a resource to be tapped, but a flow that unfortunately may be blocked by the limitations of the believer."[14]

With the popular emphasis on direct, inward experience, we can speak, as Albanese does, of a widespread mystical consciousness in America today. Mysticism in this broad sense, with its highly individualistic stance and orientation to the religious present, "reprimitivizes" religion, as she says. To reprimitivize is to restore old mythic unities that have been lost and to enhance the inner life and the subjective power of religious imagery; and in so doing God, the world, and the self are pulled together in new and creative ways. There are parallels between such unity and the rediscovery of romantic and folk traditions in other realms—in music, in health, in foods, in arts and crafts. Folk tradition emphasizes feeling and self-awareness, creativity and spontaneity. In the spiritual sense, it celebrates experience rather than doctrine; the personal rather than the institutional; the mythic and dreamlike over the cognitive; people's religion over official religion; soft, caring images of deity over hard, impersonal images; the feminine and the androgynous over the masculine. In Andrew M. Greeley's terms, religion has come to be experienced less in the "reflective" mode, and more in the "imaginative" mode, the point being that the visual and the visionary, inner realities and personal journeys, have all taken on a new prominence.[15]

At both ends of the spectrum we find apocalyptic visions of the future. Both mystics and evangelicals, along with charismatics and pentecostals, often see the world as in the last stages of disintegration before the dawning of a new era. The scenarios differ in detail, but they agree on the imminence of a worldwide breakdown and the establishment of a new, spiritually transformed community. Lifted up is a vision of a new people and of a new world.

There is also much small-group activity in both camps: Mollie in the "alternative Jewish" group, Linda with Pregnancy Distress and other groups at her church. New Agers hold festivals and create intentional communities, where like-minded individuals try to discover a deeper sense of human solidarity and the building of a new planetary society. Evangelicals speak of the "meta-church," or the small nurturing group that is a crucial part of the larger congregation. In both instances, small groups fulfill basic human needs for community and spiritual expression and help individuals to restructure their loyalties and commitments—to themselves, to others, and to causes.

An observer of the religious scene today is struck by the proliferation of groups organized around specific life situations, crises, and needs. The self-help movement is flourishing in the form of Twelve-Step recovery programs, with some two hundred different types of programs in addition to Alcoholics Anonymous—Overeaters Anonymous, Manics Anonymous, Compulsive Shoppers Anonymous, and so on. Many groups meet independently on weekdays in churches; others are sponsored by churches and have more explicit religious themes but are modeled after the Twelve-Step philosophy. Weekend seminars at retreat centers are now a burgeoning business catering to those with particular experiences—people who have to deal with terminal illness or with a family member who has AIDS, or parents grieving over the loss of a child. People of all faiths and outlooks are drawn to these seminars. All such groups and seminars generate their own spiritualities, aided by an elaborate networking through periodicals, workshops and conferences, mail-order catalogs, and religious as well as Twelve-Step bookstores.

The self-help movement is part of a larger trend of religious democratization. Not just young Americans, but members of the postwar generation in many Western countries are turning to small groups where experiences are shared and individuals support one another.[16] "Interaction ritual" is the term often used to describe what goes on in such spiritual groups, which often meet in churches or retreat centers.[17] In interaction ritual individuals speak up and tell what symbols mean to them; spontaneity and equality of participation are encouraged. Emphasis is on spiritual growth and getting help, on lay knowledge rather than expert knowledge. Such groups tend not to be permanent affiliations: they meet for a limited period of time to "work on" specific concerns, to share insights among themselves, or to explore the teachings of a particular writer. Some mixing of codes is common, drawing from Jewish and Christian teachings, Buddhism, neo-Paganism, Native American spirituality, Gestalt and Jungian psychologies, and the latest of human potential ideas, especially among those alienated from organized religion. For evangelicals and charismatics, there is less mixing out of a concern to preserve a normative Christian style, with the fusions limited largely to psychology and faith.

THE MATURING SELF

Why this strong emphasis on the self and spiritual growth? Why the movement in the direction of greater balance of commitment to self and to others? The crucial word here is *movement*—in Mollie's case it is the increasing concern to give of herself more and relate to others, and for Linda it is the discovery of the importance of her own self-growth. For both, faith is not a static phenomenon and might best be thought of as the continual activity of composing meaning. So, to rephrase the question: Why is there so much attention to the process of maturing, expanding, evolving, elaborating, growing—what Sharon Parks recently called the "motion of faith"?[18]

One might argue that the drift of American religious life has been moving this way for a long time. The older Calvinist pessimism about human nature gave way long ago to more open views of human possibility and progress. And since midcentury there have been signs of an amalgamation and functional integration in the popular culture of religious themes from both evangelical Christianity and the metaphysical traditions known as New Thought.[19] Unlikely as this blending of themes from the nineteenth and early twentieth centuries might appear, the two are in many respects quite complementary. Both evangelical Christianity and New Thought were highly individualistic in orientation but worked out their solutions of salvation quite differently. Evangelicals emphasized an otherworldly salvation, in keeping with a rural and urban working-class constituency; New Thought, more popular among the educated and more prosperous classes, stressed immediately effective cures for the problems of this life.

Today, although lines are still drawn between them in the content of beliefs, practically they have been pulled closer together, if for no other reason than because of the upward mobility of evangelicals. Evangelicals have come to taste the joys and pains of middle-class life and have had thrust upon them new psychological adjustments. Finding happiness, feeling secure, worries about being accepted by others, dealing with anxieties and stress have all taken on new dimensions in their lives. As Richard Quebedeaux describes this religious blending of traditions: "If revivalistic Christianity offered an experiential soul cure to the poor and would-be rich, New Thought offered peace of mind and emotional tranquility to those already on the way up. Salvation was mentalized."[20]

Of course, more than upward mobility on the part of evangelicals was involved in mentalizing salvation. Two broader cultural preconditions are equally important, both of which have an affinity with post-World War II generational experiences. One was the diffusion of psychological language to wide sectors of American life. Affluence opened the way for a new discourse, drawn from popular psychology, on "quality of life," the need to "keep growing," the importance of being recognized as a "real person." Beginning in the 1970s, the "self" took on new meaning as a cultural category with far-reaching implications for how Americans saw themselves, their work and careers, their marriages and families, their private and public lives. It was the age of the "inner American," to cite the title of a well-known study reviewing the subjective health of the American people from the mid-1950s to the mid-1970s.[21] Stated another way, psychological discourse brought greater focus to the interiorization of life, to the inner life of impulse and subjectivity—what William James many years ago called "the sphere of felicity."

A second precondition of the mentalizing of salvation was the rise of the visual mode of communication—the shift from printed word to image. Television culminated the transition begun with photography and film in media epistemologies from a print culture to a culture of decontextualized imagery. We cannot document with hard evidence the impact of this shift, but a close affinity exists between mode of communication and religious and spiritual styles. In a print culture, priority was given to the objective, to the rational use of the mind, which encouraged religious discourse with logically ordered content. Doctrinal debate and theological reflection flourished under these conditions, as Neil Postman has argued.[22] But in an image culture the subjective takes precedence over the objective, and the constant flow of ever-changing images replaces the coherent, orderly arrangement of ideas. Fluidity and instantaneity not only define what we know but also alter our ways of knowing. More than anything else, fleeting images have the capacity to create a sense of reality as itself shifting and without permanence, to move us from one psychological world to another—not unlike the images, insights, thoughts, and emotions that arise out of the inner life of the spiritual pilgrim.[23]

These conditions help to explain why psychological imagery is so widespread, but another factor cannot be overlooked: the demography of midlife passage. Midlife is a time of heightened sensitivities and awareness, of thinking through where one has come from and where one is going, the discovery of more of oneself. It is also a time of reassessing self and others, of balancing major polarities within the personality such as young/old, destructive/creative, giving/receiving, and attachment/separateness. Much of what we observed fits this midlife model of maturing commitments. Life is not a linear path, as we have been told in many differing ways; rather, in such threshold periods, we find new levels of depth and breadth.

A mature self expresses itself in many ways. Some of the most common among the boomers are reaching out, letting go, finding anchors, finding meaning in gender experiences, and a renewed appreciation for natural things and the body.

Reaching Out

Like the mature Mollie, many boomers today recognize that preoccupation with self can be a dead-end path. The notion of the self as private consciousness independent of people and culture is misleading. One does not "find oneself" solely by looking inward, because the search for self, for the truly concerned, directs one outside again. Lasting fulfillment in life arises out of giving, and not just receiving. Daniel

Yankelovich, back in the early 1980s, warned of a "self-fulfillment trap" in which expectations can exceed what can reasonably be delivered. He observed a growing hunger for closer and deeper personal relationships, which he described as an emerging, more balanced "ethic of commitment."[24] Now this ethic, with its shift in emphasis away from self toward greater connectedness, appears to have blossomed into full form.

Time and time again, both men and women told us that what is now important in their lives is "my marriage," "the relationship I am in," or "my children." Working class and middle class, religious and secular, evangelical and New Ager, all are greatly concerned about their marriages and families today. The settings in which boomers now find themselves shape how they feel about their own self-fulfillment. Older boomers especially have a strong sense that one's own fulfillment comes not out of some private quest, but indirectly, through commitment to others. The pursuit of self was at one time top priority for many, but now it takes second place in a hierarchy not of "needs" but of "responsibilities." Among career women who admitted that once they were concerned largely with their own lives, we found a surprisingly strong sense of obligations to others, and especially to their children. As one career woman and single mother said when asked about her duty to herself: "My friends and family are most important. I feel fairly fulfilled in my own right, so maybe I can put that on the back burner."

Another woman, a practicing Catholic named Judy, reflected on the question this way:

> What's important? My family comes first, y'know. Definitely. The self-centered "me" generation, I think, was real. . . . I think that's a part of growing up, it's a stage . . . a lot of people running around doing a bunch of stuff that didn't really connect.

When asked more directly about obligations to herself, Judy replied:

> Oh yeah, that's a piece of the pie, y'know. And you got a whole pie and I think that maybe one-eighth is probably still Judy.

Age is helping to bring about a more mature spiritual outlook. Older boomers frequently speak of their children, in one way or another, as a source of wisdom. They learn from them the most elemental, but most important things. A North Carolina man spoke about what he has learned from his children, and of how his life had changed in middle age. Now forty-four years old and married for the second time, he put it this way when asked about what was most important to him:

First of all the relationships I have with my family. My last children were born when I was thirty-eight, my twin girls . . . it certainly is a hell of a lot different than being twenty-six, when I had Jason . . . I love to watch them more. I listen to them more. I don't boss them around as much. I learn from them more . . .

He mentioned in passing the importance of his job and went on to say:

After that my interests are simply finding the way for me to sit back and bliss out and be here for the next twenty or thirty years, because as all of us who reach forty realize, shit, we are not going to live forever, and I want to slow time down. It's gone too damn fast. So that's what I'm doing now.

A single man who never knew his father reflected on the spiritual insight that can come from reaching out to others. Growing up as a "latchkey" kid with his mother, he was on his own from a very young age, "going down my own road," as he said, trying to figure out why the world is as it is. Even in early adulthood he was still very introspective. After years of searching for truth and turning inward, exploring yoga, Transcendental Meditation, and other Eastern spiritualities, he now realizes that perhaps he was looking in the wrong places. Self-growth may come not from its own pursuit, but from getting involved with people. Our interview prompted him to think out loud and to clarify his goals in life in the following way:

. . . what I'm going to do is step back and regroup. . . . If for one or two people I can make that difference, I should do it. I've been talking for a couple of years of being a Big Brother and maybe taking on one or two kids through "Save the Children". . . actually do something that's going to make a difference . . . I will probably still give up my time in the form of envelope stuffing and answering the phones for groups that I'm involved with or I see fit to do, for some of the public television stations as well as the Vietnam veterans' food bank. . . . I feel I've done enough introverted inspection of myself and done self-growth, and I think the rest of self-growth will come through helping others.

Letting Go

Another trend is "letting go," or relinquishing that which is beyond one's personal power to control. "Letting go" was described earlier as a type of supply-side spirituality distinct from that of "mastery and control," its premise being that there is an ultimate harmony between sacred reality and one's own humanity, and that such harmony is best achieved through the conformity of minds and hearts to the powers of the universe. People who are inclined toward letting go as a spiritual approach are also more likely to emphasize the positive powers within an individual as opposed to those who see only the dark and negative aspects of a sinful humanity. Often it is those who have explored many differing religions—Eastern religions, and Buddhism in particular, or who have read psychology books—who are most disposed to letting go. The theme appears to be diffusing even into the evangelical boomer strongholds, as apparent in the bumper sticker "Let go and let God" found on many of their cars.

Recent developments in American culture, and in the boomer culture especially, may contribute to this growing emphasis on letting go. If, as Roland A. Delattre suggests, mastery and control as a strategy has come to be closely aligned with a culture of consumption and a dependence on acquisition as a ready solution to almost every problem, then the second strategy—letting go—offers resources and guidance for recovery in a context in which abundance and acquisition often lead to pathological results.[25] Boomers of all kinds—upscale and poor, religious and secular, liberal and conservative—increasingly recognize a need to find spiritual renewal and recovery from addictions and compulsions. The Twelve-Step programs are flourishing for this reason, based as they are on the twin principles of letting go of that which one cannot control, and taking responsibility for one's life. The programs help individuals to clarify that which is beyond personal control and that which is not, and in so doing force them to come to terms with themselves as human beings and with their own frailties. This dual grounding of the philosophy in individual freedom and personal responsibility is found in the "serenity prayer" so central to the programs: "God grant me the serenity to accept the things I cannot change, the courage to change the things I can, and the wisdom to know the difference."

The serenity prayer affirms a basic conviction about the self, what it can do and what it cannot. Letting go is cathartic; it purges one of emotions and unreasonable expectations of controlling outcomes, and thus helps to reaffirm a stronger, more focused sense of self. And with a stronger sense of self, the individual is able to deal more constructively with the image many boomers have as "victims" in an abusive, dysfunctional world. Many people who get to "know themselves" in this way find new energy and inner strength. Even people who are not active in Twelve-Step groups discover spiritual meaning in the psychology of recovery that has come to be widely spread in contemporary society.

Perhaps the best definition of "letting go" came from a thirty-nine-year-old physical therapist, a married woman with a child living on California's central coast. She said it means "giving up something that is holding you down, keeping you from being the person you'd like to be. Maybe it's guilt or something making you feel unhappy or sad, or you are just bogged down in life." An ex-Catholic who is no longer involved in any church, she very much wants to find the harmony that comes from knowing that she is at peace with herself and the world around her. She finds spiritual renewal in belonging to a "Moon Group." This group meets every month on the night of the full moon, on a wharf jutting out into the ocean. Here she and her husband and about ten other friends celebrate a communion with Hostess cupcakes ("Rough on the outside, but creamy and soft inside," she says) and meditate quietly about nature, the stars and the planets, and whatever higher order there must be. Each person concludes the ritual by throwing a stone toward the moon's shadow into the ocean. "Whatever is on your mind," she says, "let it go." Members of the group come away, as she says, "feeling connected to something bigger."

A committed Catholic lay worker in Massachusetts, who helps operate a shelter for the homeless, speaks in more traditional religious language that testifies to the same power that comes from such self-understanding. Well-versed theologically and knowing much about the lives of Catholic saints, she tells of how in her own religious explorations, including a brief foray into Buddhism and her ongoing participation in Overeaters Anonymous (O.A.), she finally found wisdom. Wisdom lay in the realization of the self and that she was responsible, in some final sense, only for herself. Our interview with her went as follows:

INTERVIEWER: Who are you responsible for?

RESPONDENT: Myself only.

INTERVIEWER: Okay.

RESPONDENT: I used to think I was responsible for a lot of other people, and for all the problems. And since I've been going to O.A. . . . . the Twelve-Step program, I'm realizing that I'm only responsible for myself. And so I must do what I need to do and follow as God is talking to me. I used to think that kind of thinking was maybe selfish or individualistic, but I think now it is the only way I can be . . . if we know that we are responsible for ourself, then of course we have to always be desirable of self-knowledge. The saints say that. They say there's no knowledge of God without knowledge of self, no true knowledge of God.

For her, this knowledge—of God and of self—leads to others and to taking action:

And that voice inside will say, y'know, you really need to be with your son . . . or you really need to call this friend, or you really need to write this statement on abortion. So in that way, it leads you to others; but first one must be subject to God, who shows us who we are.

But action must follow knowledge of self, it is not the source of the self-understanding. For both of these women, this primacy of the self is essential. Whether it is "feeling connected to something bigger," as with the Moon Group, or being led by God's "voice inside" to others, as with this Catholic lay worker, both are saying that coming to terms with one's self is an empowering experience and an important first step in spiritual growth. Many boomers, from differing social backgrounds and with very differing religious perspectives, have learned something of the wisdom that comes from such knowledge.

Not just knowledge of self, but a greater love of self is also part of the experience. A positive identity involves a wholesome respect for, and recognition of, self. Many people we talked to, and especially those who have reacted negatively to traditional Christian teachings, feel that they were misled in being told it was a sin to love yourself. Protestants and Catholics, mainliners and evangelicals, all expressed dissatisfaction with some of the things they had been taught about the inherent sinfulness of human nature. "I think that is devastating, awful," as one ex-Southern Baptist put it, "and I think it takes a long time to readjust yourself. You have to do what you have to do for yourself, and not for other people." Letting go means many things, but one thing it means for this generation is the freedom to let go of old ways of religious thinking that are at odds with a healthy sense of self.

Finding Anchors

Others we talked to expressed the need to find anchors that transcend both self and others, to have something solid on which to base their lives. They see the choice between self versus others as a false dichotomy, and not really resolvable on its own terms. Mutually dependent on one another, the two are inseparable and best understood in relation to something larger than either of them. Some larger, overarching canopy, based on a belief in God or an Ultimate Power, can pull the two together. In response to the question about what is now most important—self or others—a very mature twenty-nine-year-old medical student, a mainline Protestant, put it as follows:

> . . . it would be an obligation to something else that would encompass both of these things. I wouldn't say one of those things over the other. I'd say that there is an obligation to something higher than yourself, something higher than myself. But there is necessarily an obligation to family and community and so on. Then there is an obligation to yourself. But I think it is all pulled together by an obligation to something, I guess to God.

Seldom does one hear such articulate statements about the hierarchy of loyalties. More often we heard testimonials about the importance of finding roots in a religious tradition, or of life in a religious or spiritually minded group. There is much interest in the discovery, or rediscovery, of religious teachings—especially by those who have been overshadowed by the established Judeo-Christian institutions. Neo-Paganism, Wicca, medieval mystics, Eastern faiths, and Native American traditions all attract interest because they are distinct, tend not to present deity in patriarchal terms, and offer fresh insights into the understanding of self. Christian saints and historical religious figures, including Mahatma Gandhi, Martin Luther King, Jr., Mother Teresa, and Billy Graham, attract interest as lives that are deeply rooted in a particular tradition. Depending on people's religious persuasions, they naturally differ in whom they select as exemplary, but boomers we talked to—be they liberal or conservative, religious or secular—seem to have little difficulty naming religious figures that they admire. For a generation for whom it is said there are no heroes, religious and spiritual biographies have a deep appeal.

Gender and Spirituality

The great changes in gender roles have churned up considerable ferment deep in the male and female psyche and unleashed new spiritual energies. A new kind of man and woman is emerging that many boomers sense and applaud but often cannot describe very well in words. Women are better able to articulate these new identities than men. Deeply caught up in the gender revolution and facing the practical problems of juggling careers and family responsibilities, boomer women find themselves today searching for new spiritual directions. Energies get expressed across the entire religious spectrum. The movement to restore the

141

female principle to religion, as Annie Gottlieb says, "ranges from all-woman Goddess worship at one pole to women's attempts to crash the Catholic priesthood at the other. In between are some fascinating experiments in balancing the female and male principles."[26]

Conventional wisdom has it that conservatives aren't feminists, but this isn't true. A Jewish woman who had converted to Orthodoxy and was planning to move to Israel spoke to us with great passion about having recently read Tamar Frankel's *The Voice of Sarah:* "Now I told you the feminist movement is not my thing, but it's really fascinating . . . this woman found all these learned women in Jerusalem . . . I'm learning so much about the women in the Torah." Many traditional-minded women have a subtle interest in, and identification with, feminist views of women. Career women often are looking for ways to deal with the tensions arising out of the conflicting demands of work and of family. It is not uncommon to hear expressions of being overwhelmed. Sometimes they turn to religion in desperation, not knowing whether or not it has anything to offer, and maybe even a bit embarrassed to admit that what they really want is some help with their own lives. We spoke with a traditional Catholic woman in a middle-management position of a large corporation, for example, who was experiencing great strains dealing with all the demands of marriage, children, and career. She had recently joined a renewal group in her parish in eastern North Carolina, and was finding the weekly meetings a "growth" experience. But when we asked about why she participates in the renewal group, she was reluctant to tell us: "I'm not sure I even want to say it." Further assured that the interview was anonymous, she went on to say:

> . . . perhaps what I'm looking for is more rules, some guidance that I'm living my life the way it should be lived or, you know, helpful hints, or how should it be improved? What should I be doing? . . . I'm struggling to find out what's right and what we should be doing. And I guess in raising children and careers and everything, I just feel like I need some more guidance.

Often the churches fail to provide the practical help and emotional support working women are looking for. As the first generation of women to enter the labor force in such large numbers, organized religion has still to find ways of relating more meaningfully to their needs.

On the more radical, feminist side of the spectrum, we find the repudiation of the dominant Judeo-Christian tradition and the emergence of the Goddess movement. "I'm a witchy woman" said a forty-year-old single mother in South Carolina, an ex-Catholic who now attends both neo-Pagan festivals and a local Unitarian church. She pointed out that there are powers of spiritual understanding that only women possess: "It is the power within a woman," she says, "as it relates to the cycles of nature." Another single mother and career woman, an ex-Southern Baptist living in North Carolina, said, "I have an appreciation for things that have to do with my body and the moon and things like that." Asked if she was involved in Goddess worship, she first said no, that she wasn't involved in any rituals, and then reconsidered her answer as she thought about a close circle of women friends she had recently joined:

RESPONDENT: Yeah, I need spirituality. Yeah, I need unity. The thing I need the most in my life . . .

INTERVIEWER: What would it be?

RESPONDENT: It's . . . a few people who I consider my family, they are my community, they are very important to me. I think we do real serious growth together. . . . That gives more meaning to my life than anything else . . . we have rituals, but we don't have them every Sunday or every Saturday or every Wednesday or every solar eclipse or full moon. Women talking about certain things to me is ritual. Even though we have not said, "Okay, we're going to talk about PMS, and then we are going to have tea and then someone is going to lead the group," there is ritual behavior surrounding talking about menstruation.

For each of these single, working mothers, Goddess symbolism is spiritually uplifting, for it legitimates female power. It affirms her own good and independent power in contrast with the usual images, enshrouded in religious traditions, of women as passive, or dependent, or as seductive and sinful. It affirms her own power of will and of harmonizing with natural energies and the energies created by others, helping to overcome all the emphasis in patriarchal culture on submission of one's own will to higher powers. The ties with nature, with the moon in its waxing, full, and waning phases, affirm the female body in its own monthly cycle. Birth, menstruation, and female sexuality are all celebrated as "women's mysteries," as spiritually empowering and a source of bonding among women. Like the promise of a full moon that comes every month, they are also a source of unending spiritual replenishment. Over against a male culture that has regarded such things as dangerous and evil, the Goddess symbols communicate a vision of life that is cyclic rather than linear; cycles of birth and death, ovulation and menstruation, are all endowed with great mystery and sanctity.[27]

The gender revolution has also given rise to a men's spiritual movement. A thirty-seven-year-old moderately conservative Protestant man we met in eastern Washington spoke of being a "kinder, better man" after participating in a men's support group. In this group they discussed portions of Sam Keen's *Fire in the Belly,* which describes war, work, and sex as a triad forming the pillars of male identity.[28] Encouraged by a growing men's movement, participants in this group look for ways to throw off the old pillars of male identity, to explore their emotions and discover the feminine sides of their lives. Exploring their feelings toward their own fathers is part of what they must often work through. For many boomer men, the void of the absent father is very real, either in their own memories or for those of their children. Usually this void was due to the demands of work, or because of divorce or desertion. Men who commit to this spiritual exploration soon discover that they are on a pilgrimage, a cycle of death and rebirth, that involves the pain of breaking out of old notions of manhood and the exhilaration of discovering new meanings.

A distinct gender difference is apparent: Women who have intense spiritual experiences are more likely to report them as "self-empowering," as opportunities for exploring who they are as people independent of their roles. Although men rediscover themselves and learn about intimacy and caring as people, spiritual exploration tends to lead them to a renewed concern for themselves in relation to wives and children. Intense spiritual experiences thus appear to liberate both men and women from their usual preoccupations. As psychologist Carol Gilligan has described it, men are led away from their ego-centered, separationist activities toward reintegration, and women are led away from nurturing and concern for attachments toward greater self-expansiveness.[29]

Natural Things and the Body

The new spiritual sensibility endows all of nature with sacred meaning. Many people speak of experiences in which they are sustained by something greater than themselves, experiences often related one way or another to the larger world of nature—saving whales, trying to protect the environment, contributing to Greenpeace, global ecological awareness, earth politics. To some, such experiences are similar to the religious concept of grace—nature is a gift full of wonder and awe. But probably for most, they are expressions of the self in its interconnectedness with all of creation. One simply finds oneself empowered to act on behalf of other beings, or on behalf of the whole. The environment provokes a strong response, if for no other reason than because individuals learn from it that they, and all other living things, are all part of a global world, that we are all in a relational web, and that "to pluck a flower is to trouble a star."[30] For a very few, there is the Gaia hypothesis, which holds that the earth is a living entity that can and will correct the imbalances that humans have inflicted on it.

One respondent tells of a spiritual experience she had on a trip to the Canadian Rockies:

> . . . God is in those beautiful mountains and meadows . . . I mean, you can just see, "Take care of me please," "Don't destroy me," "Don't litter me up," "Don't trample me," "Be careful where you step."

A woman living on a farm in North Carolina says:

> Working with animals and working with plants is very calming, just relax at it. You feel like you are in tune with the world. You appreciate things more.

Then, describing what nature has meant for her thirteen-year-old son, she uses earthy terms:

> The first time Brian had to clean the manure out of the barn it nearly killed him. And now he will go out there and get it all over his coat and everything and come in the house and he is fine. It helps a lot with their self-esteem. Lets them know that there are more things in the world than what you see on television.

The body is a source of inspiration and wonder, even to skeptics and those who are not religiously inclined. A medical doctor who does research on physiology, an agnostic struggling with his doubts, has this to say:

> I become more and more deeply moved with the magic of how the body works. It's incredibly beautiful, a profoundly beautiful creation. A religious person would say, well, obviously, God made it but I somehow don't come to that conclusion but I'm still extremely moved by it. The amazing beauty and intricacy of this organism and how it's made and how the various enzyme systems work and the beautiful interplay of all the things that go on to allow it to function properly.

For boomers, the body is more than just a source of inspiration and wonder, it is of great significance—trying to keep it in shape, trying to keep it healthy, trying to hold on to its youthful beauty. At the age when so much is happening to their bodies, they cannot escape the worries of physical decline and the inevitable relative comparisons brought on by television ads and the cult of the "body beautiful" in America. "Who is as sexy as those damned Pontiac ads make you out to be, and still has four kids?" one woman screams out in frustration. This same young thirty-year-old Southern woman tells of looking at *Playboy* magazine back when she was a child and wondering, "Wow, I'm going to look like that?" Now when she looks and sees all the pictures of younger women, she wonders when her magic moment passed and concludes, "It must have happened while I was asleep." Boomers have a renewed appreciation of the physical: of jogging, of exercising, of eating properly, of making love, of doing things with your hands, of gardening, of *tai ch'i* classes, of finding ecstasy in simple things. Interconnectedness reaches not just globally and to the larger environment, but to the daily rhythms of life, including what we eat, how we treat our bodies, the creation and expression of bodily energies. Leisure and enjoyment are invested with new meaning in a post-Protestant culture where people are more aware of their bodies, and of the rightful place of pleasure in the scheme of things. The body is not set apart from but is the basis of the spiritual and for the organizing of life experiences; it has become, as writer Annie Gottlieb says, a "medium of celebration, compassion, and community."[31]

The physical and spiritual intermesh in many ways. For a generation in which many are seeking to overcome some of the metaphysical dualisms that have long existed, the physical can be the conduit to greater spiritual awakening. The evangelical who surfs for the Lord speaks of our bodies being "the temples of God, and if they are, he would want us to respect them, take care of them, and yes, enjoy them." Another example comes from a churchgoing woman in North Carolina, who told us that "the first step for me in growing was becoming aware of my body." When asked to say more, she told us about getting involved in a group concerned with bodywork and described her responses to the leader of this group:

RESPONDENT: I had this feeling I was going to like her. She just started telling me some stuff. And I went oh, oh . . . It just opened the flood gate of spirituality for me.

INTERVIEWER: Telling you such things as what?

RESPONDENT: Things such as everything that happens to us happens for our highest good . . . And I go, 'What?' And that was the key to unlocking fear for me. If I could believe that everything could happen to me for my highest good, then I could not be afraid anymore.

INTERVIEWER: What were you afraid of?

RESPONDENT: Oh, death by knife. Husband an alcoholic. My mother has been brought up in a Southern Baptist thing and she was real fearful of hell. And real fearful of doing things wrong. But I think it boiled down to somehow I reclaimed my authority over my life. I didn't look to the church or to some male authority figure to interpret anything for me. I just reclaimed my authority over myself and my spirituality.

Reclaiming authority—that's perhaps the most fundamental of all the spiritual trends now underway. Without some reclaiming of authority, there can be no genuine affirmation of self, no real spiritual awakening. And as this example illustrates, rediscovery of the body, and of how the body is a manifestation of the self, is a vital part of this awakening.

In Part Two, we have looked at the spiritual currents now flowing in the boomer population. We described the two polar extremes as represented in the lives of Mollie Stone and Linda Kramer: an expansive mysticism versus a conservative theistic faith. The two extremes organize much of the religious and spiritual life of this generation today. Even those in the religious middle, who are neither New Agers nor fundamentalists, easily get drawn into these currents. Growing up in the sixties had a strong and lasting impact, predisposing them toward one or the other of these major meaning systems. It is hard to imagine that this great spiritual divide will not continue, at least for the foreseeable future.

But as we have also seen, there are currents flowing that cut across the great spiritual divide. The new values emphasize self-fulfillment and self-growth, inner spiritual discovery and exploration. A greater sense of self, appreciation of the body, of gender and spirituality, of reaching out to others, and of letting go are all themes that find common expression. Boomers are growing older, and many are approaching midlife and a phase of reflection that encourages greater clarity of who they are and a more balanced sense of commitment in their lives. Older boomers especially—inside and outside organized religion, both liberals and conservatives—are spiritually sensitive and seeking answers to the perennial questions about the meaning and purpose of life. As great as this spiritual divide is, it is not as vast as much of the rhetoric often implies.

We have yet to examine what all this spiritual ferment might mean for organized religion. Do any of the spiraling paths on which many boomers are traveling today lead to a return to the churches and synagogues? And if so, what are the new patterns of religious involvement? What is it about religious congregations that attract and repel boomers? These are questions that we will consider in the next section.

PART THREE

Institution

CHAPTER 6

Returning to the Fold

Let us begin this section by taking another look at Barry Johnson, the engineer from North Carolina. After almost a twenty-year absence from any church, Barry is now actively involved again in a progressive Southern Baptist church.

When asked why he has returned to church, Barry says he did so because of his children. Like so many other older boomers who abandoned religious institutions when they were growing up, he now finds himself with parental responsibilities, and with children who are growing up much faster than he cares to admit. At the time he starting attending church again, one child was already fourteen, the other nine. His wife convinced him, as he says, "Whether I bought into it or not, that I had an obligation to support some religious training, some religious upbringing, something. . . . I had to look back . . . and agree with her, because I was brought up that way." His parents saw to it that he was "exposed" to religious teachings, so why shouldn't he do the same for his children? Taking the children to church is somewhat like sending them to college—both are obligations, as he sees it, that a parent ought to take seriously.

But other things also help account for why Barry has gone back to church. For the past twenty years, he has invested much time into his career as an electrical engineer, organizing his life largely around his job and the family. Some parts of his life seem well developed, but others do not. Now, at midlife, he finds himself asking what life is all about and looking for ways to invest in himself, to develop aspects of his life beyond what he does at work and at home. Reading M. Scott Peck some years ago stirred him to thinking in this direction, and since then he has become more determined to live more deeply, and not to be so driven by external forces. He was fortunate in finding a church that helps him to heed the voice within and to cultivate the inner life.

Like many boomers in their forties, Barry thinks a lot about his life in relation to younger and older generations. For years he was sandwiched between two generations, spending much of his time devoted to the needs of one or the other. Both parents were ill and suffered for quite a while; but this past year his mother, the last of his parents, died of cancer. Thrust into a new role of family authority, he now finds himself a part of the older generation. Lately, this has had a powerful psychological impact on how he thinks of himself and of his relation to family members. He thinks a great deal about what life will be like once the kids are grown up and out of the house. At the time we interviewed him, he was feeling the heavy weight of parental responsibilities, and saving money for his kids' college education, and asking how one deals with "trying to be the provider, trying to juggle all that with my own need to find some sort of meaning in life." More so than ever before, he feels he deserves some "space" of his own. Working out the right balance of obligations under these circumstances—to family and to self—has become a pressing and a deeply spiritual matter for him.

His concern to have his own space may well be rooted in his earlier years. One detects a sober and somewhat skeptical stance toward institutional religion, arising no doubt out of his stormy experiences growing up as a white liberal in the South during the civil rights days. It was then that he had to wrestle with his conscience over what was right, even if it meant going against local customs. A sense of his own marginal identity still comes through as he talks about mainstream values and institutions in the United States today, which probably accounts for why he and his family have looked for a progressive church: He simply would not fit into many churches. Asked about what growing up in the sixties taught him, he says:

> I think it has given me a certain amount of skepticism. Like I said, the country proved itself to be fallible during that period of time. . . . And the leaders that we had proved themselves to be extremely fallible during that period of time and capable of making horrendous errors that cost thousands of people their lives. So I think one of the things I learned from that period of time is that you don't always

believe in the authority that is there. Don't always accept it as being right, even though it may be the law or it may be the accepted mainstream.

Asked further if his is a healthy sense of skepticism, he answers:

I like to think so. I like to think that it enabled me to look at policies the country has and look at values that people have, and just because they happen to be in the majority doesn't mean that I have to accept them. I think it's healthy.

His suspiciousness of institutions lives on with him, as does a strong determination to cultivate his own inner resources. Popular cultural styles inform how he speaks religiously, in the language of consumption, as something you "buy into"; religion is something about which you have options—you select it, and if it fits your needs, then you get involved. Yet his religious sensibilities run much deeper than they appear on the surface. Deeply influenced by "post-material" values such as concern for quality of life and finding meaning and purpose in life, Barry is deeply committed to spiritual concerns. He raises hard questions about life that can't be answered in simple or absolute fashion. Faith for him is not a creed, but an experience; not a set of moral rules, but a dimension of life. He abhors yuppie materialistic values and selfish pursuits. He came out of the sixties greatly influenced by its idealism: Beautiful things had happened back then that made people look beyond their own narrow concerns, that made them aware of things other than themselves. The environment, justice issues, helping people are all still important to him. By this standard the self-absorbed and greedy 1980s were a major setback to the moral virtues of his generation.

Taking his obligations to others seriously, Barry finds much meaning in his personal relationships. He can discern mystery and the sacred in his dealings with people. He likes to recount an experience he had not long ago that profoundly touched him and helped reorient his outlook. While walking on the beach during a reflective moment, he noticed a flock of birds:

You'd never see a bird out there by himself . . . just birds in a little flock . . . I thought, that's the way life is supposed to be. You are supposed to be a part of something, and if you are really going to live life, religious[ly] or otherwise, you need to have relationships with people and with . . . something . . . you believe in.

Despite his own deeply personal religious quests, religion is something deeply social for Barry. "If I was the only person in the world," he says, "I'm not so sure I'd be religious."

He goes even further. When asked how he feels about returning to church, what that experience has been like, he answers:

> I think I find God in people. I guess when I was a kid, I can remember thinking about God as being this father figure that lived up in the heavens. Had a big white beard and just kind of sat up there in a control room and kind of ran the show. Of course, as I grew up and found that things didn't seem to be running quite that way . . . I had to abandon that thought. So I've grown into thinking that I find God in people. And the most rewarding experiences I've had in church have been in relationships that have occurred, . . . where I've really got to know somebody's feelings. And I think when somebody's feelings about God comes out, that's God speaking to me through them in some way.

For Barry, these experiences also occur outside of church. Because he experiences the divine through people, he finds similar moments in everyday life when he discerns mystery and sacredness. "I find it in my kids," he says, "I find it in talking to my wife sometimes. I find it in relationships I have with people at work on occasion . . . so it tends to be varied." To experience the sacred through others in this way points to an "analogical" religious imagination, a way of seeing the world filled with God, or a set of ordered relationships that reveal, however imperfectly, the presence of God.[1] Many of the people we talked to who have returned to a serious religious commitment have such a sacramental conception involving a sense of mystery in the everyday relations of life. That we find evidence of such religious imagination on the part of a Protestant is also testimony that this mode of apprehending the presence of God is not exclusively a Catholic sensibility. It may well be that those boomers who have been thrust into a longer, sandwiched relationship between their parents and their children, and thus have had to take on extended responsibilities, think more in analogical terms.

HOW MANY ARE RETURNING?

Many in Barry's generation today, with or without his strong religious sensibilities, are exploring churches, synagogues, and other religious institutions. A fourth say they are more active now than they were five years ago, one-half say they are involved about as much now as then. As we pointed out in chapter 2, two-thirds of all boomers reared in a religious tradition dropped out of their churches and synagogues during their teens or early twenties. The average age (mean) for dropping out was 21.1 years for the older boomers, and 18.2 years for the younger boomers—in both instances at a younger age than that reported by pre-boomers.[2] Since then, many who fell away have returned to greater religious involvement; but many have not. In fact, more have *not* returned than have, suggesting that we should be careful not to overgeneralize or be misled by media hype about how boomers are going back to church. Looking at the generation as a whole today, the religious breakdown is as follows: loyalists 33%, returnees 25%, and dropouts 42%. Of the three, clearly dropouts are the largest group.

It is important to recognize that these figures are only a snapshot taken at a particular point in time. Statistics such as these fail to describe the dynamic character of people's religious lives. As we have observed, the American religious situation is very open and fluid: People move "into" and "out of" organized religion with remarkable ease. In a society where religious memberships and participation are voluntary, people freely come and go. Frequently, after dropping out people explore new faiths—often in ways that are fairly invisible, such as reading books, attending lectures, listening to audiocassettes, or subscribing to a newsletter. Previous research has estimated that roughly one out of every two Americans drops out of active religious participation for a period of at least two years or more sometime during their lifetime. Disengagement is typically a temporary phenomenon, with the vast majority—upwards of 80% of Americans—returning at some point, usually to a church or a synagogue.[3] Of the boomers we studied, those who had returned had done so on the average by age 28.7 for the older cohort, and age 24.3 for the younger cohort.[4] Some people return for a while, then drop out once more, only to return again later on. We talked with people who had been in and out of congregations in various phases of their lives as many as four or five times. That is the exception, of course, since most who drop out and return do so one, two, or possibly three times, but seldom more than three times.

Fluidity means that we often caught people during a religious upswing or downswing. Among dropouts, we often found a great deal of religious interest. Dropouts report thinking about the purpose of life and about suffering in the world as much as do the loyal churchgoers. In many instances it was simply a matter of chance that we interviewed people when they were in a dropout rather than a returning phase of their spiritual journeys. Had the interview been six months or a year later, many would stand in a different relationship with institutional religion (including others, of course, who would be dropouts now rather than returnees). For example, in a second interview with an English professor who had been highly involved in alternative religions while growing up, our double-checking about his religious preference led to the following exchange:

> INTERVIEWER: Let's see, your religious preference now is Catholic-slash-Buddhist?
>
> RESPONDENT: No. She [the first interviewer] was having trouble tracking me down on that. I've gone through a lot of phases, right now I'm leaning toward Catholic. We're probably going to register the baby with the Catholic Church cause I think the child should have some exposure to the spiritual side of things somewhere. . . . so I'd have to say I'm leaning heavily toward Catholicism.

Such language as "leaning," or "my preference is," is not uncommon. One-half of all the dropouts say that they have "checked out" other parishes and congregations that they might attend. When asked about their chances of becoming involved in a church or synagogue again in the future, 71% indicate "very likely" or "possibly"—thus indicating strong religious interest. Younger dropouts say that when they have *children* of their own maybe they will return; the older ones say they might come back if they can find *churches* that they like. Subjective considerations loom very large for those who feel deeply estranged from religious institutions—with much importance attached to phrases like "feeling comfortable with a church" or "liking a congregation." One-third of all dropouts say that they have explored other teachings and philosophies, the most frequently mentioned being Zen Buddhism or Eastern religious thought more generally.

WHY DO PEOPLE RETURN?

Why do people return to organized religion? What distinguishes those who return from those who remain as dropouts? Our description of Barry has already given us some hints of important demographic and religious factors. In our research we sought answers to these questions by asking people why they had gone back—and many told us in their own words.

Unquestionably, the most frequently cited reasons have to do with family life. The influence of a spouse and keeping harmony within the family are strong factors, but far more important is the religious upbringing of children. The presence of young, school-age children and feelings of parental responsibility for them drives boomers back to church and to enroll their children in religious education classes. Having had parents with a religious background who took them to church is obviously a crucial factor in the thinking of boomers who must now make decisions about their own children. Often the reasons for going back are cast in terms of the "needs" of children. When asked whether raising kids had influenced her to return to church, one Catholic mother put it this way:

> Yeah. Because, y'know, they need that influence. So I find myself looking for a Christian school . . . we have a Catholic church here which is kind of small.

A conservative Protestant who had dropped out of church during college, but was now married with three children ages ten, eight, and two, puts the emphasis a little differently:

> I guess I valued the upbringing of going to church, and I wanted that for my children. It was very important for them to be raised in the community of church, to be taught, especially nowadays, a moral standard to live by.

Returning to church with the family seems like a happy and pleasurable venture, yet for some people it is riddled with pain. Returning can reflect a desperate attempt to work out marital and family problems, especially when there are children from previous marriages or problems resulting from abuse or addiction. Heartache and struggle are part of the story of this woman, who had converted to Catholicism in an attempt to save her marriage and bring her family together:

INTERVIEWER: So what made you convert to Catholicism?

RESPONDENT: Well, for about a year, I was going around to all these different churches . . .

INTERVIEWER: Why?

RESPONDENT: I've got a family . . . it felt like all these people in the same house, it didn't feel like a family, and I thought, no . . .

INTERVIEWER: You're talking about your own kids and your husband?

RESPONDENT: Yeah, yeah. So I thought, it would be good for the kids. I've always seen people who go to church, they have an inner strength. And they're a family unit and that's what I wanted. So I started going around and I couldn't find what I wanted.

INTERVIEWER: You went to the Protestant churches?

RESPONDENT: I went to all of them. About the only thing I didn't investigate was Jewish. . . . And we met with the father and the sisters and . . . I don't know . . . they just made us feel so welcome and so glad to see us . . . my husband was an alcoholic and we lived with that and then he got sick. He quit drinking . . . it just seemed like the right thing to do at the time. I figured it would give us the strength we needed and something to do that doesn't involve alcohol, y'know?

A second set of reasons for returning has to do with a personal quest for meaning—for something to believe in, for answers to questions about life. Feelings of emptiness and loneliness, whether or not they are articulated in this way, lead people in such pursuits. Even among those who return supposedly for the children, as one astute pastor remarked to us, often "the children become a safe vehicle for them [the parents] to come without ever admitting that there is something in it for them." Forty-three percent of all the boomers report thinking a "lot" about suffering in the world; 31% the same about the purpose of life; 29% the same about what happens after death. If we add those who say they think "some" about such matters, between 70% and 90% give some attention to these existential concerns. No matter the religious background, current socioeconomic status, age, gender, or lifestyle, boomers—like people of all generations—think a good deal about these larger questions of meaning in life. On two of the items—about purpose in life and what happens after death—returnees think a good deal more than do dropouts. Through churchgoing, and a renewed cultivation of faith, they apparently find some answers to their questions in the form of comfort, peace, and happiness.

A woman in North Carolina put it this way:

Something was missing. You turn around and you go, is this it? I have a nice husband, I have a nice house; I was just about to finish graduate school. I knew I was going to have a very marketable degree. I wanted to do it. And you turn and you go, here I am. This is it. And there were just things that were missing. I just didn't have stimulation. I didn't have the motivation. And I guess when you mentioned faith, I guess that's what was gone.

She rediscovered faith but admits she continues to wrestle with her belief in God. Like so many others we interviewed (one-half of the boomers in the survey), she is very honest concerning her doubts about God. But unlike many, she is discerning and articulate about how her beliefs about God have changed. And unlike some whose spiritual journeys have taken them out of religion altogether, hers has led her back with a stronger existential, demythologized faith. Asked about her belief in God, the exchange goes:

RESPONDENT: I think I believe in God.

INTERVIEWER: You think? You are not sure?

RESPONDENT: No.

INTERVIEWER: You are not sure. How come?

RESPONDENT: The fairy tales. I mean, I don't believe in a God that sits in heaven, got this long white beard and he wears this robe, and you go to heaven and you go to hell because you played poker. Or, "Oops, you used coke—you've got to go." That kind of stuff. That's the kind of religion I had growing up. And those are the negative sides of it. The positive side of it is, I came back. . . . That's why I said when you said do you believe in God, and I go, I think so. I believe in the things that I hear [my pastor] say God stands for. Can I put it that way? I believe in those things. But I don't know if God is any more than that.

She gives voice to widespread feelings that old ways of believing aren't enough, and that the religious search is, in the words of a recent commentator, "*not* a nostalgic revisiting of a safe, comfortable, sentimental religiousness."[5]

A third cluster of responses emphasizes the importance of belonging to a community. Being with others, group support, sharing faith, doing things together, all are desirable—much the way Barry looks on his own involvement in a congregation. Of course, there is a considerable amount of nostalgia, and maybe even some cognitive dissonance, associated with religious belonging. Americans view religious belonging very favorably, yet great numbers of them have little involvement in religious communities. Roughly eight out of ten boomers identify themselves religiously, but far fewer—about one-half—are regularly involved in a congregation or religious group of some kind. Nine out of ten say one can be a good Christian without attending church; well over two-thirds say an individual should arrive at his or her own religious beliefs independently of any church or synagogue. Some feel there is an inherent tension between "believing" and "belonging": Assent to belief comes easily in a society where almost everyone says they believe, but communal involvement is seen as optional. They feel considerable nostalgia about the church that stems from childhood memories of families worshiping together, and some guilt because they are not more actively involved.

America, as Andrew M. Greeley reminds us, historically has been a "denominational society," in the sense that religious belonging—even if only in a nominal way—is important socially and psychologically. For many boomers this sense of community is very appealing, even to some dropouts who are unlikely ever to return. An agnostic we talked to, for example, said she would "love to be part of a religious community," but she can't reconcile belonging with her lack of belief in God. "I've always been jealous of my friends who have the faith," she goes on to say, "that allowed them to honestly be part of those things." Many look on religious groups as special, as groups dealing in something that secular organizations cannot match. Few are able to articulate very well other than in clichés and worn-out stereotypes why religious groups are special. The most succinct response we heard came from a highly committed man in Massachusetts: "I believe that the church offers something to me that I can't find anyplace else . . . that fellowship of people, of believers, the support that sustains us even in the difficult times."

For the dedicated few, an intentional religious community is a considered option. Eucharistic fellowships and home churches—small groups committed either to shared living or to celebrating a faith community—exist independently of regular congregations.[6] Here belonging takes on an even greater significance. The Catholic lay worker in Massachusetts who was mentioned earlier had this to say about living in a shelter for the homeless:

> I think we know God in community. I think whether it's a congregation or a faith community, I think there is something inadequate about seeing God in isolation. . . . you can't just love God and not love your brothers and sisters.

A thirty-eight-year-old charismatic Episcopalian from Ohio, who belongs to a home church along with his wife and children, was less able to express his feeling in words, but no less enthusiastic. When asked about why the home church to which he belongs was formed, he had this to say about its purpose: "to train people, or to get people talking about the Lord." Sharing, discipline, and fellowship—all qualities of nurturing that are found within small support groups.

These two people would not agree on very much, certainly not on politics. One a radical, liberationist-oriented Catholic, the other a conservative, charismatic Protestant, they differ in outlook about as much as any two people we talked to. No doubt they would find it very difficult if not impossible to talk to one another religiously, because their languages of faith are so very different. Yet both are caught up in a vision of belonging to a community of the committed. Both find in an intentional religious group solutions to their yearnings for a responsible self; both want a better society, though they differ in how to bring it about; both know of the spiritual growth that comes out of a supportive group experience. Both are attracted to intentional communities because, perhaps in a fundamental way, such involvement is a way to resolve the deep tensions between commitment to themselves and to others. Here they find the vital balance between the two that they are seeking.

SOME HYPOTHESES ABOUT RETURNING

Various hypotheses have been put forward about religious involvement that may shed some light on why people return to organized religion. We examined a number of these using the survey data: childhood religious socialization, parent-child relations and upbringing, life cycle, influence of spouse, education, and fear of downward mobility.

Childhood Religious Socialization

It is reasonable to expect that people with a strong religious background might, after a period of absence, return to greater religious involvement. It would be expected that religious socialization in the family is an important and lasting influence that shapes the child's belief in God and other doctrinal beliefs. Core ethical values and fundamental views of the self, of others, and of the world, as well as habits of churchgoing, are all learned in the family environment. Much research literature underscores the role of family life in shaping religious imaginations and loyalties.[7] Indeed, some of our respondents spoke warmly about their childhood years with their parents: of listening to bedside Bible stories, of families praying together, of parents and children attending religious services together.

But the impact of childhood religious socialization depends on the larger cultural climate in which children grow up. In a family-oriented climate, religious values across generations will be reinforced; however, in an environment with greater distance between the views of parents and teenagers, family socialization processes break down. Even the early childhood experiences of the older boomers may have been conducive to a breakdown of family influence. Growing up in the "aberrant" 1950s and early 1960s—a period far more conservative and conformist than the decades immediately before or since—perhaps led to a disposition toward questioning the widely held norms of patriotism, traditional family gender roles, and the complacent religiosity of the time. Given this disposition to question and to doubt, the death of President Kennedy in 1963 and the series of disillusionments that followed in the civil rights struggle and the Vietnam War helped to create a more generalized state of institutional alienation. This alienation may have undermined much of the family's influence on boomers' outlook, and especially their religious and political views.[8]

Based on our survey, the early religious socialization of the children had mixed effects. Those whose mothers and fathers did not attend religious services regularly were much more likely themselves to drop out; however, parental religious involvement makes no difference on whether or not the respondent returns. A similar pattern holds for the boomers' own religious involvement as a child. Those who were the least likely to attend Sunday school or religious services at the age of eight or ten were more likely to drop out, but their childhood levels of involvement were unrelated to their future involvement. If anything, those who never attended or attended irregularly as children were somewhat more likely to become involved later in life. Thus for this generation, parental religiosity appears to be more a factor as it bears on dropping out than on returning to religious participation. The latter is counter to what we would expect and suggests perhaps a generational break in traditional religious patterns.

Parent-Child Relations and Upbringing

A related hypothesis focuses on the character and quality of the relations between parents and children growing up. This argument is compelling both by its logic and by the amount of evidence mustered in its support. Studies indicate that social experimenters—youth inclined to deviate from conventional norms—are more likely to come from homes where relations with parents are characterized as permissive.[9] Liberal child-rearing philosophies were shown to be conducive to radical experimentation in the sixties—political as well as other kinds of experimentation. Extended to the subject at hand, we would expect permissive upbringing to be associated with dropping out of religious involvement and low rates of religious return. Often described as a generation raised on the permissive child-rearing teachings of Dr. Benjamin Spock, boomers are a prime case study for testing this hypothesis.

Data from the survey strongly support this interpretation. Those brought up in a permissive child-rearing environment dropped out in far greater numbers and are also less likely to return to church or synagogue. Those who described their upbringing as more rigid, to the contrary, did not drop out as much, and if they did drop out were more likely to return to active religious participation. A disciplined approach to bringing up children appears to instill religious values and the habits of religious observance. Whether mainline Protestant, conservative Protestant, or Catholic makes no difference: More demanding, rigid child-rearing styles reinforce religious teachings and loyalties to the tradition.

Close relations with parents growing up are also a factor of some importance. A close relationship to mother and father, like more rigid child-rearing practices, results in fewer dropouts, and a greater return among those who have fallen away. This is true for Catholics and Protestants, thus underscoring the fact that the quality of relations between parents and youth growing up was of considerable significance, independent of theological views or religious tradition.

Life Cycle

The life-cycle hypothesis, stated in its simplest form, is that people often drop out of churches and other religious institutions in adolescence and early adulthood, but then return to church once they are older, and especially after marrying and having children.[10] Barry Johnson is a good example. He dropped out during his college days, got married, had children, and some twenty years later decided to become involved again. The pattern is common in all the religious traditions.

A considerable amount of research has shown that young people fall away from religious institutions during adolescence and the early adult years, but then return to it in adulthood. As young people grow older, they settle into stable jobs and become more involved in community activities. Most marry and begin raising families. Parenthood is even more important, for becoming a parent entails responsibility for another person's moral and religious training. Society puts pressure on parents to take seriously these responsibilities and of upholding traditions—on behalf of school-age children especially.[11] As some of the previously quoted comments indicate, this theme of responsibility came through in many of our interviews.

The survey evidence provides support for the age and life-cycle argument, showing that older respondents are more likely to have returned than younger respondents. Figure 6.1 shows how specific life-cycle factors influence greater religious involvement. Reading from left to right, we see the cumulative effects of getting married, having children, and settling into community life. In phase one, for individuals who are single, without children, and are geographically mobile, only 14% have returned. Introducing marriage into the equation in phase two has little immediate effect—pushing the figure to 16%. But for those who are married and have children, as shown in phase three, we find a significant increase to 52%. And in the last phase, where all are married, have children, and are settled community residents, the figure is pushed upward to 54%. For boomers, as for previous generations, the presence of children is a strong force leading them to churches and synagogues.

Yet only 54%—slightly more than half—who meet *all* the conditions that we stipulated in the life-cycle model are now involved in religious organizations. Is this less than would have been the case, say, for their parent's generation? We do not know, but it may very well be. It is also a fact that proportionately fewer in the boomer generation fit all three conditions—marriage, children, and settled lifestyle—which means that the cumulative effect of the life-cycle factors on religious involvement will be less. All things considered, it would appear that the impact of life cycle for religion generally may have been substantially altered for this generation.[12] As journalist Kenneth A. Briggs writes, the script may have changed for boomers:

> Religious behavior has long been supposed by sociologists to follow an ingrained routine something like this: Children went to church with their parents, absorbed the particular brand of Christianity offered there, avoided church while sowing wild oats during their late teens and 20s, then married, sobered up, had a family and, having returned to their senses, came back to church with their little ones in tow.
>
> Many baby boomers followed that scenario to a T—up to and including the youthful-rebellion part. But large numbers of them apparently abandoned the script there; they haven't come back—yet.[13]

	I Single No Children Unsettled	II Married No Children Unsettled	III Married Children Unsettled	IV Married Children Settled
% Returning	14%	16%	52%	54%
N =	(51)	(50)	(71)	(124)

Figure 6.1 Religion and the Life Cycle

The old script was based on a linear conception of the adult years as a sequence of events with a prescribed timetable and rather predictable outcomes. However, in an age of greater choice—of whether to marry or remain single, to have children or not, and what lifestyle to follow—people's lives do not follow in such straight lines. People's lives develop in a more open and fluid manner. Even entry into "adulthood" is not so clearly defined today. What marks entry into adulthood—having to make car payments, getting married, having children, a steady job, physical signs of aging? The script that boomers have grown up with allows for greater variation in timing and far more flexibility in rules, roles, and relationships. One thing is certain, there is no simple master plan, no one normative prescription defining adult obligations.[14]

Influence of Spouse

A related hypothesis would be that, for married people, spouse's religiosity should have an influence on returning to religious participation. Though boomers have a much higher level of interfaith marriages than previous generations, it is still likely that spouses have a strong impact on their religious involvement. Our survey yields support for the hypothesis: If spouses attend religious services, the respondents themselves are more likely to attend. Wives have a greater impact on husbands than husbands do on wives.

Education

Another hypothesis points to the role of education. It is well known that education predicts a person's social and political attitudes. Polls and surveys have repeatedly shown that level of education is the best single predictor for distinguishing among Americans across a wide range of attitudes, values, and behaviors—including styles of religious belief and participation. For distinguishing among young Americans, education is obviously crucial, since so many of them were caught up in the expansion of higher education during the 1960s and 1970s. Far better educated than any generation before them, could it be then that those who went off to colleges and professional school are the ones who dropped out of the churches and synagogues and are also less likely to return to them?

In the lifetime of boomers, certainly, a major restructuring has occurred between religion and education in American society. Nowhere is this restructuring more apparent than in religious participation. During the 1950s, a benchmark period for religion in this country, studies showed that college-educated men and women were more likely than the less educated to participate in organized religion. The linkage between religion and class was still strong at the time, with the middle classes generally more involved in congregations and religious activities. Well-educated people tended to participate more in voluntary organizations—religious and civic groups of all kinds. Since the sixties, however, these patterns have changed. The polls show a gradual decline in religious attendance that is more pronounced among the college-educated than for any other category. Downward trends have continued, and now there are only slight differences in participation across educational lines. Either no class differences exist, or an inverse pattern is found—with working-class and lower middle-class people more active than the upper middle and professional classes.[15]

In this respect Barry Johnson is somewhat unusual. Barry can be thought of as belonging to the "new class" in his liberal political values, in his concerns about the environment and civil rights, and in his appreciation for education and technological knowledge. A gulf exists between this highly educated "new class" constituency, which is inclined toward post-materialist values and to think about religion in more personal, spiritual terms, and traditional believers, who affirm God, country, and motherhood and give voice to a consumption ethic and laissez-faire ideology. The ideological cleavage between the two embraces a wide variety of issues, including tolerance toward homosexuality, legalization of abortion, and government support for education, environmental protection, and urban improvement.[16] They differ not only on the issues, but in their fundamental outlook on life, in their priorities, and in their conception of self in relation to the world around them. One can imagine that under slightly different life conditions, Barry would not have returned to church at all—many of the technologically minded, post-materialist boomers we interviewed have not, and are not likely to in the future. We can gain some insight into his religious commitment by taking note of his style of believing: He is religious in a deeply existential way, finding encounters with God in people and in life, while at the same time he distrusts institutions. He talks comfortably about "symbols" of God and of being "pissed off" with God when his father died. His language sets him apart from his more secular friends as well as from traditional believers.

Our survey shows that returning to religion after a lapse of time varies with level of education. The return is generally higher among the less-educated boomers. It is highest for those with some college, less for college graduates, and least of all for postgraduates. The extent of return varies more by level of education than did dropping out. As youth and young adults, they dropped out rather uniformly despite levels of education, except for college graduates, who were less likely to do so than either those with more or less education. More than one-half across all educational levels are still dropouts—ranging from 53% of those with some college, to a high of 70% for postgraduates. Once they have broken ties with the institution, the chances of returning to church or synagogue are considerably less among the better educated. This may, in fact, be one of the most striking ways in which boomers are different from the previous generation: Once they have dropped out, education has fundamentally altered their chances of becoming religiously involved again.

Religious beliefs and attitudes differ greatly. For boomers as for all other Americans, traditional Judeo-Christian beliefs are stronger among the less educated. There are sizable percentage spreads by level of education for those who definitely believe in God, see temptations as the work of the Devil, and interpret the Bible literally. Education-based differences are strong among boomers, though not all that much stronger than for other sectors of the American population. It might be said that boomers somewhat exaggerate, but mostly mirror the deep divisions in belief in the society.

The impact of education on religious views is most striking, perhaps, in the attitudes toward religion and human nature. As would be expected, the better educated are more likely to hold to nonorthodox and nontraditional religious views. They are more inclined to view Jesus as a great teacher rather than as Savior: 40% of postgraduates, as compared to only 10% of those with high school educations or less. They are also more likely to hold to a religious universalism, that is, the view that all religions are equally true and good. Even among the least educated, 41% accept the premise that there are many paths to religious truth. Two items of traditional belief, the sinfulness of children and religion as preparation for the afterlife, do not fare as well among boomers, and even less so among the well-educated. Only one-fourth of boomers believe that a child is born guilty of sin, and less than half (43%) say religion prepares one for the afterlife. Among the better educated, considerably fewer hold to the traditional views on human nature and the afterlife.

Fear of Downward Mobility

Education is no guarantee of finding or keeping secure and well-paying jobs. Many boomers have discovered that they are overeducated for the jobs available, and the specter of downward mobility looms large for many of them. Born in an age of great expectations, they went to school and learned skills, assuming that jobs and careers would be waiting for them. But for many born into or hoping to join the ranks of the middle class, actual experiences have been otherwise. Even in the high-tech industry, which was supposed to be the answer to the country's economic ills, expectations of continuing prosperity and expanded possibilities have faded. Thousands of employees have been let go from Apple, IBM, and other computer firms since the mid-1980s. As a group boomers savored the American Dream; yet in times of economic recession—such as during the mid-1970s and now in the early 1990s—that dream for some comes close to vanishing. Many others are worried and have scaled down their expectations.[17]

Do the downwardly mobile, or those fearful of "falling," turn to religion? Is the rise of evangelicalism and fundamentalism among boomers related to having to scale down their expectations? Admittedly, the argument has a certain intuitive appeal and the position has long been advanced that the socially and economically deprived are inclined to find compensation in religion. American culture is rich in symbols and rituals that celebrate worldly success; in comparison, downward mobility has no public ritual face. This being the case, it might follow that those who have experienced economic failure would find in religious belief and participation a deeply personal compensation, without much public attention or ceremonial fanfare.

The one-third of all boomers who have scaled-down material expectations are more likely to have dropped out of religious organizations. We spoke to individuals who had found religious groups helpful as sources of networks and moral support when they were laid off and looking for jobs. Churches are important as resource centers in hard times. Thus there is some support for the argument that economic troubles are sending some people back to churches. However, more people facing such problems have simply dropped out; and those who have returned appear to have done so largely for support services rather than out of any deeply based religious commitment. On a variety of indicators—including born-again experiences, prayer, Bible reading, and saying grace at meals—scaling down of expectations seems to make little or no difference. It would seem, then, that economic woes and the fears surrounding downward mobility are not a major factor in the recent return to the churches.

A DISTINCTIVE GENERATIONAL EXPERIENCE?

All the previous theories capture something of the boomers' religious lives and experience, yet leave us with questions not fully answered. Why is parental religious socialization not more important in shaping the boomer generation? Why do the life-cycle predictions on religion hold for only slightly more than half of the respondents? Is education a sufficient explanation for the differences in beliefs and outlook between traditionalists and the new class? Is the fear of falling a factor of any significance in explaining if boomers return to church or not?

Something more is going on with the boomers, something far more experiential in shaping a new set of sensitivities to religious and spiritual matters. The best explanation, it seems, lies in the sixties' cultural experience. As we have seen in previous chapters, the youth countercultural values of that era swept the generation during the adolescent and teenage years. Some young people were more deeply influenced than others, but virtually all were touched in one way or another. Some, like Mollie Stone, were caught up in the cultural quake and swept out of organized religion altogether; others, like Linda Kramer, took refuge from the jolts in a resurgent Bible-centered evangelicalism; and still others, like Barry Johnson, dropped out of church but later returned. Whatever the impact of those earlier experiences, the fact is that the boomers grew up some more and some less estranged from social institutions (including the religious), and some more and some less influenced by the rise of post-materialist values.

In order to grasp more fully the current return to religion among boomers, it is important to recognize the lasting impact of this earlier

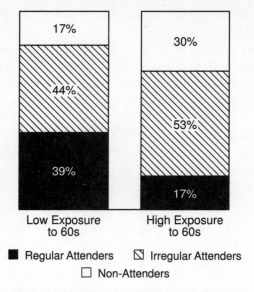

Figure 6.2 Religious Attendance in Early 20s

alienation. Whatever their childhood experiences and quest for a greater self-expressiveness, it was during their late teens and early twenties when they became alienated from social institutions. We can best demonstrate this by comparing those who were highly exposed to the cultural changes of the period and those who were not—two constituencies, it will be recalled from chapter 2, that are almost equally divided—in relation to their religious attendance when they were in their early twenties.

Despite a high involvement in religion as children, the break came in their early twenties. Among those not so highly exposed to the sixties' values, 39% were still regular attenders by the time they were in their early twenties, 44% were irregular attenders, and 17% did not attend (see Figure 6.2). But among those more exposed to the values, only 17% were still regular attenders, 53% had become irregular attenders, and 30% did not attend. Those who were highly exposed to sixties' values—and who are today disproportionately single or divorced, single parents or without children, and socially mobile—broke ties with organized religion in large numbers. Many others who were less exposed were still influenced by these values, which leads them even today to question the authority of institutions, to view religious participation as optional, and to favor greater personal autonomy in matters of belief and practice.

What had happened by the time members of this generation had reached their early twenties was crucial and would shape their future religious trajectories. If they had already quit attending religious services by that time, they were *twice* as likely never to return to active involvement again—at least during the span of time that we studied them. Eighty-five percent of those who made it through the early twenties without dropping out of their congregations have continued until now as active participants. Once again, the impact of sixties' values and experiences is powerful: *Those most caught up in the value-shifts were not just more likely to drop out, they are less likely to have returned to the churches and synagogues.* Less than one-third of the dropouts who were highly exposed to the counterculture have returned, as compared to almost half of the low-exposure dropouts.

On other measures of religious involvement today, the impact of the sixties' cultural changes shows up as well:

- Weekly attendance: 60% of the dropouts with low exposure now attend religious services weekly, as compared to 41% of the high-exposure dropouts.

- Church membership: 85% of low-exposure dropouts are now church members, as compared to 69% of the high-exposure dropouts.

- Concern for children's religious instruction: Two-thirds of low-exposure dropouts say it is "very important," as compared to 35% of high-exposure dropouts.

- Children in Sunday school or youth group: 46% of the low-exposure dropouts report involvement, as compared to 32% of high-exposure dropouts.

The evidence is substantial and convincing: How boomers experienced the new values of the period in which they grew up had a lasting impact on their religious participation. Low-exposure dropouts, with little alienation, have returned after dropping out in ways similar to earlier generations. But high-exposure dropouts, because of their greater alienation and suspiciousness of institutions, have continued to maintain lower levels of participation. They were touched in ways that carried over into their adult lives and have continued to sustain negative attitudes toward and less involvement in organized religion.

THE SELF AND THE
CULTURAL CONTEXT

We can now place Barry Johnson's experiences in a larger cultural context and begin to see that his decision to return to church is more complex than it appears to be on the surface. Many factors bear on his decision: his childhood religious involvement, relations with his parents, concern for his children, the influence of his wife, and his own midlife questions. By means of statistical procedures, we could sort out the relative significance of these factors; but based on our analyses, the combined results are not all that impressive.[18] Lacking stronger patterns for these variables, we are again inclined to think in terms of a generational *break* in the religious lives of boomers.

Experiential and cultural factors are far more important in understanding Barry's return. The sixties jarred his confidence in institutions and led him to ask questions about the meaning and purpose of his own life. These questions propelled him into more personal quests of the self—which, combined with his skepticism of institutions, would seem to be enough to sever his ties and drive him out of the church for good. Many like him were driven out. And clearly, the data from this survey show a positive relationship between a self-absorbing individualism and abandonment of organized religion. Those who stress an individualistic pursuit of self can easily leave religious organizations and turn inward in cultivating spirituality, or else they just leave. Individualism, so conceived, is an enemy to conventional religious participation.

But as we have seen, people's experiences of the sixties varied greatly, and the relations of religion and culture that emerged are extremely subtle. In Barry's case (and by inference, other returnees), two considerations must be kept in mind. One is that the sixties were not as traumatic for him as for some others—he lost confidence in the political process and became more cynical but did not, for example, break ties with his parents. He turned against the Vietnam War but did not become a hippie or drop out of school. His strong wish to become an engineer was probably a big factor in directing him into a more moderate type of social protest. Using the experiences of our characters as comparison, he falls somewhere in between Mollie Stone on the radical, high-exposure side of the sixties, and Linda Kramer on the sheltered, low-exposure side. This places him in a middle category, of more moderate experience, a position that makes it more difficult to predict whether he will, or will not, return to a church. Caught up in neither extreme of the sixties' responses, any number of factors influencing his religious future may come into play.

A second consideration is Barry's disposition toward people and the mystery he finds in human relationships. He is drawn to community, partly because he survived the sixties, but also because of his analogical imagination, which discerns the divine in human relationships. Like birds in a flock, "You are supposed to be part of something." Ultimately, it is this latter vision that predominates over his skepticism or self-pursuits and is of enormous motivational significance. As with many of his generation, he has within him a latent idealism ready to be tapped; and he seems to have found within his congregation something to commit himself to that is bigger than himself. Thus commitment to his congregation is a means of balancing his self-pursuits and desire for communal belonging.

How typical is Barry Johnson? We aren't sure, but we find similar qualities in other returnees. One interesting finding from the survey is that those dropouts who felt that God had influenced their lives—a proxy measure for "analogical imagination"—were more likely to return to active religious involvement and to report that their children's religious training is important to them. This holds for Protestants and Catholics. It also holds no matter what the level of exposure to the 1960s values—for the radical, high-exposure types, as well as for the more sheltered, low-exposure types. The capacity to perceive God as present in life and to see grace and sacrament in the world is a capacity that transcends religious tradition, at least among boomers, and may in fact have been enhanced by the boomers' own distinctive experiences. For many of them, God has broken out of the narrow confines of religious institutions and is envisioned in society and in human relationships, in experiences and imaginations arising out of everyday life.

If Barry's actions cannot in some final analysis be neatly explained, it is because the religious response is far too complex ever to be fully grasped by any single explanation, or set of explanations. It might be said that he points us to the problem of *pluralism at the level of the self*— to the conflicting languages within a person that describe his or her attraction to, and repulsion from, the church. Pluralism at this level does not permit any simple monocausal analysis. It is not simply a question of individualism versus religious belonging, not a matter of turning inward toward the self as opposed to attaching oneself to an institution. Barry Johnson shows us that human beings are complex creatures capable of combining personal, individualistic quests with a hunger for community.

The two impulses exist in some tension within the same personality, but they are not mutually exclusive; they live together in the human psyche.

Once again, personal narratives are a source of much insight. People link the impulses in many ways in the narratives they tell about their lives. The stories help to reduce the tensions fostered by pluralism and to make people's lives coherent; such accounts are always governed by what makes life plausible in its own context and are not to be judged on the basis of logical consistency or by some imposed standard.[19] In Barry's case going back to church is very much a matter of choice and of the subjective fit between his life and the religious congregation—he must work out his own identity. But it is more than this; for within the community he finds the force and mystery that sustain his religious quest and imagination about God in the world, and in turn he finds support of his religious identity. The two aspects of the self cannot be so neatly compartmentalized and separated—they are mutually dependent. Therein lies the story of his religious return, and in one version or another, why others have returned as well.

TWO TYPES OF RELIGIOUS MOVEMENT

This lengthy exploration of Barry's return to a congregation is, in part, to illustrate just how fluid boomer religious life is today. Fluidity is expressed in many ways, and not just in whether dropouts return to the religious institutions. In fact, two types of movement are of major significance in reshaping the current religious scene: one, the movement in and out of active involvement *within* religious institutions; and two, the switching into and out of religious denominations or faiths, or movement *across* religions. Barry Johnson exemplifies both of these movements, for he not only dropped out and then later became active in a church again, he has also changed denominations. He grew up Presbyterian, then attended an Episcopal church during his teenage years, and later followed his wife to the Baptist congregation where he is now active. If his cycle of dropping out and returning is not all that unusual, neither is his switching from one Protestant denomination to another. A third or more of Protestants in the United States typically switch out of the religion in which they were raised, either to other faiths or to no affiliation.[20] Among boomers, both patterns of movement appear to be greater.

The two types of religious movement often mesh together, making it difficult to sort them out. For example, a thirty-six-year-old man in southern California, a high-school graduate with only a year of college work, has the following religious biography:

- Raised as a Methodist.
- Dropped out as a teenager, preferring to play Beatles records rather than go to church.
- Attended a Lutheran church for a while.
- Dropped out and began attending Buddhist services.
- Explored the Baha'i faith and attended its meetings.
- Attended spiritual seminars on Judaism and Hinduism.
- Dropped out for a while.
- Currently describes himself as a fundamentalist Christian. He visits several churches, a Christian Church of Joy, a Baptist church, the Vineyard Fellowship, and "Once in a blue moon," he says, "I go to the Crystal Cathedral."

His is an exceptional biography, of course. Most of the people we talked to, even the most highly educated or institutionally alienated, had not explored so many differing religious alternatives. Surprising numbers of them had chosen to explore other faiths—especially Eastern religions—during phases when they had dropped out of mainline Protestant, Catholic, and Jewish congregations. If they returned to active involvement in a congregation, often this was the time of switching denominations or faiths. Among the better educated, it was not uncommon to hear stories about how their spiritual horizons had expanded during the college years—from reading books about other religions, to attending lectures, to participating in study groups sponsored by campus ministries. Often it is these earlier college experiences that they remember and draw on in their later explorations.

What are the overall patterns of religious movement for Catholics, mainline Protestants, and conservative Protestants? Put differently, where are those who were reared in these traditions today, and by what route did they get to their current destination? Let us look at the trends in both types of movement for the three differing traditions.

Catholics

Of those who grew up Catholic, 81% still identify as Catholic, which is a higher rate of retention than Protestants can claim. Nine

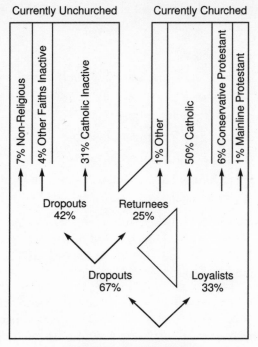

Reared Catholic (N=210)

Figure 6.3 Institutional Loyalty of Catholics

percent of those who grew up Catholic have switched to conservative Protestant, 7% to "None," 2% to mainline Protestant, 1% to "Other." Boomers who have left Catholicism have switched mainly to conservative Protestantism or out of organized religion altogether. The reasons are manifold: unpleasant memories associated with priests, disagreement with the church's position on divorce and marriage, preference for a doctrinally conservative stance combined with a more individually autonomous church setting, or preference for a more private spirituality not linked with any religious institution.

But what about the other type of movement? Figure 6.3 shows that two-thirds of Catholics dropped out while growing up, the majority of whom still identify today as Catholic but are unchurched. Like Sonny D'Antonio, the Catholic dropout in Boston, most effectively left the church in their teens or early twenties and have never returned. Returnees make up 25% of the Catholic population. One-half of all those reared Catholic are active in a Catholic congregation today, 6%

are active conservative Protestants, 1% are active mainline Protestants, and 1% are active in some other faith.

Mainline Protestants

Of those who grew up mainline Protestant, 65% still identify themselves in this way. More than one-third have switched, 17% to conservative Protestantism, 11% to "None," 6% to Catholic, 1% to "Other." The biggest exodus is into conservative Protestantism and is often accompanied by religious reasons. Like Linda Kramer, people who move in this direction cite needs for stronger moral guidelines and biblical teachings, and for a deeper Christian faith. "I got fed a lot of twinkies," was one man's way of describing his reason for leaving behind his mainline Protestant church in favor of an evangelical conservative church. Another movement is out of religion altogether, which occurs more as a secular drift than as conscious choice. Many people could not tell us why they left except in vague generalities, such as, "Church didn't seem relevant," "I developed other interests," or "I was bored." Those who leave mainline Protestantism for Catholicism do so largely because of interfaith marriages.

Looking at the other type of movement, we see in Figure 6.4 that of the 69% of mainline Protestants who dropped out when growing up, a majority are still unchurched. One-fourth identify as mainline Protestants but are inactive, 7% claim other faiths but are inactive, and 11% claim no religious affiliation. Counting returnees and loyalists, 56% meet our test as belonging to the churched population and are broken down as follows: 39% mainline Protestant, 12% conservative Protestant, and 5% Catholic.

Conservative Protestants

Of those who grew up as conservative Protestants, 80% have remained within the religious family. Nine percent have switched to more liberal Protestant affiliations, 7% to "None," 3% to Catholic, and 1% to other faiths. Those who choose a more liberal Protestant faith often mention "narrow-minded teachings" and "too much strictness" as reasons for leaving behind the faith in which they were reared. Those opting out of conservative Protestantism into the secular ranks often mention religion's seemingly "lack of relevance" and "other interests," as do others drawn away from religious communities.

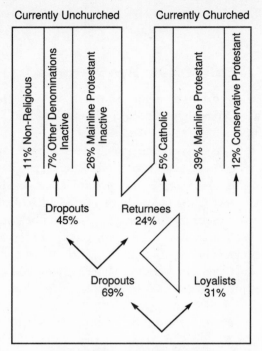

Reared Mainline Protestant (N=146)

Figure 6.4 Institutional Loyalty of Mainline Protestants

As shown in Figure 6.5, there are somewhat fewer dropouts for conservative Protestants than for the other two traditions—61% as compared to 69% for mainline Protestants and 67% for Catholics. The majority of the dropouts are still inactive today. Twenty-five percent identify as conservative Protestant but are inactive, 7% are nonaffiliates, and 4% identify with other denominations or faiths but are inactive. Returnees make up 25% of the population. Fifty-five percent are active conservative Protestants, 7% belong to more liberal Protestant churches, 1% to Catholicism, and 1% to other faiths.

For all three religious communities—Catholics, mainline Protestants, and conservative Protestants—the general patterns hold: (1) those who were most caught up in the cultural changes when growing up have become less religiously active; and (2) those who have returned to active involvement tend to have been influenced less by the cultural changes than

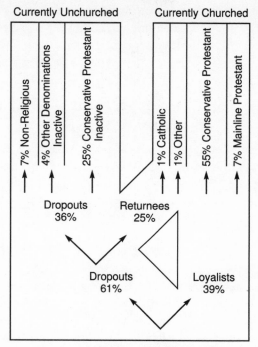

Currently Unchurched   Currently Churched

7% Non-Religious

4% Other Denominations Inactive

25% Conservative Protestant Inactive

1% Catholic

1% Other

55% Conservative Protestant

7% Mainline Protestant

Dropouts
36%

Returnees
25%

Dropouts
61%

Loyalists
39%

Reared Conservative Protestant (N=137)

Figure 6.5 Institutional Loyalty of Conservative Protestants

those who dropped out. Among Protestants, those joining conservative churches hold to more traditional conceptions of the self; those joining liberal, mainline churches hold to more open, more flexible conceptions.

LOYALISTS AND RETURNEES

With all the movement in and out of religious institutions, and the resulting split between the churched and the unchurched in all three major traditions, the question of religious commitment obviously arises: Are those who once dropped out but have later returned as committed to the churches and synagogues as those who never dropped out? Are returnees as loyal to the religious establishment once they come back?

As we saw in chapter 2, the returnees were more exposed to the sixties' values than were loyalists. They were more open to alternative lifestyles and more likely to favor abortion on demand, to question authority, and to push for women's rights. Because they were more touched by the new generational values, we might expect them to be less loyal to religious institutions. And indeed, based on the following indicators, they are *less* committed:

- Membership: 88% of loyalists are members of churches and synagogues, as compared with 82% of returnees.

- Importance of congregation: 48% of loyalists say their congregation is "very important," as compared to 43% of the returnees.

- Good Christian: 78% of the loyalists say one can be a good Christian and not attend church or synagogue; 85% of the returnees agree with the statement.

The differences here are small, but consistent. For all three major constituencies—Catholics, mainline Protestants, and conservative Protestants—levels of institutional loyalty are lower among the returnees.

Thus the two subgroups—the returnees and the loyalists—differ in how they relate to institutions and what they expect of them. Boomers have a low level of loyalty generally to traditions, institutions, and brand names of all kinds; and for returnees this is even more true. Their reluctance to make long-term commitments prompts many to postpone joining a congregation and encourages shopping around from one congregation to another, exploring whatever they are looking for. Even among those who have found a congregation in which to participate, often they do not join.[21] A disproportionate number of returnees have attended Bible study groups, spiritual seminars, and charismatic prayer services, suggesting that returnees are active *inquirers* searching after religious and spiritual meanings and experiences.

It would seem to follow that the so-called "return" of the boomers to religion is on different terms than for previous generations. Baby boomers approach congregations more as a calculated choice that consciously involves discriminating decisions among various religious alternatives, including the option of no participation in organized religion at all. Choice in matters of faith and practice, as in so many other facets of life, is as much taken for granted for this generation as were expectations of more conventional religious involvement for previous generations. In a culture of choice, the meaning of a "returning to the fold" is itself open to new interpretation; indeed, substantial numbers are not really returning, but rather are exploring the possibilities of returning.

If all this is true, we cannot really understand the dynamics of boomer churchgoing today without recognizing that loyalists and returnees represent two very different subcultures. The cultural cleavage between the two runs deep, and it shows up in congregations across all religious traditions and theological persuasions. And as Barry's own case has shown, congregations themselves have their own cultures as well, which adds even another level of complexity to our analysis. It is to this array of complexities—of subcultures and congregations—that we turn in the next chapter.

CHAPTER 7

Cultures and Congregations

In his recently published autobiography, *Returning,* Dan Wakefield describes the chance circumstances surrounding his return to a congregation. After many years of pursuing a career, through good times and hard times, and of having explored most of the seductive alternatives of the spirit and the flesh, one evening his life took an unexpected turn. He dropped in on a Christmas Eve service at a Boston congregation, and in a flash moment during the service he saw his life laid out before him in ways he had not seen it before. As if in a liminal experience, things came together for him. He became involved in a small sharing group at the church and began to explore his own spiritual journey and to see his life from a different angle. Writes Wakefield: "I started to see the deeper connections and more expansive framework offered by the sense of our small daily drama in relation to the higher meaning that many people call God."[1]

No one we interviewed spoke so elegantly, but an ex-Catholic and recent convert to the Vineyard Fellowship described very well its meaning to her:

> After my divorce, I needed to be with people and I found what I was looking for at the Vineyard Church. You don't have to dress up, I go in my jeans. The drums, the guitars, the preaching—it's all so inspiring. You really feel it . . . praising God and all. You feel good, it makes you, I think, a better person. I went with a friend and decided this is the church for me.

A computer programmer, now remarried, she describes what she likes about the congregation. Its informality, music, emphasis on experience, and clear-cut moral teachings all attract her. Feeling good and feeling she is a better person are bound up with her attitude toward this particular congregation. It's not "churchy," she says, which sums up a lot about how she feels.

Both of these accounts point to a blending of narratives—of personal story and of congregation's story. The accounts raise some interesting questions: What makes a congregation come alive for some, and not for others? How is it that people come to see their own lives in relation to the larger narratives as told through religious myth, metaphor, and symbol? Can we identify factors—about boomers and about congregations—that explain how it is that such stories come together?

AN INTERVIEW WITH A BOOMER PASTOR

We begin with a young woman pastor of a middle-class, mainline Protestant church in New England. She had this to say about what boomers are looking for in a congregation, and about what they often get:

> I think people are lonely. I think people's lives feel empty and dead for a lot of people, no matter how much money they have. I mean we haven't developed a middle-class theology to address our emptiness . . . and we are not inspired. I think there is just this kind of pervasive emptiness, and then someone our age dies, and people will come back to church. Or something traumatic will happen and they'll come. They are dealing really with life and death, crucial issues. Then we stick them on a committee—"How about being part of our building fund?" There's a gap in there. I feel we haven't developed a mechanism in which people can continue to grow with that formative search.

Once they return, whether for the children or for themselves, she observes:

> The other thing that has been happening is that many of my age group talk about coming to church, and they cry through the service . . . especially women . . . the hymns, they are just unraveled. And these are people who haven't come to church in years . . . it's empowering . . . real deep sense of coming home again . . . of something that was missing and then reaching some real deep places that people weren't even aware of.

183

Probed further about why commitment is so difficult for many boomers, she has this to say:

> . . . commitment almost always is a loaded thing. When we come down to the final joining of the church, I have found over the last five years that there is a fear . . . a fear of getting imprisoned and stifled. Almost that your spirit is going to be killed out of you. . . . I think probably we've seen too much false commitment at times, or commitment to the wrong things . . . I think it's not that this is a generation that is anticommitment. I think it's a generation that's weighing what commitment means. . . . I would almost say that the generation is more community-oriented. I would not call it narcissistic. I feel like it is trying to get away from that sense of just building up one's little reservoir of possessions. It's questioning that.

This pastor's observations strike us as on target: The self-centeredness theme has been overplayed; many boomers would like to commit themselves to something they can believe in. They are dealing with pressing life issues and searching for answers to many questions. They approach a congregation looking for spiritual sustenance and for some means of dealing with the emptiness they feel. Sometimes they get caught up in their emotions, overwhelmed by their own reconnections with a religious heritage. They want good programs, inspiring worship, and meaningful ways of serving their faith. But what does the church offer? All too often, as she says, "We stick them on a committee." Churches and other religious institutions expect them to "fit in" to existing programs and structures. Consequently, returning boomers often experience a gap between what they are looking for and what is offered to them by organized religion. Missing from many congregations is any real sensitivity to their deeper religious concerns, or a structure designed to help people to grow spiritually.

The lack of a middle-class theology for addressing emptiness is, as the pastor suggests, a serious problem for mainline religious institutions. Middle-class men and women live in a highly individualistic, competitive world and are bombarded daily by a consumer culture that tells them they are what they can purchase or possess. Commitment is a problem in the sense that boomers tend to be fearful and suspicious generally—not just toward religion, but with regard to social attachments as a whole. But they are not anticommitment, nor are they narcissistic in the self-absorbing way that term is often used. They just appear to be that way, as a result of the high levels of individualism and self-reliance within middle-class boomer culture. Because they are more focused on the self as the key social unit, rather than on the family, church, or community, they are more introspective, figuring out what to give themselves to and where to place their energies—"a generation weighing what commitment means."

Religious institutions often falter in helping boomers sort out what commitment means. In an age when theological reflection is polarized in the direction either of Mollie Stone's mysticism, with its tenuous organizational ties, or of Linda Kramer's highly structured, socially encapsulated evangelical world, potential churchgoing boomers often find little inspiration in what is held up to them as commitment in the mainline churches. Often ideas aren't very well integrated, or if integrated not very persuasive. Many churches lack a unifying perspective that links the personal and the social aspects of life; or they lack a consciousness that, as one person said, you can't "strive for wholeness personally without living in a world in which there is a loving environment, where we can breathe the air." Traditional models of piety and spirituality, often tied to outdated dualisms of body and spirit, fail to nurture. Many of the existing programs and activities in churches do not speak to them, leaving them without much nourishment and little reason to make a serious commitment to the institution.

Based on our survey, we know that boomers look for congregations with certain attractions—one being a widespread preference for churches and synagogues that are tolerant and more open than closed on lifestyle issues. Despite all the media attention given to the rise of more traditional beliefs and moral values, as found among evangelical and fundamentalist Protestants and traditional Catholics, boomers have an amazingly high level of support for tolerance and openness. In response to the question, "Do you prefer a parish/congregation with an open attitude toward people's lifestyles, or one that is more strict?" 65% of conservative Protestant returnees (63% for loyalists) and 88% of Catholic returnees (83% for loyalists) choose the first option. Among liberal Protestants the percentages are even stronger, as would be expected. The overwhelming majority of religious boomers—whether theological liberals or theological conservatives—prefer a church that is tolerant and leaning in the open direction rather than overly strict in its attitudes toward people's lifestyles. Equal numbers of conservative Protestant returnees and loyalists (48%) say they prefer a congregation that encourages believers to follow their own consciences rather than definite moral rules governing their behavior. The fact that almost half of conservative Protestant boomers oppose absolute morality in favor of a more individualistic, conscience-first approach to morality is itself a telling observation. Likewise, two-thirds of all churchgoing Catholics, both loyalists and returnees, prefer a similar type of parish. These trends toward greater openness and tolerance lie largely within the broader boomer culture, although there are changes within the religious traditions themselves in the contemporary period that dispose them favorably to these value shifts.[2]

Boomers who are religious see themselves largely in the American cultural mainstream, and not as marginal. We asked the following question: "Do you think of your congregation as being in the mainstream of how Americans live and think today, or as one that offers a distinct alternative to what most people think?" Liberal Protestants overwhelmingly (87%) say they are in the mainstream. In contrast, conservative Protestants are more internally split in how they see themselves. The loyal, longstanding church attenders are equally divided, 45% saying they are in the mainstream, 45% saying they are an alternative, and 10% saying they don't know. Among recent returnees, however, 60% claim that their conservative congregations are a distinct alternative to how most Americans live and think. Boomers now affiliating with conservative Protestant congregations, many of whom dropped out of liberal mainline churches, see themselves as belonging to a faith that is set apart from a more dominant, secular culture. They view the religious boundaries as more firmly in place.

With the exception of conservative Protestant returnees, we were struck by the extent to which boomers—of all ages, educated or not, and in all parts of the country—see themselves in the cultural mainstream. Whether in a congregation of a recognized tradition, in a new religious movement, or as a lone believer professing a faith without a group, everybody belongs to the mainstream. Old notions of "insider" and "outsider" seem to have lost much of their significance; even the notion of a religious "mainstream" is questionable, since it is common to view all religions as equally true and good. Despite differences of religious tradition, boomers share considerable common ground today. Virtually all of them see religion less in doctrinal or ecclesiastical terms, and much more in personal meaning terms, and often in vague and generalized moral terms. "It's not so much what you believe, or which religion you follow, it's how you live," as one man told us. For this man, one religion is about as good as another; there is no real basis for arguing that one is preferable to another. What matters is that people live good lives, that they try to live by the Golden Rule, and that they try to do the best they can. He was hardly alone in his outlook—everywhere we met people who spoke of religion in these terms.

While many evangelical boomers would not say that it doesn't matter what you believe, they still put a strong emphasis on the moral aspects of faith. The orthodox and the liberal, the fundamentalist and the mainliner, the born-again Christian and spiritually minded New Ager—each shares a moral conviction. A Protestant liberal characterized this generalized American approach to life in this way:

> What really matters is how you treat people in the here and now, because that's really the only thing, despite what religion teaches you, that you can ever really know about, you don't know why you're here, and you don't know what happens when you die, and so you sort of have to make the best of what you have now.

A Mormon summed up what life is about this way:

> I don't know, just be the best and do the best and treat others as if you were of them and just praise God daily and do the best you can, that's all. I don't know what else to say.

"Do the best you can" is a typically American moral injunction and is not unrelated to what a person believes; indeed, it relates to belief that is honest and sincere usually, no matter what its content. "I feel if you do your part of what matters to you, whatever it is," a Presbyterian dropout told us, "if you sincerely believe in something, whatever it can be, and if you can make just a little bit of difference, then I think that you've done something worthwhile." Believing in something and making a difference with your life go together. In American religious culture, faith produces its fruits, or at least people feel that it should, and the fruits are readily apparent to those who are able to discern them—they are visible, immediate, practical, enriching. Faiths may be substituted, one for another, and indeed they often are, but this has little to do with the religious outcome. In the words of one loyal Catholic:

> . . . the reason I'm Catholic is because I was born and raised Catholic. I would probably still be the same today with the same outlooks toward life if I was raised in a different part of the world with a different religion. I don't think that Catholicism in itself is the begin all and end all of everything. I happen to believe in it because that was what I was raised in. And I feel like you have to believe in something and that brings consistency to your life, or to my life anyway.

As this quote indicates, boomers are very sophisticated—many look on religion as simply a result of socialization, "That was what I was raised in"; or in terms of its functionality, "Believe in something that brings consistency to your life." Much of religious discourse for this generation has shifted away from the language of inner commitment to that of its outer interpretation, and partly because of the lack of a religious language that is deeply meaningful and spiritually nourishing.

THE THREE SUBCULTURES

If we are to understand what boomers are looking for in congregations today, we have to distinguish among loyalists, returnees, and dropouts. Returnees, for example, bring with them memories and expectations from their youth unlike those of the loyalists, who never dropped out of religious participation. Because they experienced a higher level of institutional alienation back in the 1960s and 1970s, religious congregations often strike returnees as strange places—with odd beliefs and practices and people who live differently than themselves. Only recently have many of them begun thinking seriously about the possibility of going to church again or what to look for in a congregation. And both loyalists and returnees must be distinguished from an *unchurched* population consisting of the large number of dropouts and a smaller number of secularists, who as youngsters were never religiously involved. This latter constituency (including dropouts and those who were never affiliated) is obviously the more secular, and thus a comparison group for understanding the cultural and religious profiles of the other two.[3]

All three are identifiable boomer subcultures. The boundaries that separate them are fairly distinct and persist today, many years after the events and experiences that first shaped them. Evidence of this abounds in Table 7.1, which shows attitudes of our respondents when they were *growing up* and *currently*, broken down for the three groups. The profiles for the three subcultures deserve attention.

Loyalists were the least likely to lose confidence in the country and to get involved in the counterculture back in the sixties and still have greater confidence in the country. They were, and still are, more committed to traditional lifestyles and family values. On the issues of abortion, marijuana, and unmarried couples living together, loyalists are far more likely than the others to hold to conventional attitudes. They are more traditional on other issues not shown here as well—respect for authority, the death penalty, cheating on taxes. They are somewhat more

	Loyalists (N=174)	Returnees (N=141)	Dropouts (N=204)
GROWING UP			
Opposed to American involvement in Vietnam War	40%	43%	51%
Little or no confidence in country	7	16	20
Smoked marijuana	32	48	67
CURRENT ATTITUDES			
Little or no confidence in country	21	26	31
Expectations about life – better than expected	66	49	47
Feel need for more excitement	17	35	34
Opposed to legal abortion	54	48	24
Opposed to legalization of marijuana	86	75	62
Not wrong for unmarried couples to live together	17	27	52

Table 7.1 The Three Subcultures

content with their lives and feel much less need for more excitement. By Yankelovich's measures they are not as highly committed to self-fulfillment as the other subgroups. Their greater happiness may be a result of their having had somewhat lower expectations for life.

The returnees fall between loyalists and dropouts/nonaffiliates on all the items. People like Barry Johnson belong in a middle category—as youths they were more caught up in the shift of cultural values than were the loyalists, but less so than those who dropped out of religion altogether. They were more likely to lose confidence in the country than loyalists, but less so than those who are still dropouts. Even today they have moderate attitudes toward social institutions—more skeptical and questioning about politics and government than the loyalists, but less so than the dropouts. They are more committed to principles of lifestyle freedom, choice in matters like abortion, and gender equality than loyalists but are not as libertarian in their moral values and lifestyles as dropouts. *Clearly, the returnee subculture is characterized by its moderate views, distinct from either of the other extremes.* Boomers knocking on the doors of the churches and synagogues today—for mainline and evangelical Protestant, Catholic, and Jewish—are more moderate in their views than either those who never left or those who are unlikely to return.

Our analysis reveals that the returnees themselves have grown more moderate in their views on abortion, drugs, and casual sex as they have gotten older. Those with families especially have moved away from earlier, more permissive views. Politically, they have grown more moderate in their views and are more likely to vote or to identify with one of the major political parties now than in the past. Compared with the loyalists, returnees also share with dropouts lower material expectations and a feeling that they need more excitement and sensation in life. Taken as a whole, the profile is suggestive. It implies that the returnees are the religiously inclined of the post-materialists—those who place more stress on psychological than material expectations, whose yearnings have more to do with personal well-being and cultivation of the inner life. More so than either of the other two subgroups, they possess a religious imagination that is at once creative and open to institutional expression.

In many congregations the returnees stand out from the others in predictable ways; they are the most visible, and often the most vocal, expression of the cultural changes of the sixties. Perhaps the biggest difference between loyalists and returnees lies not in moral outlook or lifestyle differences, but in the latter's psychological orientation to experience. Not only do they say they "feel" the need for more excitement and sensation, when asked about the forces that shape their lives, returnees are much more inclined than loyalists to speak of "new insights" they have learned about themselves. This emphasis on introspection sets them apart from others of their generation. More than anything else, it is a boundary formed by speech vocabularies: Loyalists draw on traditional moral and religious categories, whereas returnees speak in psychological or experiential terms.

Because the latter were more caught up in the value shifts of the sixties, we would expect an overt cleavage between those who left the churches and later came back, and those who never left. And indeed, many of the people we talked to hinted of such subcultural differences, and a few were very explicit about them. "I go, but I don't feel all that close to most of the people you find going there," commented a recent returnee after many years as a dropout. And a longstanding loyalist had this to say when asked if new people were coming to her church: "Oh yes, lots of them, and I find it hard to get to know some of them. Some coming now are so different from the people I remember growing up with at the church." The cleavages appear greater among liberal Protestants, but show up as well among conservative Protestants and Catholics.

SPIRITUAL GROWTH

Whereas loyalists stress *growing up* in a faith, returnees talk about *growing in* faith. When Barry Johnson speaks about what he has learned from M. Scott Peck's *The Road Less Traveled*—a book whose premise is that we operate from a narrower frame of reference than that of which we are capable—he remembers the opening line in the book stating that "life is difficult." This is a crucial truth in Peck's philosophy, and one many boomers have had to wrestle with, given their high expectations for life. It sees in life's problems opportunities to grow mentally and spiritually; problems are not to be avoided, but rather are challenges leading us to develop the skills we need to solve them. This point is not lost on Barry: "In fact, life will not become easy," he says, "until you accept the fact that it's not easy—which is kind of going around in circles, but I think I've learned that about myself. When you grow and change, don't expect it to be an easy situation." Life's difficulties have helped him to understands himself better, but he goes further in a leap of faith: Through growth and change as a person, he says, "God [is] talking to me."

Barry operates on the basic principle that one should be true to one's inner self. His story grows out of the larger cultural narrative of personal well-being so widely shared in contemporary America. In this narrative Americans seek meaning and worth in their discovery of self. The focus is on cultivating a deeper consciousness, an awareness of who one is and who one can be, as an essential first step toward well-being. Therapeutic language and metaphors give shape to his vocabulary: He speaks of feelings, of growth and change that come through his dealings with people, of new insights he has learned about himself, of healing old wounds. He has been influenced by the same therapeutic culture as has Mollie Stone, whose personal journey serves as our prime example of the concern with well-being and inner quest. Both of them look at themselves as evolving personalities, as people in the making, and both know that they must take charge of their own personal development and nurture it in the direction they want for themselves. Life is in their hands.

Yet Barry differs from Mollie in a very important way. Unlike her, he is able to connect his concern with personal well-being with a traditional religious vocabulary—with terms like love, grace, and self-sacrifice. This makes it possible for him to find a home within a church and to locate "his" story of well-being in a larger religious narrative. He has found a religious community that helps him understand his own life. To a considerable extent, this is possible for Barry because of writers like

Peck who have redefined traditional religious notions and cast them in terms of psychological growth. Old religious notions are given new meaning in ways that touch deeply in people's lives, often providing fresh perspectives on everyday life and a more developed, more positive sense of self. Religion becomes far more than a crusty institution set apart from the rest of life, more a worldview or generalized outlook than a narrowly defined sector of experience. All of life takes on spiritual significance, even a sense of mystery and of the miraculous in the process of growth. Even our interview was seen by him as a chance to reflect about his life in a psychological and therapeutic framework. At the end of our interview, he said:

> I came into this interview kind of looking forward to it, because a situation like this, I think, gives you an opportunity to get some things out from within you that you haven't thought about or talked about in a long time. To me that's always a healing process, that makes you kind of get in touch with some things that were down there festering about and not coming out and maybe bothering you a little bit until you have a chance to bring that out and think about it . . . so I got to unpack it a little bit.

"Unpacking the baggage," as he puts it, is essential from time to time. Occasionally, you must stand back and sort it all out, or otherwise religion will stifle you. By letting the "stuff pop out" when the bag gets too stuffed, you can grow and get in touch with your true self.

Returnees, concerned about spiritual growth, stress the psychological aspects of faith. One thing they look for in shopping around for a congregation is an emphasis on "feeling" religion, on bringing the experiential and belief dimensions of faith into a vital balance. Many of them never abandoned their beliefs, but often the beliefs seem disjointed from their life experiences. Congregations where the atmosphere helps to bring these two—belief and experience—into some meaningful whole are more likely to capture their loyalties. As Figure 7.1 shows, they approach congregations looking for spiritual growth. Almost three-fourths (73%) of the returnees say people should go to church not out of duty and obligation, but if you feel "it meets your needs." A psychological language of "choices" and "needs" replaces older-style religious obligations as a basis for getting involved in a congregation. Much of the shopping around occurs in an attempt to find a match between personal needs and institutional styles. For many of them, the search begins with the assumption that getting your needs met in a congregation will *not* be easy—58% see most churches and synagogues as having lost the real spiritual part of religion.

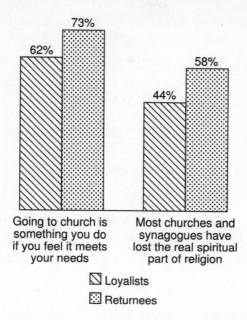

Figure 7.1 Spiritual Growth and Organized Religion

It comes as little surprise that the dropouts and nonaffiliated put even greater stress on getting personal needs met as a rationale for why anyone would go to church. Nine out of ten of those without ties to a religious institution say that you go only if you feel it meets your needs. Levels of disenchantment with organized religion run quite high for this sector of the boomer population. And within this sector we found the strongest expectations for getting personal needs met. The combination of the two—institutional disenchantment and high expectations—makes for exploration into many differing types of spiritual teachings on the part of seekers, for agnosticism and indifference on the part of the more secular-oriented, and for deeply personal religious and spiritual beliefs. Nonetheless, all groups put a strong emphasis on "feelings," on "awareness" of one's needs, on "freedom," and on "spirituality" as distinct from "religion." A disenchanted Presbyterian (now a self-proclaimed agnostic) who had broken away from the tradition put it this way: "People need freedom to be themselves, and what you need to have is an underlying basic sense of right and wrong . . . but that has to come from within."

More common among dropouts and the nonaffiliates, however, is the break with the institution combined with a strong, continuing belief in God. Our interview with a Catholic who had quit going to church, but who is still a believer, is a good example. The dialogue goes as follows:

INTERVIEWER: You're not religious, you don't feel religious?

RESPONDENT: Well, I do, I mean I'm not going to say I am an atheist . . . I have religious beliefs, but I feel that they're very personal.

INTERVIEWER: I'm interested in that. Do you feel more on a spiritual level?

RESPONDENT: Yeah. I don't feel the need to go to church.

INTERVIEWER: Is there anything from your Catholic background? I just wonder if any of that is carried through even though you don't practice it . . .

RESPONDENT: Oh, I'm sure it has.

INTERVIEWER: Do you feel like you have any kind of religious experiences other than what you would experience in a church?

RESPONDENT: Mmmm. I feel that I have a relationship with God, but it's very personal. I mean, it's not something that I feel the need to go to church for.

This exchange underscores once again the importance of the spirituality theme for boomers. In this instance spirituality is of the free-floating sort—"cut flowers," as someone told us—without deep roots in a religious tradition. Even though spirituality may be cut off from any roots, it is combined with an affirmation of traditional faith in God—a mix often expressed in our interviews.

PRIVATIZED RELIGION

Privatized faith is common among boomers, as it is for most Americans. A history of separation of church and state, a pluralistic religious order, a heritage emphasizing personal autonomy and voluntarism, and a consumer culture have all encouraged a deeply personal type of religion. On all the standard survey measures of religious privatism, Americans of all ages, of all social classes, and living in all regions score quite high. Nowhere else in the world is the term "religious preference" used so widely or in so subjective a manner as applied to religious identity.[4]

The stress boomers place on personal choice and inner feelings and truth, most certainly, encourages religious individualism and often separation from the religious institutions themselves. And a consumer approach, which leads some to shopping around for a congregation, builds on and extends a privatized conception of religion. Deeply influenced by a culture of consumption, boomers have grown up with religion made into a commodity and have looked on it in much the same way as other purchasable goods. Commercialization processes, packages, and prices almost everything in the religious market—from crosses to crystals. The consequences for religion under these conditions are enormous. Salvation as a theological doctrine, to cite just one very crucial element of religion, becomes reduced to simple steps, easy procedures, and formulas for psychological rewards. The approach to religious truth changes—away from any objective grounds on which it must be judged, to a more subjective, more instrumental understanding of what it does for the believer, and how it can do what it does most efficiently.

The same culture that simplifies and rationalizes religion also alters the very notion of the self. Under contemporary conditions the self becomes fluid, improvable, adaptable, manipulatable, and above all else, something to be satisfied—the assumption being, of course, that the self's appetite is insatiable. Parallels between the self and religion are worth observing. With a more fluid, adaptable, and insatiable self, religious identity becomes less ascribed, and more of a voluntary, subjective, and achieved phenomenon. America's religious pluralism feeds into this "new voluntarism" by demonopolizing any single version as *the* religious truth and by making a wide variety of religious options open to everyone.

But religious privatism takes many forms. If we think of privatism in its phenomenological sense, that is, as a world of meaning that has grown small, then we can begin to understand the many varieties of its religious expression. Some of the meaning-worlds in which people live may be almost exclusively personal and private, lacking in any broad social canopy of meanings; others may have a larger canopy, but it is still restricted to small worlds such as the family, the local community, or a particular social network. Among boomers, one finds enormous variety and many subtle meanings of privatism. For example, the *least* privatized in many respects are the loyalists—say, someone like Linda Kramer— who hold to more traditional formulations of faith, and by most measures are the most committed to religious institutions. They are the belongers: They have more close friends at church, they are more likely to see church as a means of becoming established in a community, and they are usually more involved in the life of a congregation. Yet the worlds in which they live can be quite parochial, and as we have seen, reinterpreted in a deeply psychological way. Others who would seem to be the *most* privatized—like Mollie Stone—are groping to break out of their own small worlds and to find a community they can claim as their own. Like her, they are now reaching out beyond themselves and are looking for ways to relate to a larger order after many years of turning inward. Certainly, privatism means something different in the two instances; but to say one is more privatized than the other is misleading.

Still another, and more common, type of privatism is exemplified by Sonny D'Antonio, the Italian Catholic from Boston who has a lot of anger toward the church. He attended Catholic parochial schools as a child and still thinks of himself as a Catholic, but he chooses not to have anything to do with the church. He remembers the fear the church instilled in him as a child when he says, "I felt like if I said 'shit' I'd go to hell." He quit going to church in his teen years, and he hasn't gone back. His view about going to church is summed up simply: "Whatever makes your boat float. . . . All I ask is, don't push it off on me." He remains a Catholic in spite of, not because of, the church.

Sonny's style of religious individualism resonates among boomers. The very words he uses in talking about religious belief have a familiar ring about them: "I'll take anybody's opinion and I'll listen to it, y'know, and we can discuss it," he says, "but don't tell me, don't ever tell me what I have to believe, cause I'll turn it around, I won't believe it." Then, catching himself in a slight overstatement, he adds: "I shouldn't say that, it's not that I won't believe it, if it makes sense to me." At one level we can read his comments as arising out of an Italian ethnic subculture known for its low levels of loyalty to the institutional church.[5] His deep feelings about priests hounding him for money and about the church refusing to marry his sister to a divorced man are not all that uncommon within an Italian-American Catholic community. Yet at another level, what he says and how he says it are peculiarly American. His comments reflect what many Americans feel very deeply about religious belief and practice. Because religion is voluntary, forced belief is not to be tolerated. But at the same time, Americans like to believe and will believe, "If it makes sense." Sonny captures something of the popular democratic, pragmatic-style religious individualism that is widespread today, and especially among young Americans.

Sonny and Barry make for an interesting comparison. Both were captured by mystery, yet one has virtually abandoned the church and the other has embraced it again. Much has to do with how they experienced the sixties: Barry was caught up in a bigger storm and questioned his southern heritage; Sonny was influenced more by his ethnic subculture, into which he retreated and found support.

Though he no longer goes to church, Sonny still holds on to much of his Italian Catholic heritage. He is a "communal Catholic," whose views and sensibilities are shaped by the rich imageries and narrative symbols of his ethnic Catholicism.[6] He believes in God and heaven and talks to his children about these things. He prays and occasionally reads the Bible. He feels that if God wants something to happen, it will happen. Much influenced by a Catholic "analogical imagination," he sees God in social relationships and in everyday life events. He thinks a lot about life, its meaning and purpose, about how things happen and why. Mystery and symbol continue to be real in his world. Even life's daily routines— like conversations with his wife—are riddled with mystery. Sometimes when his wife is talking, he says, her words don't make any sense to him at first. Then a moment later, as he thinks a bit more about what she is saying, it begins to come together and he sees how

> every little piece has its place and it all fits in. And you step back and you look at the puzzle. And that's what makes you think . . . it makes you wonder about it. If it happened once, maybe it was chance, but when it happens more than once, then I'm not too sure anymore, y'know? If it happens three times . . .

He doesn't complete the sentence—it is his way of affirming God's mysteries in the world. Such puzzles in life, including how he was saved from Vietnam by the lottery, that reveal the presence of the divine aren't to be explained.

Sonny's religious world is shaped largely around his family. "My home is my church," he insists, alluding to the religious significance of his relationships with his wife, his children, and his parents. It is in the family—his immediate family—that religious beliefs and values are taught and lived day after day. God is meaningful to him largely in this closely knit social realm; for his faith to be meaningful, it must extend to the family. His grasp of God in relational terms comes through in the following story. Sonny speaks very appreciatively of the prayer card his mother gave him the week before we interviewed him, and of how she told him to read the card every once in a while—the one about footprints in the sand:

> . . . it just basically tells you that through life, y'know, you're talking to God . . . and through all the good times, when I was looking in the sand, there were two sets of footprints, mine and God's . . . and

then when the troubled times came, I turned and looked in the sand for those footprints and they weren't there, there was only one set of footprints. "Why did you leave me when I needed you the most?" And the reply came back from God was: "I was there, I was carrying you." It was his footprints in the sand.

Despite his anger toward the church, few of the people we talked to had so strong a sacramental vision of God and world as does Sonny. In this respect he is atypical of other religious dropouts. Unlike most boomers who have abandoned organized religion, and for whom belief in God is simply a culturally prescribed affirmation, Sonny believes in a God who moves mysteriously in and about his life. He is also atypical in another respect: Sonny is far more interested in the religious upbringing of his children than most dropouts. For only one-fourth of dropouts is the concern about religious training "very important." One-half say it is "somewhat important," and the other one-fourth say it is "not really important." Whereas his concern for his children's moral and religious instruction matches that of many returnees and loyalists, he differs with them by choosing not to take his children to church, but to impart religious values at home. It might be said that he is more privatized than the churchgoers; but he is less privatized than many other dropouts and nonaffiliates in the sense that he feels he should take responsibility for his children's religious well-being. Given the great concern on the part of boomers today with family life, it is not too surprising to find a range of emerging, new patterns between institutions, that is, between family and religion.

In other respects, though, Sonny is very typical. Seventy-four percent of all dropouts/nonaffiliated say they would prefer to be alone and to meditate than to worship with others (see Figure 7.2). Less than half of the returnees and just over one-third of the loyalists opt for this radical individualist approach to the practice of religion. This gets to the heart of what is meant by religious privatism, and perhaps more than anything else describes the world of many boomer dropouts. Religion may lose its plausibility at the highest levels of societal integration, but not so for the smaller enclaves, like the family, or for private time and experiences, such as the weekend, that have come to be set apart from the public, work-oriented realms. Far from being antireligious, they opt for a deeply personal type of belief nourished more by their own private and family experiences than by what goes on in many churches and synagogues. For many boomers this type of radically individualistic religion fits in very well with a complex, highly bureaucratized society: Beliefs remain contained in private life, where they reign supreme, and do not intrude

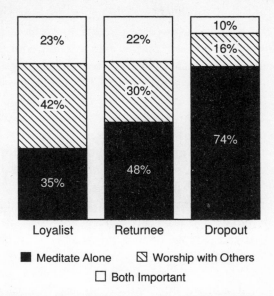

Figure 7.2 Prefer to Meditate Alone or
Worship with Others

into the broader social realms, where definitions of religious reality are contestable and can become disruptive.

Sonny's moral stance is also in keeping with how many boomers see the world. When he says, "We don't harm anybody," and speaks of helping people in the street, he expresses a conviction about human nature as basically good and affirms what is at the heart of religion as Americans have understood it—neither belief nor practice, but rather, moral standards. Aside from his family, he has a close set of "fishing buddies" with whom he shares a good deal of his life. If someone needs help, "I'll help them, not so much because of my religious beliefs, but simply because it's a human being that needs help." Beliefs aren't to be flaunted; often they fade into the background—as commentators on America have observed ever since de Tocqueville's time.[7] Sacramentalism blends with a practical utilitarianism to create a rationalist mode of moral reasoning: An act is right because it conforms to common sense. In everyday practice Sonny's moral code is not so different from that which characterizes many of his generation in organized religion—loyalists and returnees alike.

Finally, most boomers—whether active or not in a congregation—say they would likely call on a religious organization in the future. Sonny says he would go back to a Catholic church for a baptism, a confirmation, a wedding, or a funeral within the family. Even the most infrequent attenders look to churches and synagogues for celebrations of the "rites of passage," the major rituals surrounding the life stages of birth, adulthood, marriage, and death. Two-thirds of dropouts say they would like a family wedding at a religious institution; 78% would prefer to have a funeral there. They are almost as likely as regular attenders to expect these rites to be carried out for them. Boomers—no matter how estranged from the institutions—generally want the benefits of such services. Religion touches life at its critical junctures; and for those who are highly privatized, these are about the only times—and probably the most meaningful times—when they connect, or reconnect, with the institution. Like so many other things in a consumer society, these are "services" they can purchase as needs arise. For many dropouts it is all the connection with organized religion that they want, and probably enough to sustain a religious identity.

Privatized faith is common in contemporary America because it is so very congenial with a highly differentiated society. Restricted largely to the spheres of family and personal life, it encroaches very little into the larger public world, which Americans increasingly define as off-limits to religion. What one believes in private is one's own personal matter, and hence off-limits to religious institutions. With *believing* disjointed from *belonging,* it amounts to a "portable" faith—one that a believer can keep in the inner life and take along in life, having little contact with a religious institution or ascribed group. Moreover, such faith seems very natural to Americans. It is an expression of the religious individualism that is so much a part of the nation's religious and cultural heritage. Freedom, personal preference, voluntarism, individual autonomy—all are fundamental values in American religious thought. And belief in the Judeo-Christian conception of God, even a highly secularized version of the belief, adds to its legitimacy. Remembering that dropouts are our largest sector of the boomer population, larger than either loyalists or returnees, and that most dropouts are traditional believers, Sonny D'Antonio's is probably the single most common expression of faith found among boomers today.

MULTILAYERED SPIRITUALITY

There is considerable syncretism of religious belief and practice on the part of young Americans today—what is sometimes referred to as the "mixing of codes."[8] The most obvious example is Mollie Stone's free-roaming and expansive spirituality, but she is hardly an isolated instance. Spirituality of the sort she embodies takes expression in a thousand different ways, although in a less pronounced form, throughout the boomer population. Members of this generation have few inhibitions about multiple associations with vastly different groups, such as remaining a Presbyterian while at the same time exploring Zen Buddhist teachings, or a Methodist Sunday school class going as a group to hear a lecture on Goddess worship. Even more common is the phenomenon of picking and choosing beliefs from a variety of sources, which results in the "multilayered spirituality" found within organized religion: Vegetarian Unitarians, Lambs for Christ, Quakerpalians, Creation-Spirituality Catholics, macrobiotic kosher-observant Jews, and the many varieties of evangelical, social justice, gay rights, and feminist groups. Increasingly within the Protestant, Catholic, and Jewish mainline, people identify themselves by adding on layers of experiential meaning to older, less relevant religious and denominational labels.

With so much stress on experience and meaning, the psychology of faith takes precedence over systematic theological issues or concerns about social acceptance. Quests for personal fulfillment and authenticity open up new orbits of spiritual possibilities—"expanded horizons and inner explorations," as one man told us. Old boundaries separating denominations, once relevant theologically and socially, have faded as horizons have broadened; new ventures now lead many boomers, in the mainline traditions especially, into a deeper pursuit of religious and spiritual truths across traditions and across cultures. Religious identity, for them, is rooted less in a self-contained doctrinal heritage or inherited family faith than in their own experience. Doctrinal issues generate little fuss; but existential moral and spiritual concerns—how people "feel" about themselves and about life—grab them. "Labels are not important," as one commentator puts it, "it's the heart that counts."[9]

The new blended meaning systems appear to have risen in response to a weakened theistic faith. Figure 7.3 shows a clear relationship between strength of belief in God and the exploration of new beliefs and teachings. Loyalists, returnees, and dropouts, in that order, say they "definitely believe in God." With regard to the practice of meditation, belief in reincarnation, and emphasis on exploring differing religious teachings, the rank-ordering is just the opposite: loyalists are the least inclined, returnees somewhat more so, and dropouts the most inclined. Among those for whom traditional theistic belief over the past two decades has weakened, there is greater exploration into other spiritualities. This is

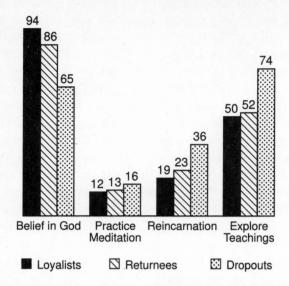

Belief in God   Practice   Reincarnation   Explore
Meditation   Teachings

■ Loyalists   ◨ Returnees   ▨ Dropouts

Figure 7.3 Beliefs and Practices (%)

true across the Protestant-Catholic-Jewish mainline, and only slightly more so among liberal Protestants than conservative Protestants. Sixty percent of the strong believers within liberal Protestantism endorse exploring other teachings, but so do 58% of conservative Protestant strong believers. Among Catholic boomers 58% of the liberationists underscore the importance of exploring, as do 44% of the traditionalists. Taken as a whole, probably no American generation has experimented so widely with syncretistic faiths as have boomers.

Probably no other generation subscribes to so many differing conceptions of Jesus Christ. Traditional Christian views of Jesus as God's Son and Savior have weakened: 46% of the dropouts say they think of Jesus as a great teacher or in some other way, but not as Savior. As one mainline Protestant dropout says:

> Jesus was a wonderful teacher, he taught us so many good things. Things never really tried, maybe. But no, I can't say I believe in him more than I believe in Buddha or Mohammed. They were all trying to help us to live a better life.

Jesus is not just a great teacher, but also a hero—someone she admires and would like to emulate. Not just dropouts, but many loyalists and returnees speak of Jesus in a way that is vague theologically, but morally uplifting. Again the strong moral component comes through in the Jesus talk. As a teacher and model, Jesus is one possibility, but there are others; and as the preceding quote indicates, the choices need not be mutually exclusive. Jesus may be the Way for some—for evangelicals, fundamentalists, and charismatics; but for mainliners, the belief shades into many differing, less particularistic versions that vary from person to person, reflecting a great variety of individual preferences. Surprisingly, many of them simultaneously draw from the teachings of several great religious figures. Except among born-again Christians and ethnic faiths, such as Orthodox Jews, the beliefs held generally by white boomers are not easily articulated save in a most personal and relativistic manner. Theological language seems to have given way to psychological interpretations. If there is one theme throughout that characterizes the languages of boomer faith, it is the subjectivist character of the affirmations: "*I* feel," "*I* have found," "*I* believe."

If cleavages emerge between loyalists and returnees, they do so largely around differences of *beliefs* or have to do with the *normative climates* within congregations. The two often go hand in hand. One returnee we spoke to, who was once deeply involved in the sixties' drug scene, describes his excitement about now attending a liberal, open-minded Sunday school class but also alludes to what is a source of real tension within many congregations. He had this to say:

> I've read a fair amount of Alan Watts, whom I love dearly, made a great impact on me. His great struggle to remain in the church and his failure to do so. I mean the letter he writes when he resigns I've read many times. It helped me, because he says a lot of what I feel about the traditional church. He just could not put it out that way anymore. There was too much joy in him, too much living in the moment for him to buy the rules that the church he had chosen was laying on so strongly.

Many returnees feel the rules that the church is "laying on" them. This should not be so surprising, since returnees are less conservative than loyalists on almost every moral and lifestyle issue. Differences between them in outlook and feelings may or may not be openly discussed, but almost always they lurk behind, and at times break into, the public conversations that can be heard in many congregations—at coffee hours, in committee meetings, in adult classes. Careful listening uncovers nuances and tones that send messages about what the congregation itself is like. This is a major reason why many returnees "shop around" for a hospitable church, and why we must now turn our discussion to the congregations themselves.

CONGREGATIONS

Every congregation has its own culture—a set of symbols, values, and meanings that distinguishes it from others. Aside from the more obvious factors that have a bearing, such as religious background, polity, and social context, congregations differ in the stories they tell about life. They are "thick gatherings," each with its own rich idiom and narrative combining elements of worldview, ethos, plot, and identity.[10] Mood, atmosphere, tone, sight, tastes, and smell are all involved, as is a sense of life's unfolding drama—from where and to where does time march. Each congregation has its own "style," its own set of encoded meanings about sacred realities. Something of this comes through in the account of the woman who belongs to the Vineyard Christian Fellowship, mentioned at the beginning of this chapter. Her story, in effect, blends with the congregation's story.

Whether the stories blend depends not just on the person's experiences and sensitivities but also on what the congregation offers. We heard many accounts of why people dropped out of church and synagogue, or finally quit looking for a congregation—they were about the failings of pastors and priests, boring and uninspiring worship services, stiff and narrow-minded people in the pews, lifeless programs, cold and unfriendly places. It is a subject about which there is much boomer talk. But we also heard about happy outcomes, about experiences that led people to want to participate in a church and to claim a congregation's story as their own. These accounts came from people of all social and economic backgrounds and all religious persuasions—liberal and conservative, Protestant, Catholic, Jewish, and assorted others, men and women, educated and not-so-educated, upscale and poor. The qualities of a congregation that make this happen are not easily described—a special pastor, priest, or rabbi, good worship, a worship service at a time other than on Sunday morning, a particular adult class where things come alive, good music, children's programs, opportunities for people to commit themselves to causes they feel are important. Often, as in author Dan Wakefield's case, it just happens.

There are no simple formulas, no simple set of criteria that will explain why some congregations attract boomers and others repel them. The chemistry between congregation and people is much more complex and far more unpredictable. Hence we have resisted trying to catalog the characteristics of growing boomer congregations, or of what young adults are looking for when they go church-shopping, preferring instead to look at several of the congregations where boomers talked to us about what attracted them to those places. We chose these congregations not because of any social background or denominational features, but simply because they illustrate some fundamental affinities between congregational cultures and boomer sensibilities.

1. "A Place Where Things Are Done Right"

In a gathering at a small Disciples of Christ church in an affluent suburb of a large midwestern city, we found that more than half the church was made up of boomers. When we asked them why so many of them were there, they mentioned the usual things: parents with children, a growing neighborhood, a hard-working pastor. One man then volunteered the following:

> . . . people of our age and income and educational level expect quality, and we offer a quality product, in the sense that things are done right . . . people sense that.

Indeed, a visitor does sense something special about the place. Most of the members are upscale, and as a congregation they work at making everything associated with church a quality experience. This means good music, good worship, good programs for children, good adult fellowship, good facilities, right down to the coffee that is served—they make sure it is fine coffee and served well! They go about all that they do in a deliberate manner, trying to make it a good experience, and to accomplish the most possible in the few hours they have together. For upscale, career-oriented boomers, efficiency and living by the watch are a part of life. With busy schedules and so many obligations, in the corporate world and at home, time at church must be quality time.

One reason the church attracts boomers is because it isn't bound by old traditions. This is a new church in a growing suburb, and it is not hampered by legacies from the past or by having many on its roll who insist on doing things the way they were always done. Though affiliated with the Disciples, it really functions as a community church, with a great deal of freedom to develop programs as it chooses. Members experiment in the worship hour with innovative presentations such as dramas and dialogues. Worship combines both traditional and contemporary themes. They are remarkably successful at developing programs around family concerns. These are largely for married couples with children, but also for married, dual-career couples without children, for single parents, and for young singles. Physical exercise is important—jogging, sports, aerobics. Doing things right means something other than "religious correctness," or doing what other churches do; rather, it is a theological affirmation about openness and acceptance.

Doing things right extends to the way they welcome newcomers in the worship service and how they go about cultivating relationships within the congregation: no name tags, no public recognition, no singling out of new people. "From the moment you come in," says one person, "you are not zeroed in on—'Well, you are the visitor here.'" Instead, the members have assigned responsibilities to meet newcomers and to try to make them feel welcome in a natural way. They respect anonymity, while stressing close, friendly ties among all participants. New people come away after their first visit knowing somebody, yet feeling that they have not been unduly exposed.

A small, intentionally minded church, the minister cultivates a personal relationship with the members: "He doesn't ask you, will you do it? He sends you a little note that says, 'Here's your duties for the next three months.'" Everyone has a job. If you join you agree to take on responsibilities. Duties are not handed down by the minister, they are agreed on. Governance of the church is characterized by an open, shared leadership style. "Baby boomers are still looking for that, no matter what we say. We are still looking to be able, a little bit, to run things ourselves," says one member. "It gives you a freer hand. You feel more ready to work for the church if everything isn't done just straight down the line the way the minister wants it."

2. "A Church That Doesn't Whack You on the Can"

In a working-class Catholic parish in Boston, boomers talk about how things have changed. They remember when parish life was so very different, before the mass was put into English and the priest did not face the people, back in the 1960s. Now people participate more in the liturgy, even the children join in. Things are done in ways that laypeople can understand. People's opinions are respected, your voice can be heard. The church speaks out more—for the poor, for the homeless, for justice causes. It's a different church.

But the biggest change is more psychological. One woman put it as follows during our group discussion:

When I was younger, I was petrified of God. There was a hot spot in hell with my name on it and a lightning bolt was going to get me any minute if I sneezed the wrong way. Of course, the Catholic church was like marriage, marriage for better or worse. In those days, if you were a good Catholic, you didn't divorce. You put up with the hell. As kids, we grew a resentment. Religion during my time was very cut and dried. This was the way it was. To me, religion and the God that I was raised with kind of combined.

Now, she says, she has been reoriented and has a much different conception of God: "I am learning about this God, and he is not really going to get me."

Another person says:

I think the church teaches more spiritual things than direct religion now. It breaks that fear. Even coming back now, I've felt like that commercial, "Come back to Jamaica." It's like, come on in. The door is open. It ain't like giving you a whack on the can coming to church.

The church that doesn't "whack you on the can" is a church that respects people. It recognizes freedom of conscience and relies less on fear. It is less authoritarian, and more democratic. It is a church with tradition, yet not closed to change. All are trends set in motion by Vatican II, but having a progressive priest helps. The priest in this parish encourages lay participation and shared decision making. He pushes hard the point about personal obligations and taking responsibility for one's own actions. Even with the children at confirmation, he has been known to say, "I don't care if you make it or not," to underscore that church is a commitment they must want and that they must freely give. His teaching hasn't fallen on deaf ears, in part because people in the parish relate so well to him. They understand choice and the responsibility that goes with it. As one of them says, it's like having to choose between going to mass and going to a Patriots' game—conflicting loyalties for a Catholic in Boston!—but, "At some point you have to take responsibility for yourself."

The connection between taking responsibility and boomer experiences is not lost on these parishioners. Asked about what influenced them most when they were growing up, they mention first, the Pope's visit to Boston, and second, Woodstock. The choice of events is telling; both are symbols of great significance to them, and both capture something of the profound changes during their lifetimes. Asked further about the impact of Woodstock, a parishioner says: "That's still a big thing now." And another person quickly adds:

> I think the whole idea of it really changed us all. I think a lot of people just got together and said to the government, you can't just control us. We are going to take some action ourselves. And that was good. We can really do that. We can stick together and change things.

And that's what they've been doing ever since—taking action and changing things.

3. A Temple That Invests in People

A Reform Jewish temple in a Los Angeles suburb prides itself in being different—"not just another temple," declares the membership chairman. "We have something to offer these people," he says, referring to the fact that most of the new members are boomers and at least half of the active congregation is under forty-five years of age. "Two things we offer: family emphasis, and [the opportunity to] relate to Judaism in your own way."

The temple combines traditional Jewish and contemporary spiritual themes in various ways. Many of the married returnees want to celebrate Jewish traditions but often prefer to do so in *havurah* groups. These small groups, made up of couples and their children, get together for dinner and for home-centered celebrations and readings of Jewish stories. At present about a dozen or so of these groups meet monthly. The temple encourages the small groups because they offer members a chance to learn about Judaism and give them considerable freedom to interpret the tradition as they choose. An advantage of the groups is the informality and small size that allows people to discuss freely with one another and with the children what the stories mean—"It's very warm and open," says one person. The groups encourage the breakdown of sexism as well: "Men can light candles and instead of just women doing the serving, we all serve food," says another person. The temple holds family *Shabbat* services once a month, and special children's programs more frequently, adding to the family motif that is so prominent within this congregation.

The congregation is remarkably open in allowing people to relate to Judaism as they like—some leaning to Conservative Judaism, and even some toward "meditative Judaism" and the mystical tradition. Those who are not members of the temple participate freely with those who are.

Some know very little about Judaism and are exploring what the rituals mean, others know a lot and observe inherited rituals in traditional ways. "There's a sense people have here of 'working at' Judaism," comments one member, implying an open stance toward the meanings of Judaism and toward spiritual growth. A boomer-style pragmatism comes through also in the "interfaith workshops," which are held regularly and function as support groups for those in mixed marriages. The workshops are a venture in exploring Judaism, human relationships, and how to deal with contemporary life. "Unlike in some places, where there is great worry about this, here we try to turn it into an asset—after all, mixed marriages are an opportunity to expose people to Judaism," comments an ex-Catholic, who is now in charge of the workshops.

4. A Church Where There's a Lot of Freedom in the Basement

In a large, progressive church in North Carolina, people feel a great deal of freedom to practice their own style of believing and belonging. People's comments convey something of the church's climate. Someone who was deeply involved in the sixties' counterculture and didn't think he would ever fit into any church told us:

> . . . this church calls me a Christian. And lets me be a part of their family in their search. Tolerates my excesses and my obnoxiousness and learns from me, too. I am part of the family here, whether or not I am a member. . . . That's what's wonderful about this church—they tolerate a wide range of belief. Here we have this wise man, Jesus Christ, who they won't push down your throat as the Son of God . . . they don't hit you over the head with it . . . the teachings of Jesus, the teachings of Buddha, the teachings of Confucius are all ways for us to free ourselves and let us see God in each other and in the world around us. Let us find ecstasy in simple things, meals, relationships especially, family and business, pure and simple. So that's what this church let me do.

A more traditional believer feels equally comfortable in telling us how he has found meaningful boundaries for his faith in the congregation:

> I've listened to a lot of Joseph Campbell, Bill Moyers, and that. I've been very interested in comparative religion and that type of thing. The spirituality movement. And I've come to the conclusion there's enough here, while this is not the only answer, there is certainly enough here for a lifetime of whatever I need to do.

When asked about how the church can relate so well to so many, another person called attention to what goes on in the church "basement"—experimental classes, courses in the new spirituality, and groups of all kinds (Twelve-Step, women's, quest, healing, Jungian analysis, peace and justice, support, sharing), and how they all look on the Bible and Christianity as "keys" to spiritual fulfillment, not as absolute, closed answers. Some churches, he observes, use the Bible and religious teachings as whips to force you into believing a certain way. They have answers for everything, more answers sometimes than questions. But not this church. Here there is a range: Some people lean toward traditional belief, others would call themselves Christian but are unsure of what they believe, still others are exploring new spiritualities. What they all share is a conviction that everyone must grow in faith, each in his or her own way, and that life is a journey with new religious and spiritual possibilities, waiting to be discovered. And for just about everybody, there is a group—"Choices unlimited," as one member put it.

In this place, with its latitude and so many ways of relating, there is inevitably some tension between the two floors—between the pulpit and the basement. Not serious tension, but enough that participants can identify "levels of"—almost the subconscious delving into—faith exploration. The picture is an intriguing one: a religious establishment meeting on Sunday morning in formal worship, and recovery and sharing groups meeting in the basement on weeknights and weekends. A kind of ecclesiastical upstairs and downstairs! Upstairs is official religion, truth as handed down and defined by authorities; downstairs is religion *à la carte,* grass-roots spirituality, *bricolage,* truth as people know it.

5. A Church with a Big Heart

Attending a worship service at a predominately black Catholic parish in downtown Los Angeles, a visitor will discover it to be a very special place. The service combines African music, Southern Baptist hymns, and chancel dancers. Red, black, and green African-American freedom flags hang over the altar, and a portrait of Dr. Martin Luther King, Jr., hangs under a stained-glass window. During the service women read from scripture and girls serve as acolytes. People frequently clap and applaud and say, "Amen." They hug and kiss one another. Many in the congregation wear African *kufi* hats and clothes.

It is a special place in several respects. African-Americans, Hispanics, and a handful of whites mix together. Many of them are young—the average age is thirty-five.[11] Many of the newcomers present belong to the boomer generation: men, women, and lots of children, adding to the excitement and liveliness of the congregation. Large numbers attend a service that allows them to be proud of their ethnic roots, and at the same time, to belong to a community that enacts Christ's Last Supper and invites all people to participate. "Here you can be African-American and celebrate Christ," a member says, "and have fun and be happy doing it." The sense of joy expressed at the worship service arises out of a feeling that this is their celebration, a mass they can call their own. Plans are underway as well for a Saturday evening jazz mass, and there is already a monthly healing service.

The congregation is a special place of concern for the surrounding community. Far from being preoccupied with otherworldly hopes, they are strongly committed to social action. In more than forty lay ministries, parishioners—many of them boomers—volunteer their time and services to work with teenagers, pregnant girls, high school dropouts, jobs, housing, drug problems, alcoholism, overeating, elderly care, AIDS patients, and gangs. A group of men have organized the "Godfather Club," which tries to get young boys off the streets and cultivate stronger ties with them. They know they must reach out to the young, educate boys in African-American history, and provide male role models. During the L.A. riots, the church was a center of activity, reaching out not only to help those in need, but trying to ease tensions between African-Americans and Korean-Americans. A member expresses the concerns of a young and caring congregation:

> We're doers. We have to go to the people, for they are our people. We live or die together. We must help our people. . . . That is what this church is about.

Asked about how and why the parish is special, he says: "We are a congregation with a big heart."

In these and other congregations, a boomer presence shapes new styles of believing and belonging. Wherever they get seriously involved, boomers change the atmosphere of churches and synagogues, create new agendas, and force issues that otherwise would be overlooked. Some congregations actually describe themselves as "boomer congregations" because of the disproportionate numbers and influence, usually of returning boomers; but in most instances the congregations boomers attend are not identified in this way. Rather, they go to congregations that have something distinctive about them—good worship, good programs, a particular social cause, a warm and accepting environment. Whatever the religious background, integrity is crucial.

And in all these places there are conflicts—latent, if not always man-ifest—between the loyalists who never left and the returnees who have just come back, and between boomers and an older generation. How these tensions and strains all work themselves out affects the ethos of a congregation. Often the tensions and strains take a heavy toll on indi-viduals. At the psychological level, the pressures arising out of gender, family, and identity issues can be deeply wrenching. It is to these under-lying tensions that we now turn.

CHAPTER 8

"It's Hard to Find a Religion You Can Believe Totally In"

Talking to boomers, one hears many stories about religious struggles—over beliefs, over feelings of anger, guilt, fear, and over relating to religious organizations. One hears the stories inside and outside of congregations. This is hardly the first generation to have such struggles with religion, yet many feel "bruised" over gender and lifestyle issues and are more forthright in expressing their feelings about them. One thing that has certainly come out of boomer culture and its transformations of self is a more assertive stance toward all things that stifle the human spirit—including religion. This often leads to a wholesale rejection of any religious involvement, a clean break with the institution. Just as often, however, people will simply try to find ways to reconcile their feelings or accommodate those aspects of religion that bother them. Boomers expect some rough edges and are prepared to deal with them. They talk about religion as something that has to be "worked out," "adjusted to," or "lived with." Like other things, religions have their pros and cons, aspects you like and aspects you don't. A practicing Catholic who disagrees very strongly with her church's stand on birth control and abortion puts it this way, "It's hard to find a religion you can believe totally in."

RELIGIOUS STRUGGLES: FROM ABUSE TO MILDER FORMS

Some stories of religious struggle verge on horror, as did those we heard from ex-churchgoers in the state of Washington who belong to Religious Abuse Anonymous, a Twelve-Step program for those who feel judged, shamed, or somehow manipulated by religion and who seek healing from it. Religious abuse occurs, we were told, whenever people experience undue pressures from religious authorities or rigid doctrinal positions or the loss of a healthy identity. Religious abuse, according to this group, is an addiction that can have a lasting grip. They offer victims of religious abuse the necessary support to break its hold, and at the same time encourage people to find a spiritual faith that leads to wholeness and freedom. In today's climate of concern about abuse in its many forms, healing from religious abuse has emerged as a spiritual quest.

Here are some of the symptoms of religious abuse, according to our informants[1]:

- obsessive praying, talking about God, quoting scripture
- thinking the world and our physical bodies are evil
- refusing to think, doubt, or question
- excessive judgmental attitudes
- isolation from others
- unrealistic fears, guilt, remorse, and shame
- thinking only in terms of black and white—simplistic thinking
- excessive fasting and compulsive overeating
- belief that sex is "dirty"
- cries for help: physical and mental breakdown
- attitudes of conflict with science/hospitals/schools

An ex-fundamentalist spoke of "breaking my codependency," by which he meant that he no longer thought of God as father ("a white guy with blue eyes") and of himself and others simply as dumb sheep. He had worked his way out of a strict, hierarchical understanding of his relationship with the divine. An ex-Catholic said, "Finally, I'm through with my guilt. I'm a woman, I'm beautiful, I'm sexy, and God, the universe, whatever, loves me." She had developed a positive self-image after years of suffering from guilt and low self-esteem. Both tell wrenching stories of psychological pain and self-deprecation that, if not created by religious indoctrination, were at least legitimized by it. In many instances people who speak of religious abuse have also experienced other forms of abuse: sexual abuse, physical abuse, verbal abuse, and the like. They are struggling simply to feel better about themselves.

Support groups for religious and related abuse have mushroomed in the past decade. In one large city, the newspaper listing of support groups numbers over a hundred, categorized under such rubrics as "singles," "homosexuals," "women," "men," "parents," "physical," and "adolescents." Under the "religion" rubric alone there are the following:[2]

- Crossroads in Faith: for men who batter women and children.
- Evangelicals Concerned: for gays and lesbians reconciling their spiritual lives with their sexual orientation.
- Shield of Faith: for people hurt in religious groups.
- Recovery: for sexually abused children.
- Sexual Assault Support: for adolescent victims of sexual assault.
- Therapy-Support: for adult incest victims and victims of physical abuse.

These are not specifically boomer groups, of course, but young adults do make up a sizable proportion of the participants.

Breaking out of old imageries and relationships, group members help one another to develop new, more positive ones. They cultivate a holistic spirituality, a playful and celebratory view of life, a psychology of acceptance and forgiveness, and a positive conception of themselves and of others. Those who have had such intense experiences are adamant about inclusive religious language; they insist that faith is a process involving, among other things, liberation from distorted and hurtful words and expressions. The languages of "letting go" and "levels" of spiritual growth and self-empowerment are common discourses. The therapeutic languages, drawn from the cultural narrative of well-being, are adapted to the fears, anxieties, guilt, and shame often fostered by traditional religious teachings and practices. Distinguishing between religion and spirituality, or between the outer and inner aspects of faith, is an important theme and helps individuals to find a more enriching, favorable connection with the divine. Self-worth and self-esteem are elevated to top priority in thinking about what is most important in a person's life. Some turn their backs on all churches and synagogues and vow never to return again because of bad memories; but some do search out new congregations in hopes of finding a home—usually in more liberal religious environments.

As in all such recovery groups, letting go of the old and taking hold of the new is the central psychological process. Taking hold of the new doesn't mean "you just become a loner," as one man put it; rather, he went on to say, "Finding an open-minded and supportive congregation is a must, if you are to survive after leaving the program." This suggests that the program does not simply revel in selfishness or self-absorbing narcissism, but instead encourages connecting with others and finding community. Often people talk about such connections in psychological terms—using words like empathy, communication, or relevance. Inner definition and ego strength are essential first steps that have the potential to lead to a renewed social self. But for these ex-religion addicts, the recovery experience is midwife to a new shared experience.

Most stories of struggle are not of this intensity. Even under the best of conditions, however, contemporary religious pluralism creates difficulties among committed believers—especially, perhaps, for committed believers. In a society where there are so many competing versions of religious truth, some psychological dissonance is almost inevitable. Boomers, of all people, know there are others who believe differently from them. How can a person hold fervently to her own faith when so many others believe equally as fervently in theirs?

In a highly individualistic culture, there is also a problem in how religion is defined. Because religion is seen largely as a personal "preference," something chosen by a free and autonomous individual, as a subjective reality it exists over against an external and often distant institution. A psychological approach to religion exacts a price: A burden falls on the individual to "work out" personal religious questions, often without much help from the institution itself. Consequently, individuals must match their own personal preferences with institutional realities, that is, they must find a church "where you can feel comfortable," to cite Linda Kramer's words again. This involves a psychological voyage of sorts and a series of cognitive and emotional negotiations, of trying to fit one's own needs and preferences with an institution and what it is perceived to offer or stand for. Especially in a time of enormous religious and cultural change, when normative expectations are in flux, these burdens become greater.

When we add to this the institutional dislocations felt by members of this generation, it becomes apparent why struggle is a big part of boomers' stories. Many of them are still "working out" their relationships with an ambivalent religious past—which, like all ambivalences, attracts as well as repels. They are attracted to idealized versions of religious truth, repelled by their actual experiences with religious institutions. In some respects they are like outsiders: They find cultural narratives about the biblical covenant and America's role in the world as alien to their experience; they feel at odds with the stories, unable to claim them as their own. The narratives are not fully meaningful and often are seen as deceptive and exploitive. In response, boomers reject the narratives altogether, or embrace them wholeheartedly; or, perhaps most likely, they modify the stories in light of their own experiences and give them a more nuanced interpretation.

People who consider becoming involved in a congregation often experience a fundamental clash of two conflicting yearnings: on the one hand, to hold on to one's own individuality, and on the other, to be a part of a larger faith community. Aside from the values of freedom and autonomy of American culture, the estrangements many boomers experienced in the 1960s and 1970s encourage autonomy and a psychological distancing from religious institutions. Dropouts resolve these issues through their defections, but many of those who have remained in, or returned to, religious institutions try to find ways to deal with their struggles. This is not to imply an enormous angst besetting the boomer population, but rather to suggest that many young adults feel bruised in their relationships with religious institutions and must overcome negative feelings. Often the more introspective and self-reflective ones feel they must "work out" their religious and spiritual identities around the confrontations they have had with religion. This can result in lingering memories of bad experiences, or in distorted perceptions that are slow to give way. Sometimes it results in negative religious references: "I can tell you the church I don't go to," one man said when asked about his religious preference. In all of this, there is the potential of much soul-searching, and the possibility that deeply felt concerns may not be fully resolved. It is a source of much of this generation's spiritual quest.

WOMEN, CAREERS, AND SEXIST LANGUAGE

Boomer women, especially the working, career-oriented women, struggle with religion more than do their male counterparts. Seventy-five percent of the women of this generation are in the paid labor force, either full-time or part-time (with the remaining 25% largely homemakers).

One-half of these women work full-time. Many of them are like Carol McLennon, the Catholic woman from southern California, who hasn't always worked outside the home but does so now to help with family finances and to save toward college costs. With four children to educate over the next ten years, the McLennons are already worrying about how they will meet these obligations. It is not an uncommon worry among the older members of this generation, many of whom now have children in junior high and high school. And many of the women—whether single or married, working outside the home or as homemakers—grapple with their feelings about how women are received in religious organizations.

Many women's stories carry an undercurrent of negative feelings toward religion, though it is not always expressed explicitly as anger. Often the feelings are displaced, as when one single mother told us, "I knew things were screwy as a kid. God was a man, and all the ministers were men. Strange, I thought, but that's the way it was." Religiously conservative women are more likely than others to express their feelings in a subdued manner. Often they are concerned about how they say things and how others might interpret what they say—with the choice of words, tone of voice, and type of expression all taken as an indication of a person's own deep feelings. Laughter or a giggle is sometimes the best clue of psychological tension in an otherwise proper display of religious appearances.[3]

Other women are much more forthright and care far less about what they say. An ex-Episcopalian and self-described feminist said: "I was turned off. We would say there is no health in us in the prayer, and we confessed this, of course, always to a God who is a he. Wouldn't you know?" Sexist language came up more than any other single concern among women. Words that ignore the existence of women alienate and cut them off from a wholehearted affirmation of their personhood and continue to remind them of the evils of patriarchy and sexism. Women feel starved spiritually with symbols and rituals that fail to include them and nurture them as whole people. One woman we talked to told us she was so starved in a church that she decided to take a leave for a while to get away from "all the God-he talk" and rituals that remind her every Sunday that it's a man's church. Though still a member of her church, she deliberately does not attend services and has joined a women's group in order to explore her feminine spirituality. She describes her leave from church and her new adventure this way:

> . . . the church has been good for me. It's been a real catalyst. But I have come to find out that it doesn't corner the market on spirituality . . . it's a time of really getting in touch with the feminine side that

has not been acknowledged for maybe five thousand years. And it's like a reawakening . . . getting in touch with some feminine energy. All my life has been a patriarchal kind of thing. And it's just a balance. It's like ultimately I want it to be this male/female balance. But if you look at what I've had for thirty-five years, it's been patriarchal male authoritarian stuff; and so for me to be meeting in a circle of women who are honoring their intuitive side, honoring the Goddess, the feminine counterpart of God, it's balancing it.

Carol McLennon has not left her church and probably never will, but she struggles with it as much as anyone we met. She'll tell you about the Catholic church's shallowness, its hierarchical authority, its rules. She is disgusted with the way women are treated, and how laypeople generally are overlooked. She is not alone: Nine out of ten Catholic boomer women prefer a church where the teachings are in the hands of both the hierarchy and the laity. This was one of the strongest findings from our survey of Catholics—true for both women and men. Women demand a say in determining the morality of abortion, and of views on divorce and remarriage, and in practical matters like how parish funds are spent. The democratization of decision making is regarded as essential in all social institutions—including religion. Authority bears directly on the role of women in the church:

> . . . the church is two hundred years behind the times, I mean, they're so ancient. I'm talking about Pope Paul John II. Lightyears behind. And if they just stopped thinking rules and what's gone in the past and just listen to who they are, y'know, it would be so much freer and so much more open. It's the walls. We build so many walls between people, so afraid to give up the rights of the ordained to women, as if only men have a hold on spirituality.

On the issue of ordination of women, Carol reflects very well how Catholic boomer women think. Eight out of ten favor the ordination of women. Mainline Protestant boomer women favor it even more so than Catholic women. Conservative Protestant boomer women favor the ordination less—but even so, more than a majority support it. The right of women to the ministry in all these faiths is overwhelmingly supported. Likewise, over three-fourths of boomer men support the ordination of women. Gender equality and career opportunities for women are deeply rooted values for this generation, values that lead them to be supportive of women's movement into jobs and careers outside the home, and at odds with religious establishments that resist opening doors for women.

But there is more to Carol McLennon's discontent than just access to jobs and careers and the church's authoritarianism. Her frustration is with its failure to understand the demands placed on her as a woman. She wishes she had more support than she does in her congregation. Besides working part-time, she is a wife and a mother of four children, she takes care of an aging mother who lives with her, and she is very active in her Catholic parish. Actually, work, family, and faith all mesh pretty well for her—on the surface, at least, she seems pretty happy with her life. Yet she voices deep feelings about playing "the roles of supermom, superwife, and superworker, to the point of being totally exhausted." The demands placed on her can get heavy, and sometimes she seeks help: She has gone to workshops dealing with family life; she and her husband have participated in a Marriage Encounter weekend (a program of spiritual renewal for couples). Even though her marriage is solid and her family life is very rewarding, still she feels the church could do much to provide support for working women. Full-time working women everywhere express these feelings: the need for child care, mother's night out, and women's sharing groups.

One thing is very clear: Boomer women of all faiths find the existing programs in most congregations, including many of the older, gender-based men's groups and women's groups, inadequate to their needs. Rather, they look for more specific types of programs organized around career concerns, women's issues, and lifestyles. There is a distinct generational break here between boomer women and the older women. "Let's talk about the bastards—the men—I have to work with every day, all the stuff a woman has to put up with," said an angry working woman, "but I'm not interested in those stitch and bitch groups of women sitting around at most churches."

The frustration working women feel about juggling jobs, children, and marriage is rooted in the demands of the overlapping roles, and also because boomer women have no previous role models to emulate. "Our mothers didn't have as many options as we do," comments a middle-class career woman, pointing out that women today must work out for themselves how to combine their many roles. Boomer women are in this respect on society's frontier, having to redefine their roles and to forge new identities. And this hasn't come easily, without ambivalence or guilt. A woman from Ohio spoke of the role strains she has experienced:

> I was raised to be a wife and mother and I had my place in society, and I felt very certain about that. And then just at the point where I was getting married and having children, all of a sudden I was getting the message that I was supposed to have a career. Things were changing. I felt guilty on both sides. If I wasn't working, I felt guilty

because I wasn't fulfilling my potential. If I was working, I felt guilty because the children weren't getting my care.

Contemporary culture contributes to the frustration by holding up an image of the superwoman as "energetic" and "competent," as one who has the personal skills of putting it all together, not as one who has been forced, as Arlie Hochschild points out, to adapt to an overly demanding schedule.[4] The superwoman image appeals to many boomer women because it helps them to think of themselves as unusually efficient, organized, and confident, and as Hochschild argues, because it is a cover-up to the emotional crises and conflicts that women often feel very deeply.

Trying to juggle the roles of wife, mother, and work forces decisions about what to really put yourself into, and Carol is quick to point out that work is the area that gets slighted. She likes being a wife and mom. Like many other married women who work with only a high school education, she values family life more than work. Less than one-third of the working women with a high school education that we surveyed agree that "commitment to a meaningful career is one of the most important things in life." Among college graduates who have jobs or careers, more than half agree with the statement about the importance of careers. Family-versus-career priorities thus vary by level of education. Those investing in family tend to be more involved in religious activities, while those committed to careers have less time and energy for religious activities. Despite the prevailing cultural images, most boomer women know that they cannot really be superwomen and that they must make hard decisions about the roles they value and where to place their energies.

Working has a predictable impact on religious involvement. Women holding down jobs and careers are more likely to drop out altogether or attend religious services irregularly. They are less likely to pray regularly, to say grace at meals, or to report having memorable religious experiences. Working women obviously have less time to devote to religious activities—a factor that was sometimes mentioned in our interviews. But more is involved than just time considerations. As the first generation of women to work and pursue careers in great numbers, they also find social and psychological benefits from working that individuals in the past often derived from religious involvement. Jobs and careers are a source of values and identities, and act as an affirmation of their own worth as people.

Gender differences have long been recognized in American religious life, with rates of participation in religious activities and personal religiosity higher for women than for men. Religious institutions have given support to a gender-specific division of labor—breadwinner and

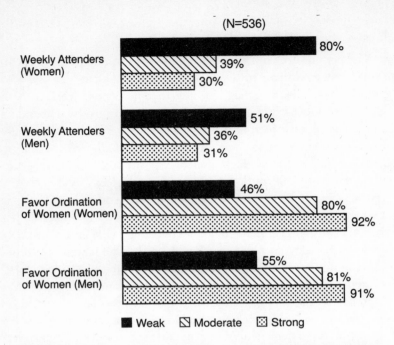

(N=536)

Weekly Attenders (Women)
- 80%
- 39%
- 30%

Weekly Attenders (Men)
- 51%
- 36%
- 31%

Favor Ordination of Women (Women)
- 46%
- 80%
- 92%

Favor Ordination of Women (Men)
- 55%
- 81%
- 91%

■ Weak   ◨ Moderate   ▦ Strong

Figure 8.1 Commitment to Gender Equality and Religion

provider for males, and moral and religious nurturer for females. This role for women was encouraged by cultural narratives emphasizing the good woman as a "helpmeet"; that is, as wife and partner to the man and as mother to her children. But as women of this generation have moved into the labor force, the gender gap in religion has narrowed. For well-educated men and women in career lines especially, the gap has declined.[5] As a new image of woman emerged—as autonomous, as competent, as a person, not defined by her husband's role or her responsibilities in the home—the older, gender-based religious styles have collapsed. Working women now structure their lives, including how they spend Sundays, more and more the same as do working men, obviously underscoring the fact that the conditions of work, and not gender, have the greater influence on religious life.

The greatest religious differences today are not between men and women, but between "feminists" and "traditionalists." By feminists we mean men or women who endorse egalitarian attitudes toward gender roles; and by traditionalists we mean those more likely to favor more conventional attitudes. The two constituencies differ on many aspects of personal religiosity as well as institutional commitment. Figure 8.1 shows, for example, a 50-point spread in attending weekly religious services between women scoring "weak" and those "strong" on an index of gender role egalitarianism.[6] Eighty percent of the traditional women are regular church attenders, but only 30% of those strongly committed to egalitarianism are regular attenders. A similar pattern obtains for the ordination of women, with almost as much percentage spread. Among men we find much the same. Fifty-one percent of the traditionalists attend religious services regularly, as compared to 31% of the nontraditionalists. Fifty-five percent of traditional men support women's ordination, as compared to 91% of the men strongly committed to egalitarianism. Ideological differences arising out of the women's movement and other social and cultural changes of the 1960s and 1970s are a major cleavage today among boomers. And it is clear that these ideologies have a direct impact on boomer involvement in and attitudes toward churches and synagogues.

GAYS AND LESBIANS

When Carol McLennon speaks of life as a struggle—"death and resurrection"—she knows about it close to home. A woman who has confronted the sexism of the Catholic church, she must also deal with other gender issues. Her teenage son is homosexual. When she tells of his attempted suicide and of the family's experience with this, her voice is filled with compassion:

> . . . he had to sort all those things out and it was something he didn't come to me about, or either of us about. It just kills me to think that he struggled all that time and it never crossed my mind that one of my children would be homosexual. . . . I never talked to my kids about being anything but heterosexual.

When asked if she had learned anything from the experience of dealing with her son, she responds:

> I have learned that we are all to be who we are. And by being who we are, we add to other people's lives. For those who aren't like us, we become a challenge to them. That was a very uncomfortable issue to deal with, and yet it has opened me up not just to homosexuals but anybody who's different.

Characteristically, Carol is able to find something positive in all of this. She is a more sensitive person now as a result of the experience. Asked if her parish was any help during all of this, she says: "Yes and no. They're both a thorn and a comfort." She received support from close friends in the parish, but the parish as a whole did not respond in any really sensitive way to their family crisis.

All of the mainline Protestant denominations now are grappling with issues of homosexuality and the related question of ordination of gays and lesbians to the ministry. Three denominations have been forthright in supporting gays and opening the way to ordination: the Unitarian Universalists, the United Church of Christ, and the Disciples of Christ. In the main, however, the churches still see homosexuality as morally and religiously deviant. Some formally excommunicate "practicing" gays; most do not ban but simply disapprove of sex outside marriage. The Roman Catholic church takes the position that any sexual activity outside marriage is sinful. For gays, who by law cannot marry, religious acceptability means abstaining from any sexual practice. "It puts us in a position of saying our sexuality is immoral," a gay man told us. "You can't be in favor with God unless you are straight." In some churches gays are forming their own organizations, hoping for eventual, full acceptance. The More Light program for Presbyterians, Integrity for Episcopalians, Affirmation congregations for Methodists, and Dignity within the Catholic church are all efforts led by gays seeking inclusion. Congregations here and there celebrate the union of a gay couple in a joyous "gay commitment" ceremony. Jewish gays and lesbians have formed their own temples in many big cities. In a fight that extends across faiths, gays and lesbians push for a place within religious communities that for centuries have excluded them, and to claim the great religious narratives as told within these communities as their stories as well.

Despite the efforts of some to find a home within the churches and synagogues, many others have given up trying to do so. In frustration, many gay people have left traditional congregations, some to join predominately gay organizations such as the Metropolitan Community Church, and others opt for spiritual support groups. Disillusionment with organized religion within the gay community runs deep. A poll in 1989 found that half of all gays surveyed nationally consider themselves to be "not very" or "not at all" religious. Almost one-third of gays polled nationally believe that church attitudes toward gays have become less favorable over the past twenty years.[7] In times of spiraling expectations for change, frustrations mount.

The pain for gays and lesbians arises, fundamentally, out of the lies, denials, and self-hatred forced on them by religious teachings on morality and views of homosexuality. A person's sexual self becomes filled with shame and a chasm created between sexual identity and spirituality. A thirty-four-year-old gay Catholic at Chicago's Jesus Day festival spoke of the pain of growing up always trying to be what others wanted him to be, and of the self within him that wanted to get free. There was the double life of being with boys publicly, and of knowing the same boys privately. There was a double life spiritually, the open mass and communion with God, and the more agonizing private confessions. Today he remains a Roman Catholic and attends mass occasionally but is sustained mostly by his career as a counselor and voluntary work on a citywide committee on lesbian, gay, and bisexual concerns. He reads Sufi mystics and believes that God gives all people the capacity to grow, to discover, to create, and that gayness is a special spiritual quality that will in time break through and maybe even help to redeem the brokenness of the world. His deepest spiritual needs are met, he says, not by the church or in formal worship, but in personal meditation, in writing, and in conversations with people who share his experiences.

SINGLE PARENTS AND BLENDED FAMILIES

The symbolism of religion and family has long been closely intertwined, with religious beliefs and sanctions shaping norms of sexual practice, marriage, and child-rearing. These teachings on family life are at the core of Judeo-Christian religious heritage. Recent debates over abortion, homosexuality, and no-fault divorce, combined with attacks by the religious right on the "new morality" in the 1970s and 1980s, made the public even more aware of religious pronouncements about family-related matters. And more recently, in the 1992 presidential campaign, "family values" were thrust into political debate. The television program "Murphy Brown" took on symbolic significance in that debate after then Vice President Dan Quayle attacked the program, which portrayed an unmarried woman choosing to keep her baby—sparking much discussion about what constitutes a family today. Not surprisingly, in an age when the "Ozzie and Harriet" family of the 1950s has virtually vanished, and many new forms of family life and living arrangements have emerged, there would be tensions. Fully aware of these older normative standards, boomers recognize that a gap exists between what "is" and what many think "ought" to be in regard to family life.

This phrasing—what "is" and what many think "ought" to be—is crucially important. Given the sensibilities of boomers, the gap that exists is one that was created not by divine mandate, but by the generations.

"Life is really different for us today," a single father from Denver told us. "Older people in the churches seem to forget how it has changed." Ever aware of themselves as a generation set apart by their size and experiences, boomers know, and if pushed will say, that in some matters—and especially sexuality and lifestyles—things are just not the same as they used to be, and that many of the older connections between religion and family don't hold very well anymore.

Consider Oscar Gantt, the African-American from North Carolina who is disillusioned with his church. Much of his disillusionment has to do with the church's lack of commitment to social causes, but family considerations are of some significance. Oscar is a single parent raising three children. He is living with a woman but has no immediate plans to remarry. In this situation he feels a bit rejected by people at his church and especially by his mother, a loyal churchgoer. He describes his feelings as follows:

> I feel that I'm faithful to Christianity, but I've done some things that people around me, I guess, would consider immoral, sinful, and they still have trouble embracing the things I've done. In fact I don't think my mother visits me too much because I am living in a situation in which I am not married and stuff like that. But I don't share her views on that, and I know her views are rooted in her religion. But it doesn't work for me that way. I still believe what I believe, and I can't see living my life any other way.

While few people seem as distraught as Oscar does over living together ("and stuff like that"—whatever that means!) many boomers in this situation don't feel welcomed in religious institutions. The sense of rejection may be greater in the South for the divorced, for single parents, and for those living together, as the following comment from a Southern Baptist woman would suggest:

> When you are divorced—I don't know how it is up North, and it may be better up there—but down here you are like a diseased person if you go to church. You can't go in a class with the married people. You can't go in a class with the single people. They put you in what they call Singles Again classes, which is sort of like lepers.

The feelings of estrangement from religious organizations on the part of those who are not married is widespread. Well over a majority of the divorced and separated feel that the rules about morality in churches and synagogues are too restrictive. They are less involved, and especially if they have no children, compared with those who are married. The truth is that religious institutions are bastions of bourgeois-style familism:

Those who deviate in some way from the "Ozzie and Harriet" family simply don't fit in very well.

Boomers know well what has come to be called the *blended family.* A high rate of divorce combined with relatively high levels of remarriage have created more complex, divorce-extended families, which in many respects are resourceful and adaptable, as family forms go.[8] Neither are they viewed as deviant in the way that divorce and single parenting tend to be by middle-class American standards. But blended families can and do create religious strains. Tensions come about as a result of the added complexities of human relationships. A divorced Catholic woman who no longer attends mass threw up her hands in dismay over how her daughter was caught in the shuffle between parents—a shuffle bearing on the child's religious life:

RESPONDENT: The gal that [my ex-husband's] seeing now, who's also divorced and has children, is very Catholic. It's bad enough that we have joint custody and Sylvia's with me three or four days a week and with him three or four days a week. She's also in day care because both of us work. Then on weekends this gal has her kids, and he and my daughter spend the weekend at her house. Then on the weekend that her ex has her two children, she comes and stays with my ex and my daughter at their condo. So there's like . . .

INTERVIEWER: So what happens Sunday morning?

RESPONDENT: There's like three families involved here. Every other Saturday Sylvia comes home to me, and then on the opposite week she's with her dad until noon on Sunday. Well, it turns out, she goes off to Sunday school with this other woman and her children. While my ex stays home and reads the paper or does whatever he feels like doing. And I almost feel like it's something that alleviates him or gives him some more free time, while this other woman is basically responsible for my child. But I can't really speak up and say I don't want her attending Sunday school, because then I look like the bad guy.

Tensions get even more compounded when there are mixed-faith marriages. They often run high even for first-time marriages, since choices must be made about how to raise children. These choices require decisions that the partners themselves often find difficult, and which can cause dissension among grandparents and other family members. In Jewish-Christian marriages, for example, couples often find differences of faith irreconcilable, especially during the December holiday season, when tensions that have simmered all year boil over. Nearly one-third of these marriages end in divorce, compared to only 17% when both partners are Jewish, according to a recent survey.[9] At the same time, however, the number of mixed-faith marriages is increasing. Half of all young Jews marrying today choose non-Jewish partners—double the number who married outside the Jewish faith twenty years ago.[10] In this same period, Protestant-Catholic marriages have skyrocketed as well. Where there are second marriages, the extended families that are created—with multiple sets of children and step-kin—expands enormously the possibilities of mixed faiths within the kin network.

Taboos against interfaith marriages may have lessened, but many families find themselves coping with the strains they create. Some of the strains are indirect, such as guilt from not getting children baptized or taking them to church or synagogue for religious training. A Methodist married to a Catholic described what had happened in her family:

> My first daughter was baptized Catholic. I never baptized the other two. I always to this day feel kind of guilty about that. But we just can't seem to agree.

Interfaith marriages can lead to a further watering-down of the contents of faith, as is the case for this family:

> I told [my husband] the other day I think I am going to start taking them to a church down the street that is just a regular Christian church, and that is my goal—to just have them raised as regular Christians. I don't want them to feel they have to conform to any set rules, but I want them to be raised knowing Jesus and God and the things I learned in Sunday school. What all children should get— that rounded kind of Bible.

Blended families that are religious easily become settings for an expanded, and potentially stressful, confrontation with a pluralism of faiths. As an example, a divorced mother whose family connections are all quite religious describes how, during the course of a year, her eight-year-old son makes a round visiting four differing churches:

1. With father: He goes to a Southern Baptist church.
2. With paternal grandparents: He goes to a United Methodist church.

3. With maternal grandparents: He goes to the Catholic church.

4. With mother: He goes to the Calvary Chapel.

At present, she thinks it's good that he is getting so much exposure (and so much churchgoing). Yet she wonders what all this religious variety will mean for him. When he gets older, what faith will he choose? If no one faith is impressed on him as a child, will he abandon all of them? What, then, will he believe?

The survey makes clear just how many parents in the boomer generation might realistically ask such questions. Eighty percent of the first-time married population say that members of their families share similar views about religion. In the case of mixed-faith marriages, presumably one spouse has converted to the faith of the other, or they have both switched to another faith, or somehow they have found ways to blend their distinctive beliefs, rituals, and traditions into a common family pattern. However, for those married more than once—the blended families—the proportion with similar views in the family drops to 65%. With more complex, divorce-extended families, the likelihood of a shared faith declines. Blended families pray less, read the Bible less, say grace at meals less. They have less to share religiously, at least as a common, unifying tradition.

Not too surprisingly, the emergence of new family types corresponds closely with the greater religious individualism of contemporary society. Family life in the past was hardly immune to a broadly based cultural individualism; but until fairly recent times, American families did resist its encroachments by maintaining family-based religious norms of belief and practice. When we asked if families should attend church or synagogue as a family, or should family members make individual choices about religion, 45% of boomers opted for the latter—a sizable percentage, considering how values and symbols within the institutions of family and religion have long been fused together. But the emphasis on religious choice *within* the family varies by family type: It is greatest among the separated and divorced (58%), next highest for those married more than once (50%), and least for first-time married people (36%). As boomers have been remaking family life, they have been redefining religious norms within the family. Just as there is no longer a single culturally dominant family pattern to which the majority of the American population conforms, so increasingly there is a great variety of religious and secular styles.

ON BEING A "GOOD CATHOLIC"

For all Carol McLennon's love for the church, she has been at odds with the church throughout her adult life. Ever since she decided to get a tubal ligation and not have any more children, she was estranged from church authorities. The estrangement never quite goes away, partly because people continue to remind her: "And people will still say to me, 'How can you do that? You're Catholic and that's against the church.' " However, Carol has not been driven out of the church. Nor does she accept second-class citizenship within the Catholic community. Having to defend her actions, to others and to herself, she has grown in her understanding of faith and of the church as people. One very important result is that she has come to know what it is like to be true to her conscience, which, according to Vatican II, is the highest arbiter of moral decision making. She describes how reliance on her conscience has made her more self-reflective and self-assured:

> . . . it gave me a whole different outlook on the church. I can't live by what the church says, y'know? I have to check my own self out with God. And yes, I listen and, yes, I read. And you go through the Bible and you don't have Jesus saying to people, look what you did! That's wrong!

Many Catholics in Carol's generation, women more so than men, have long been disaffected from the church over the teachings about birth control as morally wrong. One of four Catholic women in our survey who dropped out of the church said that the teaching on sex-related issues was the major reason. Women in their thirties are particularly concerned about the contraception issue, since many of them are at the age where they must make decisions about having children, or if they already have children, whether or not to have more. Still others, like Carol McLennon, stick with the church by defining sexuality issues as "private," and thus treated as a sphere of life removed from the authority of the church. Despite her feminist leanings and deep personal struggles, Carol is incredibly committed, still a loyalist after all these years. Given all the wrenching experiences that she and many other Catholic women have had, how do we explain why many of them leave the church and still others stay with it?

Vatican II itself figures very prominently. This historic event came at a crucial moment for older boomers like Carol: It occurred during their impressionable adolescent years. In the early to mid-1960s, they were at the age to be making decisions on their own to be Catholic when the democratizing reforms of Vatican II were just beginning to be felt. At the time there was considerable optimism that the church was moving into the modern era—an awareness, as writer Garry Wills put it, that "the Church" *can change.*[11] For young Catholics caught up in the social unrest of the sixties, it was as if the major institutions of American life—family, political, military, and religious—were in the throes of change. When Carol speaks of her years growing up as a "transition time" and a "really rich era," she expresses the great optimism of the times, and her conviction that "there was a real change in our behavior from then on." By coincidence, many social and religious changes came together during the mid- to late 1960s to produce great hope and expectancy about a new world and a new church in the making.

Much of the optimism about the future was dampened in 1968 with *Humanae Vitae,* the encyclical reaffirming traditional views on birth control. Because the encyclical followed so closely on Vatican II, sending a message that seemed contrary to the spirit of the liberalizing trends, many Catholics were left confused and ambivalent toward the authority of the church.[12] Already there was a growing disenchantment with the authority of the church, hence the encyclical reinforced trends toward greater religious autonomy and encouraged further privatization of views on sexuality. The encyclical was a trigger for questions on a range of women's issues—birth control, abortion, divorce, remarriage, the ordination of women. Since that time there has been continuing disaffection over the church's position on such issues, declines in institutional commitment, and greater individual reflection and autonomy. This latter has occurred for those we would most likely expect to feel some dissonance over sexual and lifestyle matters. At the time that D'Antonio, *et al.,* did their national survey of Catholic laity in 1987, three groups particularly reported that their commitment to the church had weakened because of these teachings: Catholics in their thirties, college graduates, and the most affluent. All three groups were more likely to question the church's teaching on artificial contraception and related sexual matters.[13]

Carol is more reflective and critical of the church's position on such matters than many of the Catholics we spoke to; however, the dissatisfaction among young Catholic women is found in all social sectors, among white-collar and blue-collar, among college graduates and high school dropouts, among singles and married women. Evidence of a "fomenting feminism" within the church is readily discernible in many quarters, leading recent commentators to speak of "new Catholic women" and a "new social reality" for Catholic women.[14] The rise of a feminist agenda signals far more than just a women's movement. The development of gender concerns comes at a time when there are many other major cultural changes, and together they fuel a fundamental shift in the definition of a "good Catholic" from the one promulgated by the church hierarchy. These deeper cultural shifts in normative expectations of religious life is perhaps the really big story of generational change.

Financial support of the church and weekly attendance at mass are two behaviors that traditionally were seen as benchmarks of "good Catholics." Among Catholic boomers, however, 88% think that a person can be a good Catholic without contributing money regularly to the church, and 85% think that a person can be a good Catholic without going to church every Sunday. The erosion in these traditional expectations signals a massive shift toward a more personal, freedom-of-choice approach to defining religious norms.

In more recent times, controversies have grown over other issues bearing on who is a good Catholic. Two teachings of the church that have stirred much private anxiety and public debate are those on abortion and on divorce and remarriage. Eighty-one percent of boomers state that a person can be a good Catholic without having to obey the church's teaching on divorce and remarriage. A smaller but still quite substantial percentage thinks the same about abortion. Over two-thirds (68%) deny that one must obey the teaching on abortion in order to be a good Catholic. Despite a deep-seated conflict between pro-life and pro-choice constituencies, a decisive majority of Catholic boomers do not regard one's position on the issue as determining whether one is a good Catholic.[15]

Interestingly, Catholic baby boomers, after disagreeing for the most part with two of the church's obligatory practices and two of its moral teachings, demonstrate overwhelming support for a social justice commitment. Only 19% say that a person can be a good Catholic without being concerned about the poor. Older boomers especially, those most rocked by the social and cultural upheavals of the sixties, emphasize the importance of justice in the redefining of religious norms. Described as the Catholic church's "best kept secret,"[16] the social teachings emerge as far more meaningful to boomers than the more traditional practices or moral teachings. Boomers care the least about the teachings on which the church is most vocal; members of this generation care greatly about those teachings on which the church is less vocal.

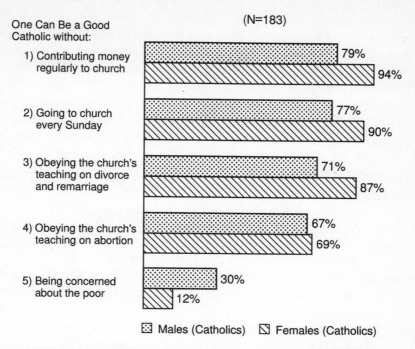

One Can Be a Good
Catholic without:

(N=183)

1) Contributing money
   regularly to church — 79% / 94%

2) Going to church
   every Sunday — 77% / 90%

3) Obeying the church's
   teaching on divorce
   and remarriage — 71% / 87%

4) Obeying the church's
   teaching on abortion — 67% / 69%

5) Being concerned
   about the poor — 30% / 12%

⊞ Males (Catholics)   ◫ Females (Catholics)

Figure 8.2 Definitions of a "Good Catholic" by Gender

The force of a "fomenting feminism" in reshaping normative religious styles comes through on most of these key considerations. Figure 8.2 shows Catholic boomer women to be more liberal in their definition of a good Catholic than are men on the importance of contributing money regularly, of attending church weekly, of being concerned about the poor, and of obeying the church's teaching on divorce and remarriage. Gender differences here suggest continued conflict in a church where males have traditionally formulated the policy and the women have carried it out. These differences will continue to be played out, no doubt, on parish, diocesan, and national levels as women become more empowered and have even greater potential for influence.

On the question of abortion, there are no significant differences by gender.[17] More than two-thirds of the men and women agree that a person can be a good Catholic without obeying the church's teaching on abortion. The absence of a gender gap relative to the abortion issue might appear as peculiar, but in actuality it may illuminate the deep and sometimes acrimonious debate within American Catholicism and among

Catholic women themselves on this issue. It shows just how deeply the new gender values have taken hold in the boomer population. On this and another issue as well—the question of church authority—boomers have strong opinions.[18] Both men and women want greater participation in decision making at the parish level. An astounding 95% of Catholic baby boomers say that the development of church teachings ought to be in the hands of the hierarchy and laity, not in the hands of the hierarchy alone. Young Catholics—men and women, well educated and poorly educated, conservatives and progressives—are insisting on a more lay-involved, democratic church.

SPIRITUALITY AND RESPONSIBLE ACTION

In her book *Do You Believe in Magic?* Annie Gottlieb speaks of how this generation has moved beyond guilt and rage and of the coming politics of love. She is not describing some nostalgic return of the sixties, but rather a turning away from a preoccupation with self to a greater concern for others. The politics of love has to do with a basic orientation toward life, a reconnecting of spirituality and justice. This new consciousness finds expression in many places—in the compassion generated by liberation theology, in the Catholic bishops' pastoral letters on economic life and nuclear arms, in the women's movement and its revamping of religious priorities, in the social activism of the evangelicals known as Sojourners, in the struggles of gays and lesbians for a religious voice, in the Jewish quarterly magazine *Tikkun,* whose name means "to mend, repair, and transform the world," and in many local congregations where the emphasis is on getting involved in hands-on social activities and causes.

Oscar Gantt especially embodies the struggle many boomers, and especially Protestants, feel about the priorities within many churches. Aside from Oscar's struggles with religion over his lifestyle, in a more basic way the problem with his congregation is a loss of spirituality, and of any genuine connection between spirituality and everyday life. He is "turned off" by the church's own routines, by its ritual dryness and conventionality. "I want it to be more than just an experience of attending church, hearing a sermon, some good singing, and then going home." For many in Oscar's generation, this type of routinized religiosity cut off from everyday life either drives them out of religion altogether, or they look for better congregations, or they struggle within it.

What he sees around him in the churches is a great deal of complacency. Many churches, which once spearheaded a civil rights movement, now seem to have turned away from a social agenda. In its place there is an emphasis on raising money for building new churches, buying bigger and better pews and more fancy windows. Has the church lost its soul? How can it reclaim its role as a spiritual force in the lives of the people? The answer lies not in religion's outer forms, for there's plenty of that around: "Some of these folks are the most religious people in the world, they attend church faithfully and read the Bible all the time."

As with so many boomers, the distinction between religion and spirituality is very real to him. He distrusts outward forms that lack inner meaning. Such outward forms alienate when cut off from feelings and compassion. Much of what's wrong with organized religion arises out of this split between form and feeling. Speaking of many religious people, he has this to say:

> You don't see in their lives an embodiment of the spirituality of the faith. They don't adhere to those things that give the faith its force. They can't embrace that commandment to love the neighbor as themselves. I see this happen all the time with folks who are pillars of the church, but then cannot be a good neighbor. To me, the development of the spirit allows you to embrace your neighbor. You become the embodiment of that commandment.

Many others feel about religion as does Oscar. When we asked Protestants, "Who is a good Christian?" we got answers very similar to those Catholics gave us on the "good Catholic" question. Eight out of ten say one can be a good Christian without attending religious services regularly; seven out of ten say the same without contributing money regularly to a church. But on the social justice question—in this instance, caring about the poor—the figures are much different: 14% of conservative Protestant boomers and only 8% of mainline Protestant boomers say one can be a good Christian without concern for the poor. Mainline boomers put even greater emphasis on social justice than on accepting the divinity of Christ for defining who is a good Christian! Older boomers are somewhat more likely than younger ones to say that justice is important; women more likely than men. The evidence makes clear that as a generation, regardless of faith, boomers write off much of religious conventionality as being essential, and regard justice concerns, or love for the neighbor, as far more integral to defining the religious life.

The struggle is to get beyond the facade, the external shell of religion, to its "embodiment," or the link between spirituality and responsible action. Action here need not be thought of simply as the most radical of social justice causes; it can mean many things—spearheading a civil rights movement, as in Oscar's vision, or working on behalf of Pregnancy Distress, as in Linda Kramer's vision. In either case what is important is that it be an authentic expression of a deeply felt conviction. They may disagree about what is a responsible expression of faith, but both have respect for action deemed to have integrity and a genuine expression of commitment. Boomers are willing to make commitments that express their deepest convictions; what they have difficulty doing is giving of themselves to programs and causes that do not connect with their own lives.

Many in this generation have deep-seated yearnings—across all religious traditions and across all social categories. If anything, white Protestants expressed more such yearnings than any others. White Protestantism as a heritage probably suffers more than the others in its loss of a transcendent faith and its resulting desacralization of life. The heritage benefits from an older establishment status and a broad social basis; but religiously, it has become largely a cultural faith lacking in power to sustain strong and compelling religious convictions. More than half of all Protestant boomers feel that the churches have lost the spiritual part of religion. Conservative boomers feel that way more than mainliners. Women feel it more than men. The returnees, those searching for a religious home, feel it more than the loyalists, and even more than the dropouts. Forty-eight percent of mainline Protestant and 76% of conservative Protestant returnees agree that the churches have lost spirituality, while at the same time, interestingly, they look for congregations where they might find it. Many of the conservative returnees left mainline congregations out of disillusionment, but the numbers would suggest that many are returning to congregations similar in theology and in style to what they left behind. The disillusionment is widespread, which is perhaps why there is so much movement in and out of congregations to begin with. In all the searching and shopping around, some find what they are looking for in a church, but many do not and drop out.

"BUT WHAT IF THE CHURCH DOESN'T CHANGE?"

The yearnings are all real enough across a wide religious spectrum of the boomer population. If all the psychic energy now going into adapting to religion or into resolving feelings about religion could be gauged somehow on a meter, it would amount to an astounding psychometric. Staggered by its proportions, an observer of the contemporary scene must ask, "Why?" Why do they not just drop out? Why opt to stay within religious institutions if it involves so much struggle?

A satisfactory answer to the questions would have to include consideration of how boomers' relationships with organized religion were jarred in earlier years, and of the dynamics of adjustment that were set in place. Psychologically, religion functions both as a world-maintaining and as a world-shattering force, to use Peter Berger's terms.[19] Religion is world-maintaining in providing a conception of the social order that is stable and unchanging and a way of looking on life as meaningful. It is world-shattering in the sense that in the presence of the divine, all social arrangements come to be understood as human constructions and devoid of any inherent sanctity. In the case of the first, religion legitimates and creates an integrated world; with the second, religion relativizes, "demystifies," and "debunks" that world. The two aspects of religion function as powerful and conflicting forces.

If, as has been argued, "outsiders" have religious stories of greater world-shaking force than "insiders," then perhaps we have a clue about why so many boomers stick it out with religion.[20] The experiences many of them have had force them to think of themselves as "outsiders," as people whose stories tell of "the way it is" and of the self-deceptions within organized religion. Like veterans who have been through a war together, they have their own bruises and pains. They explore the religious world from a more marginal position, approaching it from the vantage point of their own historical and cultural experiences. Yet theirs is a religious world—or better put, a recreated religious world—because in the midst of so much world-shattering, reaching out for its order and stability is a means of human survival. The power of religion lies in its capacity to create humanly significant worlds. In the most basic of ways, religion provides an anchor, a mooring amidst chaos. "You have to have something to hold on to," as one of our more reflective respondents said, "or else you lose direction in a world where everything seems so relative, so unsure." More than just a mooring, religion is for many boomers, to change the metaphor, actually a yardstick around which and against which to pattern their lives. They reject many of religion's teachings or conventional practices, yet organize their own tailor-made religious worlds around them. They are who they are, and believe as they do, in part because of who they are not, and how they don't believe.

This working out of ambivalence is summed up by the woman who was quoted at the beginning of the chapter. A practicing Catholic who disagrees with her church on women's issues, she both rejects and accepts her religion. She rejects much of her church's teachings, yet claims the faith as hers.

Speaking of the church, she says: "There still has to be a lot of change."

"Getting back to issues of the body, what about birth control and abortion?" queries the interviewer. "Do you feel that has to change, too?"

"Yeah, yeah," she says.

"But what if the church doesn't change?" the interviewer persists.

"You know, the reason why I like it," she says in a rather matter-of-fact manner, "is its strong guidelines. It's been around and it definitely knows where it's coming from. Even though maybe you don't believe in all of it." Ambivalence toward the church may drive some people out, but not her. Despite her struggles with religion, she has learned to deal with her feelings. Many boomers would agree that it's good to know where religion is coming from—then you can know what it is you are struggling with.

PART FOUR

Conclusion

CHAPTER 9

Transforming America's Religious Landscape

Writing a quarter-century ago, Martin E. Marty described the search for a new spiritual style in secular America. An astute observer of religious trends, Marty detected in the midst of the 1960s' religious and cultural upheavals a powerful ferment and the evolution of a "new language of the spirit." He wrote:

> In search of spiritual expression, people speak in tongues, enter Trappist monasteries, build on Jungian archetypes, go to southern California and join a cult, become involved "where the action is" in East Harlem, perceive "God at work in the world," see Jesus Christ as the man for others, hope for liberation by the new morality, study phenomenology, share the Peace Corps experience, borrow from cosmic syntheses, and go to church.[1]

With a slight change of emphasis, his words might just as easily apply to the boomer generation today. Its members are still spiritually "open" and exploring a range of new languages—both inside and outside the religious establishment.

Marty's comments are worth pondering. The connections between his observations in 1967 and the current scene run even deeper than might appear on first glance. Marty was writing, as he notes, at a time when spirituality as a term had been abandoned. In the frenzy of post-World War II church expansion, "religious" language captured the day,

241

and a theological and ethical agenda crowded out spiritual concerns of the religious establishment. Debate over the "death of God" and controversies over civil rights, poverty, and the war in Vietnam drew the attention of religious leaders and inspired activist causes. Life in the secular world was celebrated; social concerns took precedence over personal faith. So preoccupied were the religious elite and avant-garde with secular and worldly issues at the time, that theologian Paul Tillich spoke of "the almost forbidden word 'spirit' " and of the spiritual dimension of life as "lost beyond hope."[2]

Yet, as Marty argued at the time, spirituality did not disappear. Rather, it went underground and took expression outside of the religious establishment. The quest for a spiritual style expressed itself in many ways: in popular books of the time such as Pope John XXIII's *Journal of a Soul* and Dag Hammerskjöld's *Markings;* in new religious movements such as the Eastern mystical faiths; in the rise of cults and communes; in experimentation with ESP and LSD. Signs could be seen in many places of deep stirrings, of new visions, and of an aroused consciousness. Neither urgent nor obsessive, the stirrings were simply a prod in the direction of what Tillich had called "the unity of power and meaning," toward a more holistic conception and experience of life. The spiritual cravings sought to overcome the anomie and disintegration that marked so much of social and political life, and to create a new order of meaning combining the inner and outer life and characterized by harmony between the temporal and the eternal, the human and the divine. Those who felt the deepest stirrings were led, as Marty wrote, by "a desire to see life transformed, the *charisma* of leaders transferred to followers, and roots given to personal and public life."[3]

PATTERNS FOR THE 1990S

Today that quest finds a more mature expression. Those growing up at the time and who reacted against the bland religious establishment of their youth continue in their explorations. The search for a spiritual style goes on, but now the quest is in clearer focus.

Looking back on that generation's experience, we begin to see how the larger story unfolds. As children in the 1950s, they were as involved in religious institutions as any generation. Then as youth in the late 1960s, they dropped out in record numbers. It was not really until the 1970s, as they dropped out of the religious establishment, that we began to grasp just how great had been the impact, and how their defection was restructuring the American religious landscape. In the 1980s we grasped better how some in the generation had turned to born-again evangelical and fundamentalist faiths, some to New Age beliefs, and even more had simply defected from religion altogether. Now in the 1990s, when many in this generation are rearing children and facing midlife, we observe yet another phase of their religious and spiritual saga. Now we have enough distance to grasp the broader evolving patterns and understand the role this generation is playing in reshaping the American religious scene.

Four patterns of change during these years show us how the religious landscape is being transformed: the reemergence of spirituality, religious and cultural pluralism, multilayered belief and practice, and transformed selves.

The Reemergence of Spirituality

If, as Marty says, spirituality as a term was abandoned in the 1960s, clearly it reemerged in the 1980s and 1990s. Spirituality reappeared not simply among the elites, but as a grass-roots movement. It seems reasonable to expect some connection between the experiences boomers had as children in a religious establishment that had lost much of its spiritual dimension, a youthful revolt against that establishment, and today's spiritual ferment. It seems likely the sources of the youthful revolt against conventional religion of the late 1960s and 1970s reach back to an early era of childhood experiences; certainly, the "return to spirituality" that emerged with the youth of the sixties has now taken more mature form. Spirituality has been restored to its rightful place, in the way people think, talk, act, and live. It can be argued that in its spiritual quest this generation, contrary to much that is said about its secularity and self-obsession, has reclaimed something fundamental to the American religious experience. The generation may well be remembered, in fact, as one that grappled hard in search of a holistic, all-encompassing vision of life and as a spiritually creative generation.

One sign of this maturing spirituality is its new depths of meaning. The term itself now conveys much more clarity and creativity: Boomers speak of creation spirituality, Eucharistic spirituality, Native American spirituality, Eastern spiritualities, Twelve-Step spiritualities, feminist spirituality, earth-based spirituality, eco-feminist spirituality, Goddess spirituality, and men's spirituality, as well as what would be considered traditional Judeo-Christian spiritualities. Having passed the stage of groping for a new language of spirituality, now such languages flourish in ever more highly focused, tailor-made varieties. New vocabularies compete with the older theological terms, forcing philosophical and theological systems to assimilate them. The diversity of spirituality reflects, of course, a consumer culture, but also a rich and empowering melding of traditions and existential concerns.

Also, there has been movement in the direction of overcoming old dualisms in Western culture through renewed appreciation for the core teachings of the great wisdom traditions about life, suffering, the body, the natural world, and the interrelatedness of all things. Awareness that ours is a global world, memories still of the Holocaust, and the abiding threat of nuclear annihilation all serve as reminders of interconnectedness—in its most positive and destructive senses. A growing consciousness of the relational web in which people live is closely related to a sense of self and of the importance of having a vocabulary of spiritual practice that can be shared with others. Global awareness and environmental consciousness have both provided "checks" on an unbridled obsession with self and helped to shape a more balanced perspective. Vocabularies of spiritual practice differ greatly, whether for evangelicals, mainliners, or religious individualists; but underlying all of them are common themes born out of this generation's experience.

Pluralism Now for Real

The postwar generation grew up with pluralism of all forms—cultural, religious, lifestyle. Its members were not exposed, except possibly as young children, to the religious culture that the preceding generation of Americans had known as constituting the core of the American experience; instead, boomers came into adulthood at a time when the "mainline" Protestant churches were losing their hegemony over the culture and were competing with other faiths for a place in the sun. After the 1960s, and after Vietnam and Watergate in particular, the old normative faiths linking public and private piety had fallen upon hard times. Hence, as adults, the new generation has not known a strong religious center in American life. Religion was whatever one *chose* as one's own, whether of the denominational Protestant, Catholic, or Jewish variety, or the radical quests of a Mollie Stone or the resurgent evangelicalism of a Linda Kramer. Pluralism, as this generation knew it, also included the privatized faith of a Sonny D'Antonio and nonreligion, or the more secular faith of a Pam Fletcher.

Boomers have not just known pluralism, they deeply value it. Tolerance and respect for others are widely affirmed as basic values, to be honored in religious as well as other contexts. For them, the American practice of speaking of religion as a "preference" assumed a taken-for-granted quality. What else could it be but a personal choice? No generation in America's history was ever more exposed to or more devoted to pluralism as a social and religious reality.

Multilayered Belief and Practice

As Marty observes, much of the old spiritual style prior to the 1960s depended on homogeneity, upon assent to the details of a grand theological or philosophical system. But this has all changed in the intervening years. Greater attention to spiritual quest, an expanded number of religious options, and a consumer culture have all contributed to "multilayered" styles of belief and practice. With a syncreticism and eclecticism made possible by so many alternatives, boomers continue to recognize, as Marty says, the "merits of borrowing" from other traditions and figures. The diffusion of belief in reincarnation is a case in point: With one-fourth of boomers affirming reincarnation today, there is an obvious blending of religious themes from other traditions with more historic Christian beliefs.

Boomers are more open than recent generations about such mixings and matchings, though not necessarily more so than in earlier times in America.[4] They are the dominant carriers of a remarkable religious voluntarism today, in keeping with the popular culture of choice. Consumer choice in religion shows up not only in the obvious ways but also in very subtle ways. One man we interviewed thought it nothing out of the ordinary to describe himself as "primarily Catholic," and to tell us that while he attends mass weekly, he also belongs to an ecumenical prayer group in his neighborhood and frequently worships at a local evangelical church because of its "good preaching." While his configuration of practices may not be all that common, his open attitude toward creating his own set is not unusual. This *pastiche*-style of spirituality shows up in countless forms. It is also expressed in people's choices of heroes or people they admire. The heroes are seldom restricted to a person's own faith tradition. One white Protestant we spoke to named as his heroes Mother Teresa, Martin Luther King, Jr., and Mikhail Gorbachev. Asked why these three, he replied that if they could come together in one place, "They would respect each other." Contemporary pluralism demands spiritual models of tolerance and openness, while at the same time encourages principles of integrity and conviction.

One can only speculate, but based on our observations, it appears that the blending of religious themes is spiritually rejuvenating. "I have my own faith," said one person. "It includes Jesus, yes, and meditation, and helping out at Transition House for the homeless—not a bad mix, is it?" New mixings and matchings release creative energies and refocus people's lives. Because these constellations are meaningful, they give expression to deeply personal religious feelings—"my own faith." It may well be that it is this personal quality combined with an openness to many differing existential concerns that makes for a spiritually creative generation. In other historical periods, deeply personal, syncretistic-style faiths have been a source of spiritual vitality and empowerment.[5]

Transformed Selves

When Marty made his observations, there were widespread signs of self-exploration, more searching than serious reaching out to others. Even today boomers are chided for a lack of commitment. But as we have argued, boomers will commit themselves to religious activities and organizations, including traditional congregations, where they feel there is some authentic connection with their lives and experiences. Authenticity, celebration, spiritual growth, cultivating a center that holds their lives together, rearing children, meaningful action in the world—these all motivate commitment. Generally, there appears to be more of an "ethic of commitment" today along the lines Yankelovich described in the early 1980s, recognizing that genuine self-fulfillment requires giving to others, having relationships that last over time, and sharing of lives. There is more concern with the expressive and the sacred, and awareness that these two can only be fully realized in a web of relationships that transcend the self as an isolated object. As Yankelovich proposed, greater commitment on the part of young adults would involve two steps: one, a change in strategy, away from obsession with inner needs and a cultivation of shared meanings; and two, a genuine concern for the well-being of society as well as themselves.[6] In our judgment there has been movement in both directions since he wrote.

It is important to recognize, however, that the boomer style of commitment is different from the older, more culturally prescribed patterns of institutional activity. The changed views of self—toward a more psychological, more dynamic conception—is central to this new style. Boomers are hungry to find ways to commit themselves, if they can find personal enhancement, or extension of their own selves, in whatever they do or in however they give of themselves. This blend of giving and receiving is evident in so much of what they do—in family life, in community activities, in religious and spiritual life. We observed it in places where we didn't expect to see it, such as in a discussion on what you can do to improve society. For example, in a "Reaching Out" forum we attended in Oakland, California, where a largely boomer audience of over a thousand people attended sessions for a ten-week experiment in community service, we listened to Ram Dass (known as psychologist Richard Alpert in the 1960s) and other religious and spiritual figures debate such topics as:

- Can you still make a real contribution to society— something that makes a profound difference—in a nation whose heroes are Bart Simpson and Madonna?

- Can you walk by the poor and the homeless on the street and keep an open heart? Is it politically correct to invite them home for a shower and a Big Mac?

- If you choose to help the disadvantaged, can you do it for long without feeling burned out, or becoming as depressed as those you seek to help?

The agenda is a 1990s-style social and political activism, which differs from the activism of a few decades back in its greater concern with the self. An emphasis on "open heart" and "feeling," that is, the self and its fulfillment, is very much at the center of the discussion of commitment, as is also the case in a more specifically religious and spiritual context. Whether in a Twelve-Step group, a family *Shabbat* service, or a Methodist Sunday school class, one hears this interweaving of languages—to self and to something beyond—in a way that resonates differently than in the past. At a deeper level, new understandings of a more enhanced self are given expression in the languages. A revised giving/receiving pact permits a continued calculation of what the self should receive, but now it is a sense of self in relation to others; or it may be that the emphasis on fulfillment provides, as one commentator has argued, a language that justifies what people do when other values or circumstances are actually responsible for their actions.[7]

All these trends—a more focused spirituality, experience with pluralism, selective mixing of traditions, and new styles of commitment—are deeply entrenched in popular culture today. With one-third of the

American population in the boomer generation, they set normative styles that influence the rest of the country; their values and practices create the norms to which others respond. Moreover, the trends may be reinforced in the coming years. Between now and the turn of the century, year by year, the thirtysomething population turns into the fortysomething population. Considering that the peak of the baby boom births occurred between 1957 and 1958, then in the latter years of this century and the early years of the next large numbers of boomers will enter into their forties.[8] Boomer demography thus assures a large supply of young adult Americans passing through the midlife transition over the next dozen or so years. If developmental psychologists are correct about these years being a crucial time of reflection and reassessment, it should follow that the nation will continue to experience considerable religious and spiritual ferment.

While every generation undergoes a midlife passage of sorts, for boomers it is perhaps more traumatic. For a long time they knew only a youth culture—everybody around them, seemingly, was young, they were a persistently adolescent generation. "We have dieted, jogged, and exercised so much," comments boomer writer Lynn Smith, "we look and actually *think* we are five to ten years younger than we are."[9] True or not, the illusions of youth are wearing thin for those who grew up in a time when the future was open, when they could be and do whatever they wanted. Now that future is no longer so open, the options more limited. For boomers in midlife, as psychologist David Gutmann says, "It will be brought home that everything is *not* possible, that they have made their choices, and they will have to live with them. This is not a generation who wanted to feel they made final choices about anything."[10] Much depends, of course, on the economic conditions of the 1990s as to the range of choices open, but the inevitabilities of aging and a sense of a future closing in will no doubt provoke religious and spiritual concerns. Already, the reality of death has hit home—through the loss of parents and the specter of AIDS. Already, the reality of economic uncertainty is deeply unsettling, coming as it does at a time when many of them have children to educate. Already, the reality of their own aging bodies has set in. As one older boomer woman put it: "We are beginning to face the three Ms—mortgages, menopause, and mortality."

Looking even further into the future, we find reasons to expect that boomer trends will have a long-lasting influence. The changing patterns of family and religion for boomers and their children are crucial. High rates of interfaith marriage and continuing large numbers of blended families will result in new generations of children with weak institutional religious ties. Denominational boundaries within Protestantism will likely erode further, as increasing numbers of Americans grow up knowing very little about their religious heritages. Better known will be the general faith traditions—Roman Catholicism, Judaism, Islam, and Protestantism clustered into its liberal and conservative camps. A highly privatized and relativistic approach to religion, already practiced by large numbers of boomers, will probably become even more widespread in a society that has no strong religious center. Both privatism and relativism in matters of faith and practice will be sustained in a culture where the importance attached to choice is so deeply rooted. Spirituality will naturally be subject to fads and fashions, quick-fix techniques that promise easy solutions. The self-help movement itself risks loss of credibility with its endless proliferation of Twelve-Step groups and perpetuation of the notion that ours is a society of victims.[11] Even so, it seems unlikely that there will be any great turning away from concerns with the self and its spiritual quests.

Changing values will have a continuing impact as well. We have emphasized the value shifts of the 1960s and 1970s—that is, the countercultural values, later described as post-material values—as creating the context for understanding the religious and spiritual transformations. Our simple index of exposure to the counterculture proved to be a good predictor of who would drop out of religion, and whether or not that person would still be uninvolved twenty years later. The index was a good predictor as well of a person's current moral and lifestyle values. The index itself is not as important as the value shifts that it sought to capture. We look on these shifts, in keeping with the debate today on post-materialism and post-modernism generally, as a major alteration in the way Americans relate to social institutions, and hence as resulting in a significant break in how religious cultures and identities are transmitted. In our view the value shifts were not a temporary aberration—a sudden outburst of hippies and flower children—to be followed by a return to the normalcy of the past. The counterculture came and went, but many of the values associated with it, such as libertarian aspirations, greater egalitarianism, ecological consciousness, and an enhanced concern with the self, are all now deeply entrenched in American life. The evidence points to an enduring pattern of changing American values. A major study of the children born to countercultural parents shows, for example, that even though they behave fairly conventionally, they are more aware than other children of such issues as women's rights and ecology.[12] The parents taught strong values to their children, values that continue to set the children apart from others. Even the children from families that became more conventional in appearance and lifestyle as time passed believed more in gender equality and environmental causes than did their friends from families that had always been conventional. The point is that the 1960s ushered in cultural changes that have lasted and are now being transmitted to the next generation. What was once on the cultural margins now permeates the cultural mainstream. Much of what the parents' generation struggled for is taken by their heirs as the accepted values by which we live.

And this country is not unique: Political scientist Ronald Inglehart documents a "culture shift" toward post-modern values of egalitarianism, peace, environmentalism, and quality of life in a dozen or more advanced industrial societies during the post-World War II years.[13] His graphs show age-related shifts in people's attitudes and values across national boundaries. The new value commitments are passed on to the next generation with a great deal of fervor and conviction on the part of boomer-age parents. There is evidence of widespread religious changes as well.[14] Cross-cultural research shows fundamental declines in institutional religion associated with these changes in values; but more than just this, it shows a heightened sensitivity to questions about the meaning and purpose of life and to spiritual concerns generally. Despite high levels of alienation from institutional religion in countries like Great Britain, France, Belgium, and Sweden, concern for the sacred never goes away. The hunger for meaning in an emerging global world in which many of the old barriers of ideology have collapsed is expressed in many places around the world. Among those most caught up in the new values, we find a restlessness and spiritual yearnings. As Inglehart puts it, "Postmaterialists have *more* potential interest in religion than Materialists."[15]

THE RESTRUCTURING OF RELIGIOUS COMMUNITY

Clearly, major restructuring of religion is underway, particularly the reshaping of religious communities. We have argued that the religious and spiritual concerns of this generation run deep, far deeper than a simple notion of "return to religion" would imply. Our view is that the generation is so deeply spiritually divided that only segments of that population will ever "return" in the traditional sense, that is, settle comfortably back into conventional religious routines. Other segments will be involved in various types of group activities, some self-consciously describing themselves as religious or spiritual, and others not. Those participating in such groups may or may not view themselves as related to the existing religious establishment. As we observed in a previous chapter, we can think of the religious establishment today as involving an ecclesiastical upstairs and downstairs—a divided house where often there is little communication between floors. Because of this fracturing along spiritual lines, we can speak of the generation's search for a spiritual style as all-encompassing, reaching to the very depths of peoples' lives and giving birth to new forms of community.

Of course, not all of the religious landscape is caught up in so great a transformation. For a sizable number of boomers, life goes on pretty much as it always has, and without any great rupture in their experiences or links with organized religion. The loyalists that we have described, for example, are very much embedded in traditional religious life—in its ritual, in its communal activities, in its friendship networks. For them, congregations do provide what Bellah and his colleagues call a "community of memory."[16] Here they find continuity of faith and a language by which they can express their understanding of themselves, largely in familiar religious and cultural terms. Traditions pull at all of us, and for many boomers these are powerful forces, in no way to be minimized. Congregations are familiar places where they find meaning and belonging and a spiritual home.

Yet many others have little sense of community or memory associated with congregations. They may experience a latent nostalgia to return to a warm childhood religious experience, but as Christopher Lasch reminds us, nostalgia and memory are two quite different things. Nostalgia idealizes the past, and a frozen past at that; but memory links the past with a living present. Speaking of memory, Lasch writes in *The True and Only Heaven:* "It draws hope and comfort from the past in order to enrich the present . . . it is less concerned with loss than with our continuing indebtedness to a past the formative influence of which lives on in our patterns of speech, our gestures, our standards of honor, our expectations, our basic dispositions toward the world around us."[17]

But what about those for whom there is little religious memory? Disillusionment, as Lasch points out, is a source of nostalgia because it divides the past from the present; and for that reason it might be said that boomers are vulnerable to a nostalgic sensibility. Their experiences of disillusionment and severed memories give rise to hopeful expectations. For whatever reasons, they often turn to small groups and lifestyle enclaves in search of a quality of belonging and attention to specific issues they fail to find elsewhere. This quest for community takes many forms—adult education classes, Twelve-Step groups, caucuses, sharing groups, workshops, yoga classes, therapeutic groups, the Goddess movement, women-church, the men's movement, and scores of special purpose organizations. It cuts across denominational and faith lines, finding expression in evangelical, conservative churches on the cultural right as well as in New Age circles on the cultural left. It occurs within and outside of the religious establishment. In all these ways, boomers try to rediscover a connection to a meaningful community. Community, of course, is an elusive term and can mean different things to different people; but in practical terms it refers to a group of people who share their lives and communicate honestly with one another, "whose relationships go deeper than the masks of composure and who have developed some significant commitment to 'rejoice together, mourn together, and to delight in each other,' " as M. Scott Peck puts it.[18]

It is these qualities that boomers look for—sharing, caring, accepting, belonging. The qualities themselves often are more important than the places where they find them: People find others with similar concerns while carpooling children to Sunday school, but also in Adult Children of Alcoholics meetings; women can explore spirituality in a support group at church or in a Goddess study group; there is sharing in an evangelical prayer group or in group meditation; people come together in social justice work as well as in a group on visualization and dream analysis; people join in celebration at Jesus Day as well as Earth Day. Community varies in its forms, but the qualities that make for its appeal are much the same. In all of this, what is most important is that people forge a link between their own experiences and religious and spiritual teachings. The yearning is about finding a connection between life and meaning, and about finding your own voice and expressing it.

Both the gender revolution and the self-help movement are having an impact on community formation. Older hierarchical, domination-submission models of the individual's relationship with the divine are brought into question.[19] Women's groups emphasize a sense of self that relies on relationships, and thereby refocuses the religious and spiritual experience as something that happens with others, and away from the more traditional one-to-one relationship with the divine. The men's spiritual movement encourages greater sharing of experience as well, though usually in a more traditional setting than is the case for feminist theology and spirituality. The mushrooming of groups organized around not just gender but specific life situations and needs (divorce, abuse, single parenting, abortion, justice, and so on) is a powerful force in the direction of reshaping the experience of the divine. In all these instances, the notion of solitary spiritual journey is seen as inadequate: The group experience is itself sustaining and empowering and a means by which individuals come to know and to relate to the divine.

On all fronts new patterns of religious community are emerging—from Protestant to Roman Catholic, from Muslim to Jewish, to even the more amorphous New Age movement. Mainline Protestant congregations have internalized the pluralism of contemporary culture and lifestyles, and thus house a wide array of special purpose groups. Membership in such groups has grown dramatically in recent decades, for both those of the "right," such as healing ministries, prison ministries, pro-life groups, and charismatic groups; and for those of the "left," such as antinuclear coalitions, pro-choice groups, holistic health groups, therapy groups, and positive-thinking seminars.[20] Many boomers identify more strongly with one or another of these special purpose groups than they do with the denominational or faith heritage in which the groups are found. Often they share more with people of similar outlook and concern in another church than they do with other members in their own, more heterogeneous congregations. For this reason it is fairly easy to switch from one congregation to another across traditions.

In some churches small groups, or even adult classes, take on greater meaning in people's lives than do the larger congregations themselves. One woman we interviewed in a midwestern church had the following to say, both about her church and an adult class of which she is a member:

> I think it's difficult for me to grow spiritually in an organized church. I have a hard time with a lot of dogmas. They don't match what I feel on a spiritual level, so I keep looking and looking. The thing about the Serendipity Class is we are exploring lots of different things. We've been talking about the concept of evil and Satan and all that, but any view is accepted. We will talk about it. People will argue with you, but you are perfectly free to express what you think and how you feel about things. In the course of talking back and forth, it helps us all to clarify it for ourselves. And we still may walk out not really agreeing on it, but we may have come a little bit farther in our own personal spiritual journey. That's what for me is so appealing about this class.

Despite all the attention given to the rise of megachurches, the giant-sized evangelical and charismatic congregations, the more remarkable change today in conservative Protestantism is the emergence of the meta-church: the flourishing of small groups within the larger structures. Boomers are often attracted to large churches because of the diversity of programs and the varied ministries they offer; much of the attraction has to do with the range of small groups, dealing with Bible study, prayer, compulsive eating, family life, singles' activities, abortion counseling, exercise and weight lifting, and the like. Evangelical and charismatic churches are more successful than other churches in maintaining a self-contained community linking small groups and the larger congregational life, but not at the expense of accommodating the social and psychological needs of boomers. Seminars on "boomers and church growth" are common training for church leaders; there is a deliberate attempt at catering to boomers and at making congregations, in the words of one writer, "user friendly."[21] Evangelical and charismatic faiths will no doubt continue to attract many in this generation, due in part to how they allow people to "feel" and "express" their religion, but also because of how they accommodate choice and life concerns in a framework that sets some limits. Frustration with a society that offers too many choices virtually assures a need for meaningful boundaries and clarification of priorities.

Growing numbers of young Roman Catholics, Muslims, and Jews are turning to small groups. For Catholics, many of these small groups are far more than Bible studies or prayer groups; they are small gatherings in people's homes increasingly taking on parish functions and committed to the celebration of the Mass. They function as faith communities that come together to enrich each other's family and work lives. Often the emphasis in these communities is on liturgy and providing "Gospel values," including social justice work and finding ways to be more than mere support groups for self-actualization. Young Muslim women "reinterpret" their traditions with an aroused feminist consciousness, forcing a confrontation of ancient and contemporary worlds. A new generation of men and women seek to define their lives as American-born Muslims and to claim their place in the nation's changing religious world. Many Jews with young children attend "tot *Shabbat*" on Friday nights—informal services designed for unaffiliated Jewish boomers and their children, many of whom know very little about the tradition. Many young Jewish women have a growing interest in new, less traditionally female forms of spirituality. With the creation of new rituals, stories, and blessings, many belong to groups where they can share the richness of women's experiences, what Reform Rabbi Laura Geller has called the "Torah of our lives as well as the Torah that was written down."[22]

In meditation centers and the loosely based network of spirituality movements, there appears to be growing emphasis upon group spirituality. Individuals come together ("ceremonial circles") to share spiritual experiences, often without formal leadership. They discover one another through their languages—in speaking of "energy," of "vibrations," of *"chakras."*[23] They incorporate ritual practices and encourage a collective search for answers, thereby building a sense of community. Often the circles are catalysts for social change: They speak out and take actions in support of environmental causes, planetary healing, and animal rights, and against nuclear power plants. Though seemingly individualistic, such spirituality breaks into community as people look inward toward themselves and outward toward a socially transformed world.

Where all of this small-group activity leads is anyone's guess, but probably religious communities of the future will look like loose federations made up of many smaller communities. Small groups will continue to have a vital place in religious life because of the trend toward shared authority and the opportunity they afford for shared experiences. Boomers are not likely to give up their proclivities toward sharing with one another. Nor will they forsake their more expressive religious styles. Celebration and festivity are a part of their legacy. The two—community and celebration—are both features of religious life which may gain in importance as the boomer population ages.

RECONSIDERING RELIGIOUS INDIVIDUALISM

Throughout this book the relation of the individual to community has been a preoccupying theme. We have tried to show that the American religious context provides many angles through which to explore relations of these two. Boomers, as we have seen, have nuanced experiences: Carol McLennon, Pam Fletcher, Mollie Stone, Linda Kramer, Barry Johnson, Sonny D'Antonio, and Oscar Gantt each represent a different version of how individual and community relate. Taken all together, we have a rich mosaic of patterns and possibilities.

Commentators like to criticize boomers for their self-centeredness, greed, narcissism, and lack of commitment. They are often held up as examples of what has gone wrong in an American society where individualism runs rampant, eroding social and institutional loyalties. Religiously, it is said, they are too preoccupied with themselves to join churches, synagogues, and mosques or to get involved in their programs. They are more self-serving than self-giving and would rather distance themselves than commit themselves. If America is already highly individualistic when it comes to matters of faith and religious belonging, then how this generation relates to religious institutions is nothing less than alarming. Since 80% of Americans already agree that "an individual should arrive at his or her own religious beliefs independent of any churches or synagogues," then boomers must push these figures up truly into the frightening zone.

When critics speak of Americans becoming too individualistic, often they have in mind implications for community. They argue, or presume, that individualism results in the breakdown or loss of community. The assumption is that the two are antagonistic to each other, as if the two are locked into a zero-sum relationship: the greater the level of individualism, then the less the sense of belonging. Yet this is far too simple a way of posing the problem. Today's spiritual quests are the working out of the tendencies deeply rooted in an Emersonian conception of the individual who must find God in herself or himself, and of an experience with the divine affirming that she or he is known and loved in a personal way. Now as in the past, such inclinations have encouraged an assertive self, not necessarily independent of community but one that insists on "working out" the individual's relation to and meaning of such involvement.[24] Americans not only pick and choose what to believe, by and large they also set the terms governing involvement in religious communities. Especially in a time of heightened spiritual activity, we would expect a more rampant subjectivity, but also the possibility of new, emerging forms of community giving expression to personal enhancement.

"Temperament, and not theology, determines the self's stance in religion," writes Harold Bloom.[25] Perhaps an overstatement, yet there is truth in the assertion. We find ample evidence in our own representative boomers. Carol McLennon, for example, is an individualistic, post-Vatican II Catholic, but she is probably a more deeply spiritual person, and perhaps even a more committed Catholic, because of her own struggles with the church. Knowing what it is she rejects about the church has helped to make her even more affirming about what she likes within Catholicism. Oscar Gantt is enjoying some freedom from the church these days, but he is working out a new balance in his life that may yet produce a more satisfying and enduring religious commitment. His search is not over. Barry Johnson, who is very involved in his congregation today, is also carving out some space for himself and looking to a redefinition of who he is and of his commitments. As all three experiences suggest, these men and women are forging new styles of an "ethic of commitment" that involve neither a stifling of the self nor an obsession with it; they have grown as people, each in his or her own way. In a sense individualism has made it possible for all three to stay in a religious community. Because they have the freedom to "work out" a more satisfactory balance between self and community, they have found richer meanings for their lives and more fulfilling identities; thus they are able to remain in, or close to, a congregation, without having to abandon the faith community altogether.

For Linda Kramer as well, a case can be made for a more subjective, self-enhancing mode of evangelicalism. An individualistic religious culture has made it possible for her to find what she is looking for and to forge a meaningful identity for her as a woman. And as we have seen, Mollie Stone's journey is taking her in a search for community. The American assertive self often leads people into groups and established institutions. It leads people out as well, as with Pam Fletcher, but it might also be said that our religious culture makes it possible to hold on to a religious identity while at the same time rejecting all close ties to the institution. Sonny D'Antonio is a good example, still a Catholic despite his distance from any religious community. American-style individualism is not all bad; it is the source of much religious and spiritual vitality, of personal accommodation and adaptable religious life.

Contrary to those who argue on behalf of a neo-communitarianism as the solution to the problem of individualism in contemporary culture, we opt instead for a more pragmatic approach to the linkages of individuals and communities. Rather than holding out for community as traditionally defined and for conventional forms of institutional commitment, we would encourage a more functional and more variegated conception of moral and religious community. It simply is not true that boomers aren't interested in either community or commitment: They were galvanized in youth into strong solidarities and passionate commitments and are still capable of them. What is true is that existing religious institutions do not always give expression to their deepest feelings and commitments.

Narcissism as a psychological condition is a frequent target for attack, yet this seems misplaced. Rather than attacking the narcissistic self as the source of the problem of individualism, we think a better solution lies in recognizing the close association between narcissism and religion, and in capitalizing upon the current signs of a "transformed narcissism" among members of the boomer generation today.[26] To underscore the close relation between these two is to recognize that narcissism has features clearly compatible with the positive, reinforcing role of religion: a person's need for affirmation, for encouragement, for support, for expressiveness. A transformed narcissism is a more mature form of narcissism that has a more direct link with these elemental psychological needs. Psychologist Heinz Kohut describes this more mature narcissism as having the following capacities: for personal creativity, for empathy, recognition of one's own finiteness, a sense of humor, and wisdom arising out of the acceptance of one's own limitations.[27] All these are capacities bearing a remarkable resemblance to Peter Berger's "signals of transcendence"[28] in a secular world. And we might add, all are capacities of the older boomers approaching midlife.

In all of this, there are two fundamental points. One is that these capacities or signals do not depend on religious institutions—they arise out of life. The sacred may or may not be mediated through existing institutions and is not to be limited to the layers of social customs and history surrounding organizational expression. A second is that a transformed narcissism is not only compatible with a religious orientation but may well be crucial to the continuing role of the sacred in a secular society. The freedom to develop one's own talents or interests, flexibility and adaptation to new life conditions, an emphasis on the whole person, empathy with others, confrontation with one's own mortality, a sense of irony in life and the capacity to laugh at it, and asking how one's own creativity may contribute to the well-being of others may all undergird a sense of the sacred. Shame, not guilt, may be the psychological condition that is a crucial entrée to the boomer mentality. Indeed, it may well be, as psychologist Donald Capps argues, that the rise of the narcissistic self is bringing about a new emphasis on God as the "accessible Self," in which case openness and availability of the sacred become all the more important. Inaccessibility is problematic to spiritual well-being in the contemporary culture. And of necessity, accessibility must involve alternative ways of experiencing the sacred. As a computer programmer who happens to be an evangelical put it, without any prompting on our part: "We all access God differently."

As the 1990s unfold, new styles of balancing concern for self and commitment to community may take a clearer form. The sacred may become more accessible, leading to the creation of new social forms and the possibility even that existing religious institutions may themselves be transformed. Many of the fears that a corrosive individualism is eating away at America's social fabric may yet prove to be unfounded, or at least improperly focused. Younger boomers, for example, are less anti-institutional than older boomers; and as they approach the parenting years, they may return to the churches and synagogues in even greater numbers. Having achieved an easier blend of pragmatism and idealism than their elders, they may be better able to relate to existing institutions and to transform them subtly in directions more in keeping with their lives. Also, recent evidence suggests that Americans who are the most self-oriented, or individualistic, are also the most likely to do things to help others.[29] While the relationship between individualism and charity may not be a strong one, still it goes against the grain of much thinking about how Americans live and act today. And it is true as well that America's institutions, including the religious, are adaptive institutions; they absorb and accommodate cultural changes with remarkable resilience. The pace of change is sometimes slow, but we would expect them to adapt in the direction of allowing individuals to relate in more meaningful ways. As in all times, trends in cultures and traditions have the power to reshape the face of institutions; and in turn institutions, if they are to survive, must embody and extend those cultures and traditions.

Furthermore, a strong religious individualism need not necessarily loosen ties to institutions. It can work the other way as well—to "tighten up or clarify commitment to institutions," as Penny Long Marler and David A. Roozen put it.[30] Americans will increasingly make religious and spiritual choices on the basis of their preferences, which will help to emancipate faith from ascriptive loyalties. Personal autonomy rather than family heritage or religious background will increasingly be the basis on which one relates to the sacred. What a person chooses rather than is born into will be decisive. This should produce more self-conscious religious constituencies and greater clarity of the alternatives available in an amazingly diverse religious market. Boundaries separating faith communities should become clearer. Given the great value boomers place on choice and having alternatives, the sheer force of boomer culture should push religious institutions into clearer focus along these lines.

Boomer-style individualism and culture may be, in fact, just what it takes to lead some congregations to a renewed health. Many of the old-line Protestant congregations especially, which put a great deal of emphasis on social action in the 1960s, may be transformed spiritually by returning boomers. We observed congregations where this seems to be occurring. A quote from a member of a United Church of Christ congregation in Colorado is insightful:

> . . . there is a tension here in this congregation between the heritage of our tradition, which is outward looking, and all of this inward reflection that's new to this tradition. I think it's a needed corrective. But we haven't lost our commitment to public morality. There is still a very strong sense that this church is part of the broader community and that what it does, it sets an example. But I think we needed that corrective because I think we got so outward oriented that we weren't sure what was holding that together.

The vision is that of a new vital balance of spirituality and social action, of the sort many boomers are looking for. Where congregations are open to new spiritual vision, or in places where boomers "invade" in large numbers, they will play a crucial role in reshaping their future. They will provide leadership moving in new directions, or at the very least, bring to them a change of sensibilities that in time promises to create "new wine in old wineskins." A United Methodist in the Midwest, a member of a congregation known for its openness and for attracting boomers, had this to say:

> . . . thirty years ago you see the newsreels of ministers standing up and saying rock-and-roll was the work of the devil and anybody that was dancing was going to hell. Last night this church had a fun night. The theme was the fifties. Our daughter got up there and danced with blue suede shoes. It just strikes me as odd that here we are thirty years later, and what was being condemned is now part of an activity taking place in a church. I think that is part of the reason that some of us that may have dropped out have come back, because it's a different church today than it was thirty years ago.

As boomers age we can expect increased attention to *creating* new forms of community. A more settled life, the end of child-bearing, and greater concerns about health and well-being should all create conditions for more community. Boomers will likely invest their energies in those institutions where there is freedom to create—be they religious or otherwise. They may actually reach out to one another in ways we have yet to imagine. "Networking" may become a deeper, more encompassing concept than it is now.[31] Already there are signs of a rediscovery of village forms of life, of a co-housing movement, and of cooperatives. Out in the future will come an elderculture with a concern to preserve values and traditions—including, no doubt, community as a cherished value.

One expectation already advanced is that the creation of community inspired in their youth may blossom again in their old age.[32] They may have unfinished business to return to once they are no longer absorbed in careers and rearing families.

This speculation aside, we can say that, despite the language of individualism, a concern for community is already very real to them. The sense of group identity known from the time of their youth has not been lost on them in their more individualistic, more competitive middle years. In fact, many may yearn nostalgically for its return. Many whose consciousness had been formed by the sixties told the author of a study on loneliness in America that at one time they "had a feeling of belonging to something larger than themselves, whether the antiwar, women's or civil rights movement or the youth culture."[33] The feeling was gone but not forgotten.

THE END OF ALL OUR EXPLORING

Whatever the future holds, this generation's struggle over values and commitment is not over—if for no other reason than that the memories of the past live on as reminders of who they are and where they came from. Mountains may not be moving now, as they were during the years when the boomers were growing up, but boomers haven't forgotten mystery and excitement. Nor have they confronted all the challenges life will present them. The quest for a spiritual style continues into the future.

As a generation they grew up on folk music: They sang of love, of justice, of a new tomorrow, of peace and protest. Today they know the hopes, joys, frustrations, and heartaches of life, the stuff of which country music and folk ballads are made. They are deeply enmeshed in the narrative tradition—for at heart they are storytellers, and like all storytellers, they know that life is an open-ended plot. They have a narrative perspective on commitment, which locates its meaning in their unfolding lives. As long as there are years to live, their narrative of life will continue to evolve, open always to reinterpretation and emendation at each stage along the way.

Struggle will continue to be a big part of this narrative, but as a theme it can easily mislead. For beneath all the rhetoric of distrust and distance rests another, far quieter rhetoric—that of the soul. In their innermost beings, the "children of the sixties" know that religion, for all its institutional limitations, holds a vision of life's unity and meaningfulness, and for that reason will continue to have a place in their narrative. In a very basic sense, religion itself was never the problem, only social forms of religion that stifle the human spirit. The sacred lives on and is real to those who can access it.

Far from having been in vain, their explorations have served to bring them to a greater wisdom. Life takes on richer meaning for those who are wise enough to know that in exploring, life begins to look more like an ever-evolving spiral than a vicious circle: "You can't come full circle unless you are dead. You come around, but it is a spiral. You come to the same position, but your height is different," as one person told us. He spoke for many others whose understanding of life is undergoing transformation, those for whom T. S. Eliot's refrain has special meaning:

> We shall not cease from exploration
> And the end of all our exploring
> Will be to arrive where we started
> And know the place for the first time.

Epilogue

As this volume went to press in the fall of 1992, we checked back with the seven people whose lives are described in these pages. Two or three years had passed since our interviews, and we wanted to know if their lives had taken any new directions.

Barry Johnson still attends the same Southern Baptist church, but not as actively as he once did. ("Needed some space for myself," he told us.) For a while he and his wife were in marriage counseling, but now "things are better." Finding space and working things out in the marriage are top priorities. When we talked to him late one afternoon he had just come in from jogging—"spiritual time . . . something you just got to give yourself." His son had left for college the week before, and he inferred that this was another reason why he has been reflecting more than usual about things lately.

Linda Kramer holds firm to her evangelical faith. She still listens to Dr. Dobson on the radio and "enjoys" his insights into psychology; she is active as ever in small groups at her church. She spoke of how she "enriched" her life by following the guidelines of the Bible. As her children grow older, she worries more about them being exposed to "all the violence and pornography on television." If anything, she has become more pessimistic about the moral and spiritual state of the country—"it will take more than re-electing George Bush to turn things around. . . . The country is going down the drain if people don't wake up." An ardent pro-lifer, she prays the courts will overturn *Roe vs. Wade*.

Pam Fletcher reports that her life continues much the same. Her daughter goes to church with friends occasionally, which seems not to bother her, providing "that's what she wants to do." The in-laws no longer pressure her about taking the children to church—"they finally gave up," she says with a chuckle. Asked if she thinks of herself in any way as spiritual, she replies, "No, not really." Family life remains uppermost in her concerns.

Sonny D'Antonio is still working hard and enjoying his family. We had difficulty getting through to him; only after a second letter asking that he answer a few questions (plus a check for $10) did he respond. His views on Catholicism have not changed.

Oscar Gantt is now married. He and his new wife have five children, two of his and three of hers. He still hasn't found a church that he likes—"everything is for me, me, me. . . . What happened to churches doing things to help people?" He seldom goes to any church anymore. When he does, it's usually to his mother's AME congregation, "to get a fix once in a while." Islam continues to fascinate him, although he is unsure whether he would ever convert.

Mollie Stone remains a single mother and has moved with her children to another town in Massachusetts. Her "bad experience" with the man she was living with when we first interviewed her (the father of her third child) is why, she says, she now attends Co-Dependents Anonymous once or twice a week—"That's mainly what sustains me, plus this other group I'm a part of." She has not found the alternative Jewish celebration she was looking for when we first talked, but speaks fondly of a small group that meets in a nearby church, a group she describes as made up of "New Agers, open-minded Baptists, and humanistic Jews."

Carol McLennon now works full time to help out with the family finances. Her older son, who is gay, moved to Oregon last year. She is not attending Mass regularly in her Catholic parish at present; "Some churches are dysfunctional," she explains when asked about her frustrations with the parish leadership. Her two junior-high-aged daughters are involved in a Baptist youth group. Carol and her husband, Brad, sometimes go to that church, but more often they go to a nearby Episcopal church. Liturgy and the Eucharist remain important to her. "The church is conservative around here," she says, "but each parish is different. . . . I might find my Catholic church yet."

A generation of seekers.

Appendix: Data and Methods

The data on which this study is based were collected in four stages: (1) general survey, (2) follow-up survey, (3) in-depth interviews, and (4) group interviews. Two of these stages involved telephone interviewing and the other two face-to-face interviewing. The first three phases were closely interrelated, since the same individuals were tracked in our interviews. The fourth phase was somewhat independent from the other three in that, except in one instance, group interviews did not include people who had been sampled in the first three phases.

GENERAL SURVEY

This initial phase of the research was conducted as part of a joint project with Phillip E. Hammond. With support from the Lilly Endowment, the two of us (with the assistance of John Shelton Reed) designed a survey on four states: California, Massachusetts, North Carolina, and Ohio. These states were selected to maximize regional variation.

The survey was conducted by Focused Group Interviews, Inc., (FGI), a private research firm located in North Carolina. Using random-digit dialing, the firm sampled 2,620 households in the four states. Potential respondents were screened by year of birth, so that only those born between 1928 and 1963 were interviewed. These birth years were used in order to sample two cohorts, pre-boomers and boomers. Only one person in each household was interviewed. We used a stratified sampling process in order to get approximately equal numbers in each of the four states. The procedure yielded the following number of completed interviews for the four states:

	Female	Male	Total
California	360	295	655
Massachusetts	343	312	655
North Carolina	397	252	649
Ohio	394	267	661

The interviews took place during the fall of 1988 and the spring of 1989. Overall response rate was 60%—somewhat lower than we expected. In Massachusetts especially the response rate was low. Potential respondents who initially refused to participate were recontacted and offered five dollars to participate. This incentive changed few minds, however. Much of the interviewing was done in the fall of an election year, which may account for the low response rate, since many polls were being conducted at the time. We simply do not know if, and to what extent, the response rate introduces systematic bias into our data. Fortunately, our samples reflect quite well the census-based educational, income, and occupational breakdowns from the four states, which would suggest that this is not a problem.

Respondents were asked more than eighty questions on their social background, religious participation, moral values, and attitudinal items. The FGI staff used random listening procedures to ensure that all questions were carefully monitored, and to assure maximum validity of coding and completeness. Interviews took about twenty minutes. Edited questionnaires were keyed directly to disk, and entries were professionally verified.

In the final analysis, we selected (somewhat arbitrarily) the birth years from 1946 to 1962 as the boomer category. Sixty-one percent of the total, or 1,599 cases, fell into this category. We defined older boomers as those born from 1946 through 1954 (802 cases), and younger boomers as those born from 1955 through 1962 (797 cases).

FOLLOW-UP SURVEY

We conducted the second phase, a follow-up telephone interview, with 536 of the boomers who were interviewed in the first phase. Because we were more interested in older boomers, these interviews were conducted with respondents born between 1946 and 1960, or from a pool of 1,300 cases. We selected every third case for a follow-up interview, with the following exceptions: (a) all Jewish respondents

266

were included; (b) in California, all Catholics were included; in Massachusetts, all Protestants were included; in North Carolina, all Catholics were included; in Ohio, all those claiming no religion were included. These interviews were conducted within three to nine months after the first interview. Overall response rate was 81%.

These interviews averaged about twenty-five minutes in length, with an additional battery of more than fifty closed-ended and open-ended questions exploring religious biographies in greater detail. Bruce Greer, Mary Johnson, Karen Loeb, and Elizabeth Souza, under the supervision of Andrea Leibson, conducted the interviews at the University of Massachusetts.

IN-DEPTH INTERVIEWS

Based on the follow-up interview, we selected sixty-four cases for face-to-face interviews. We made these selections not on any strict random basis, but generally so that we would gain more in-depth information on the three constituencies of interest to us: dropouts, returnees, and loyalists. These interviews were about equally distributed in the four states. Interviews were for an hour or more; we used a semistructured set of questions, but with freedom to explore topics of interest to the respondent.

These interviews sought to explore more fully the respondents' reasons for religious participation, or lack of, and their religious biographies generally. We tried to gain in-depth information about people's life courses and their own narrative interpretations. Since information from the previous two telephone interviews was available to the interviewers, they were able to ask questions of clarification and further inquiry. These interviews were taped and transcribed. Bruce Greer, Mary Johnson, Karen Loeb, Marilyn Metcalf-Whitacker, Elizabeth Souza, and the principal investigator did the interviews.

GROUP INTERVIEWS

In the final phase, we held group interviews to discuss religious and spiritual topics of interest to boomers. We held fourteen group interviews, some with as few as four or five people, and others with as many as twenty people. Usually these were conducted in churches in the four states where we did the other interviewing, but additional group interviews took place in Colorado, Connecticut, Florida, Texas, and Washington. In addition to church groups, one interview was in a synagogue, two were in Protestant seminaries, and one was at a New Age festival. Most of these interviews were taped and transcribed.

Notes

INTRODUCTION

1. Paul C. Light, *Baby Boomers* (New York: W. W. Norton, 1988), 19.

2. After 1945 the number of annual births jumped considerably. A million more births took place in 1947 than in 1945, and for the next seventeen years the annual average was 4,035,000. The number of births began to decline in the early 1960s, and in 1964 reached a low level comparable to 1947. By the mid-1970s, births had fallen to just over 3 million per year, only slightly higher than in the early 1940s. See Leon F. Bouvier, "America's Baby Boom Generation: The Fateful Bulge," *Population Bulletin* 35, no. 1 (April 1980).

3. Karl Mannheim, *Essays on the Sociology of Knowledge* (New York: Oxford University Press, 1952). Also see Norman B. Ryder, "The Cohort as a Concept in the Study of Social Change," *American Sociological Review* 30 (1965): 843–61. As noted in the text, "cohort" refers to an age strata in society, whereas "generation" carries more of an emphasis on its self-conscious collectivity and solidarity. For a cyclical interpretation of American history from a generational perspective, see William Strauss and Neil Howe, *Generations: The History of America's Future 1584 to 2069* (New York: William Morrow, 1991).

4. See Howard Schuman and Jacqueline Scott, "Generations and Collective Memories," *American Sociological Review* 54 (June 1989): 359–81.

5. Annie Gottlieb, *Do You Believe in Magic? The Second Coming of the 60s Generation* (New York: Times Books, 1987).

6. See Todd Gitlin, *The Sixties: Years of Hope, Years of Rage* (New York: Bantam Books, 1987) for perhaps the most penetrating and balanced treatment of the period. Other recent accounts include Peter O. Whitmer (with Bruce VanWyngarden), *Aquarius Revisited: Seven Who Created the Sixties Counterculture That Changed America* (New York: Macmillan, 1987); Peter Collier and David Horowitz, *Destructive Generation: Second Thoughts about the Sixties* (New York: Summit Books, 1989); Jack Whalen and Richard Flacks, *Beyond the Barricades: The Sixties Generation Grows Up* (Philadelphia: Temple University Press, 1989); and Lauren Kessler, *After All These Years: Sixties' Ideas in a Different World* (New York: Thunder's Mouth, 1990). For a fascinating, insightful account by a journalist who wrote extensively about the period, see George Leonard, *Walking on the Edge of the World* (Boston: Houghton Mifflin, 1988).

7. Andrew M. Greeley, *The Catholic Myth* (New York: Charles Scribner's Sons, 1990), 44. He draws upon Geertz's work. See Clifford Geertz, "Religion as a Cultural System," in *The Religious Situation 1968,* edited by Donald Cutler (Boston: Beacon, 1968) and "Ethos, World-View and the Analysis of Sacred Symbols," *Antioch Review* 17 (1957): 424–34.

8. Aside from the earlier work of Freud and Jung, Erik Erikson's writings are especially important here. See his many writings, but particularly *Identity: Youth and Crisis* (New York: W. W. Norton, 1968). For a good summary and interpretation of Erikson's theory of the stages of life, see the biography by Robert Coles, *Erik H. Erikson: The Growth of His Work* (Boston: Little, Brown, 1970). Popular treatments of midlife transitions and their growth potential are found in Gail Sheehy, *Passages* (New York: Bantam, 1977) and Daniel J. Levinson, *The Seasons of a Man's Life* (New York: Knopf, 1978).

9. John F. Roschen, "The Baby-Boom's Second Journey into Self: Finding Faith at Midlife," unpublished paper, 1990. For a similar, more journalistic assessment for why questions of faith and spirit have emerged at this time, see John Wheeler, "Themes for the 90's: A Rebirth of Faith," *The New York Times* (December 31, 1988): 23.

10. Robert N. Bellah, Richard Madsen, William M. Sullivan, Ann Swidler, and Steven M. Tipton, *Habits of the Heart* (Berkeley: University of California Press, 1985).

11. Robert Coles, *The Spiritual Lives of Children* (Boston: Houghton Mifflin, 1990), 39.

1. THE LIVES OF SEVEN BOOMERS

1. Daniel Yankelovich, *New Rules: Searching for Self-Fulfillment in a World Turned Upside Down* (New York: Random House, 1981).

2. The major work is Robert N. Bellah, Richard Madsen, William M. Sullivan, Ann Swidler, and Steven M. Tipton, *Habits of the Heart* (Berkeley: University of California Press, 1985).

3. Clifford Geertz, *The Interpretation of Cultures* (New York: Basic Books, 1973), 52. See Roger G. Betsworth, *Social Ethics: An Examination of American Moral Traditions* (Louisville: Westminster/John Knox Press, 1990) for an elaboration of American cultural narratives.

2. A TIME WHEN MOUNTAINS WERE MOVING

1. See "TV Mirrors a New Generation," by Jeremy Gerard, *The New York Times* (October 30, 1988): Section 2.

2. David Sheff, "Portrait of a Generation," *Rolling Stone* (May 5, 1988): 55.

3. The three items were worded as follows: "In your late teens and early twenties, did you ever (a) attend a rock concert? (b) smoke marijuana? (c) take part in any demonstrations, marches, or rallies? The three are moderately intercorrelated, ranging from 0.20 to 0.41 (Pearson correlations).

4. The terms "challengers" and "calculators" are taken from Douglas A. Walrath. See his *Frameworks: Patterns for Living and Believing Today* (New York: Pilgrim Press, 1987), chapter 3.

5. Annie Gottlieb, *Do You Believe in Magic? The Second Coming of the 60s Generation* (New York: Times Books, 1987), 18.

6. These data are reported in Paul C. Light, *Baby Boomers* (New York: W. W. Norton, 1988), 168.

7. William Atwood, "How America Feels," *Look* 24, 1 (January 5, 1960): 11–15.

8. Loren Baritz, *The Good Life* (New York: Alfred A. Knopf, 1989), chapter 5.

9. Light, *Baby Boomers,* 160–61.

10. Seymour Martin Lipset and William Schneider, *The Confidence Gap* (New York: The Free Press, 1983), 296–98.

11. Joseph Veroff, Elizabeth Douvan, and Richard Kulka, *The Inner American: A Self-Portrait from 1957–1976* (New York: Basic Books, 1981), 141.

12. Sheff, "Portrait of a Generation," 52.

13. Landon Y. Jones, *Great Expectations: America and the Baby Boom Generation* (New York: Ballantine Books, 1980).

14. Jones, *Great Expectations,* 51–52.

15. Ronald Inglehart, "The Silent Revolution in Europe: Intergenerational Change in Post-Industrial Societies," *American Political Science Review* 65 (December 1971): 991–1017. Also see his expanded argument in *Culture Shift in Advanced Industrial Society* (Princeton: Princeton University Press, 1990).

16. Veroff, Douvan, and Kulka, *The Inner American,* 528–29. Many others have written about the cultural shift toward the subjective and the personal. See especially Christopher Lasch, *The Culture of Narcissism* (New York: Norton, 1979); Peter Clecak, *America's Quest for the Ideal Self* (New York: Oxford University Press, 1983); and Robert N. Bellah, Richard Madsen, William M. Sullivan, Ann Swidler, and Steven M. Tipton, *Habits of the Heart* (Berkeley: University of California Press, 1985). Also see Penny Long Marler and David A. Roozen's "From Church Tradition to Consumer Choice: The Gallup Surveys of the Unchurched American," in C. Kirk Hadaway and David A. Roozen, eds., *Church and Denominational Growth* (Nashville: Abingdon Press, 1993). Their paper and conversations I have had with them, especially at a conference in spring 1991, were very helpful in shaping my own views on trends in religious individualism.

17. Daniel Yankelovich, *New Rules: Searching for Self-Fulfillment in a World Turned Upside Down* (New York: Random House, 1981), 4–5.

18. Yankelovich, *New Rules,* 5.

19. Michael Maccoby, *Why Work?* (New York: Simon and Schuster, 1988), 103.

20. Sheff, "Portrait of a Generation," 54.

21. Ralph Waldo Emerson, "Nature," in *Selected Writings of Emerson,* edited by Brooks Atkinson (New York: Modern Library, 1940), 36.

22. Philip Rieff, *The Triumph of the Therapeutic: Uses of Faith after Freud* (New York: Harper & Row, 1966).

23. Betty Friedan, *The Feminine Mystique* (New York: W. W. Norton, 1963).

24. Loren Baritz, *The Good Life* (New York: Alfred A. Knopf, 1989), 238–39.

25. These statistics are reported in *U.S. News and World Report* (July 11, 1966): 65 and in *Ladies' Home Journal* (June 1990): 186.

26. Elaine Tyler May, *Homeward Bound* (New York: Basic Books, 1988).

27. Arlie Hochschild (with Anne Machung), *The Second Shift: Working Parents and the Revolution at Home* (New York: Viking, 1989).

28. Considerable research has documented these declines. For a review and interpretation of the declines, see Robert Wuthnow, *The Restructuring of American Religion* (Princeton: Princeton University Press, 1988), 153–72. Wuthnow describes a much broader "education gap" emerging in the sixties than had existed before.

29. Wuthnow, *The Restructuring of American Religion,* 157–58.

30. Light, *Baby Boomers,* 123.

31. M. Kent Jennings and Richard Niemi, "The Transmission of Political Values from Parent to Child," *American Political Science Review* 62 (March 1968): 169–84.

32. Dividing the survey into four cohorts, those born between 1926 and 1935, between 1936 and 1945, between 1946 and 1954, and between 1955 and 1962, the differences in childhood religious involvement vary not more than 2 points.

33. For a case study of the losses within the United Methodist Church, see Warren J. Hartman, "Our Missing Generation," *Discipleship Trends* 5, no. 4 (August 1987).

34. For the four cohorts described in endnote 32, the percentages attending once a week or more when the respondents were in their early twenties are as follows: born between 1926 and 1935, 54%; born between 1936 and 1945, 46%; born between 1946 and 1954, 29%; and born between 1955 and 1962, 27%.

35. On the basis of a review of religious periodicals that we conducted, we found that every generation expresses great concern about what is happening to the young and their religious faith. Our review suggests there was an outpouring of concern in the 1920s, but more so in the 1960s. See Jonathan A. Dorn, "Sodom and Tomorrow: Will the Young be Morally Good," unpublished paper, 1989.

36. Norman B. Ryder, "The Cohort as a Concept in the Study of Social Change," *American Sociological Review* 30 (December 1965): 843–61.

37. See Light, *Baby Boomers,* chapter 5.

38. J. Conger, "Freedom and Commitment: Families, Youth, and Social Change," *American Psychologist* 36, no. 12 (1981): 1477–1478. Also see May, *Homeward Bound,* and Arlene Skolnick, *Embattled Paradise* (New York: Basic Books, 1991), chapter 2.

39. Craig Dykstra, Editorial, *Theology Today* 46 (July 1989): 127.

3. MOLLIE'S QUEST

1. Matthew Fox, "A Mystical Cosmology: Toward a Postmodern Spirituality," in David Ray Griffin, ed., *Sacred Interconnections* (Albany: State University of New York Press, 1990), 16.

2. A voluminous literature describing middle-class, bourgeois religious beliefs and values was written in the 1950s and early to mid-1960s. This would include Roy Eckardt, *The Surge of Piety in America* (New York: Association Press, 1958); Martin E. Marty, *The New Shape of American Religion* (New York: Harper & Row, 1959); Peter Berger, *The Noise of Solemn Assemblies* (Garden City, NY: Doubleday, 1961); Gibson Winter, *The Suburban Captivity of the Churches* (Garden City, NY: Doubleday, 1961); John Robinson, *Honest to God* (Philadelphia: Westminster Press, 1963); Pierre Berton, *The Comfortable Pew* (Toronto: McClelland and Stewart, 1965); and Harvey Cox, *The Secular City* (New York: Macmillan, 1965). For a review and interpretation of this literature, see Benton Johnson's "Liberal Protestantism: End of the Road?" in *Annals of the American Academy of Political and Social Science* 480 (July 1985): 39–52.

3. For a history of the African-American churches, see Sydney E. Ahlstrom, *A Religious History of the American People* (New Haven: Yale University Press, 1972), 698–714; and Liston Pope, "The Negro and Religion in America," in *The Sociology of Religion: An Anthology,* edited by Richard D. Knudten (New York: Appleton-Century-Crofts, 1967). For a more recent interpretation of changes and summary of contemporary interracial religious practices, see C. Kirk Hadaway, David G. Hackett, and James F. Miller, "The Most Segregated Institution: Correlates of Interracial Church Participation," *Review of Religious Research* 25 (March 1984): 204–19.

4. William James, *The Varieties of Religious Experience* (New York: Macmillan, 1961). The lectures on which the book is based were given in 1902.

5. See Roland A. Delattre, "Supply-Side Spirituality: A Case Study in the Cultural Interpretation of Religious Ethics in America," in Rowland A. Sherrill, ed., *Religion and the Life of the Nation* (Urbana: University of Illinois Press, 1990), 84–108.

6. Aside from Emerson's influence, New Thought movements in the nineteenth century embodied this assumption of spiritual abundance. Perhaps the most significant of these movements was the Unity School of Christianity, founded by Charles and Myrtle Filmore in 1889. Today its headquarters are located in Unity Village near Kansas City, Missouri. Its magazines, including *Thought, Unity,* and *Daily Word,* and its radio programs, reach millions of Americans regularly. Unity teaches, to quote Delattre, "that goodness, health, and prosperity rather than sin, pain, and poverty are the natural condition of humanity and the companions of true spirituality" ("Supply-Side Spirituality," 92).

7. Lucy Bregman, *The Rediscovery of Inner Experience* (Chicago: Nelson-Hall, 1982).

8. Precise figures on how many people are involved in Twelve-Step recovery programs are not obtainable. A recent estimate is that 15 million Americans are involved in 500,000 meetings across the nation. See the *Boston Globe* (April 29, 1990).

9. Sanaya Roman, *Spiritual Growth* (Tiburon, CA: H. J. Kramer), 9.

10. M. Scott Peck, *The Road Less Traveled* (New York: Touchstone, 1978).

11. These data are reported in George Gallup, Jr., and Jim Castelli, *The People's Religion: American Faith in the 90's* (New York: Macmillan, 1989), 77. Greeley found in the General Social Survey for 1984 that some 67% of Americans

thought they "were somewhere you had been before but knew that was impossible." Two-thirds also said they felt that they were in touch with someone far away from them. See Andrew M. Greeley, *Religious Change in America* (Cambridge: Harvard University Press, 1989), 59.

12. Research shows that whereas affirmation of belief in God and life after death has declined only slightly, uncertainty has increased. If asked about doubt or uncertainly, the number of people saying they have questions appears to have increased. See Bradley R. Hertel and Hart M. Nelsen, "Are We Entering a Post-Christian Era? Religious Belief and Attendance in America, 1957–1968," *Journal for the Scientific Study of Religion* 13 (December 1974): 409–19.

13. Andrew M. Greeley's research on images of God is worth noting here. He finds, using General Social Survey data, considerable variation in the responses of Americans to such images as Father, Mother, Master, Spouse, Judge, Lover, Friend, King, Creator, Healer, Redeemer, Liberator. Also, he shows that the images relate to voting behavior, social and political attitudes, and happiness. See his *Religious Change in America,* chapter 9.

14. David Ray Griffin, *God and Religion in the Postmodern World* (Albany: State University of New York Press, 1989), 52.

15. Fox, "A Mystical Cosmology," 24.

16. Two studies on Catholic Pentecostals (or Charismatics) underscore these personalistic themes: Meredith B. McGuire, *Catholic Pentecostalism* (Philadelphia: Temple University Press, 1982), and Mary Jo Neitz, *Charisma and Community* (New Brunswick, NJ: Transaction Books, 1987).

17. Quoted in Fox, "A Mystical Cosmology," 21.

18. This image might best be described philosophically as *panentheism,* as opposed to *pantheism.* Pantheism teaches that "all is God and God is all," as opposed to "all things in God and God in all things." Panentheism does not deny the transcendence of the divine, as does pantheism.

19. Wilfred Cantwell Smith, *Faith and Belief* (Princeton: Princeton University Press, 1979), 12.

20. Tex Sample, *U.S. Lifestyles and Mainline Churches* (Louisville: Westminster/John Knox Press, 1990), 48.

21. Abraham H. Maslow, *Religions, Values, and Peak Experiences* (New York: Viking, 1970), viii.

22. Daniel Yankelovich, in *New Rules: Searching for Self-Fulfillment in a World Turned Upside Down* (New York: Random House, 1981), offered this as a profile for the group he called the "strong formers," those who were most caught up in the quest for self-fulfillment. He estimated this extremely committed group to represent 17% of the population.

23. Robert Wuthnow reviews this argument as it applied to radical youth in the sixties in *The Consciousness Reformation* (Berkeley: University of California Press, 1976), 184–88. Also see Richard Flacks, "The Liberated Generation: An Exploration of the Roots of Student Protest," 104–26 in Richard Flacks, ed., *Conformity, Resistance, and Self Determination: The Individual and Authority* (Boston: Little, Brown and Company, 1973); and Kenneth Keniston, *Young*

Radicals: Notes on Committed Youth (New York: Harcourt, Brace and World, 1968), 278–88.

24. Ernst Troeltsch, *The Social Teachings of the Christian Churches* (London: George Allen and Unwin, 1931), 730.

25. For a review of the New Age movement, see Catherine L. Albanese, *America: Religions and Religion,* 2d ed. (Belmont, CA: Wadsworth Publishing, 1991), chapter 11, and J. Gordon Melton, Jerome Clark, and Aidan A. Kelly, *The New Age Encyclopedia* (Chicago: Gale Research, 1990).

26. Wuthnow, *The Consciousness Reformation,* 125.

27. The phrase belongs to Catherine L. Albanese. See her *America: Religions and Religion,* chapter 8.

28. The term *bricoleur* was introduced by Claude Levi-Strauss in *The Savage Mind* (Chicago: University of Chicago Press, 1966) as "someone who works with his hands," to emphasize making do with whatever is available. It has come to be used more broadly to mean the creation of an outlook by reordering and putting together that which is usable. See Jeffrey Stout, *Ethics After Babel: The Languages of Morals and Their Discontents* (Boston: Beacon Press, 1988), 74–81.

4. WALKING WITH THE LORD

1. Carol S. Pearson, *The Hero Within* (San Francisco: Harper & Row, 1986).

2. Nancy Tatom Ammerman makes this point. See her *Bible Believers: Fundamentalists in the Modern World* (New Brunswick, NJ: Rutgers University Press, 1987), 8.

3. It is estimated that 1.5 million children are enrolled in Christian schools. See Melinda Bollar Wagner, *God's Schools: Choice and Compromise in American Society* (New Brunswick, NJ: Rutgers University Press, 1990), 9.

4. For an analysis of how this operates in a small-town setting, see Arthur J. Vidich and Joseph Bensman, *Small Town in Mass Society* (Garden City, NY: Anchor Books, 1958), 313–15.

5. A good description of the differences between evangelicals and fundamentalists is found in Ammerman, *Bible Believers,* 3–6.

6. Far less is written about evangelicals on the left. On the Jesus People and left-leaning evangelicals, see Richard Quebedeaux, *The Worldly Evangelicals* (San Francisco: Harper & Row, 1978).

7. The items are moderately intercorrelated, in the 0.3 to 0.4 range. Unfortunately, we did not have an item on premillennialism to include in the index.

8. Gallup reports 31% of Americans are evangelicals, a figure that he says has been fairly stable since the mid-1970s. See George Gallup, Jr., and Jim Castelli, *The People's Religion: American Faith in the 90's* (New York: Macmillan Publishing Company, 1989), 93. Data on fundamentalists are much more difficult to come by. On one survey in the early 1980s, Gallup found that 40% of Americans believe that the Bible is the "actual word of God and is to be taken

literally, word for word." See his *Public Opinion 1980* (Wilmington, DE: Scholarly Resources). If this is any indication, the number of Americans with fundamentalist leanings is quite sizable.

9. Robert Wuthnow, "Religion as Culture," in David G. Bromley, ed., *Religion and the Social Order: New Developments in Theory and Research* (Greenwich, CT: JAI Press, 1991), 280.

10. George M. Marsden, "Preachers of Paradox: The Religious New Right and Historical Perspective," in Mary Douglas and Steven Tipton, eds., *Religion and America* (Boston: Beacon Press, 1983), 151. Also see Wade Clark Roof, "The New Fundamentalism: Rebirth of Political Religion in America," in Jeffrey K. Hadden and Anson Shupe, eds., *Prophetic Religions and Politics* (New York: Paragon House, 1986), 18–34.

11. Richard Quebedeaux, *By What Authority: The Rise of Personality Cults in American Christianity* (San Francisco: Harper & Row. 1982), 85.

12. Marsden makes this point is his essay, "Preachers of Paradox."

13. See James Davison Hunter, *American Evangelicalism* (New Brunswick, NJ: Rutgers University Press, 1983), who emphasizes that though conservative Protestants lost the theological battle in the 1920s, they continued to share the moral values with most other Americans until the 1960s. Also see Phillip E. Hammond, "The Curious Path of Conservative Protestantism," *Annals of the American Academy of Political and Social Science* 480 (July 1985): 53–62, for a similar interpretation of the rise of a militant religious conservativism in the 1970s.

14. Loren Baritz, *The Good Life* (New York: Alfred A. Knopf, 1989), 306.

15. James Davison Hunter observes considerable change, for example, in the views of young evangelicals on "casual petting" and "heavy petting." See his *Evangelicalism: The Coming Generation* (Chicago: University of Chicago Press, 1987), 56–64.

16. Judith Stacey offers an interesting account of how, in a study of working-class families, she found a remarkable blend of formal patriarchal principles and informal egalitarian practices, and a feminized doctrine of heterosexual love combined with ideas from the human potential movement. See her *Brave New Families: Stories of Domestic Upheaval in Late Twentieth Century America* (New York: Basic Books, 1990), 113–46.

17. James Davison Hunter, *Evangelicalism: The Coming Generation,* 65.

18. Peter Clecak, *America's Quest for the Ideal Self* (New York: Oxford University Press, 1983), 9.

19. The notion of a "new voluntarism" is discussed in Wade Clark Roof and William McKinney, *American Mainline Religion: Its Changing Shape and Future* (New Brunswick, NJ: Rutgers University Press, 1987), chapter 2.

20. For a review of how boomers are divided on a variety of issues, see Paul C. Light, *Baby Boomers* (New York: W. W. Norton, 1988), chapters 3 and 7.

21. Gallup and Castelli, *The People's Religion,* 167–79.

22. Hunter, *Evangelicalism: The Coming Generation,* 73.

23. The argument is that generational effects are not permanent, that age-related differences are really the result of life-cycle effects. See Ted G. Jelen, "Aging and Boundary Maintenance among American Evangelicals: A Comment on James Davison Hunter's *Evangelicalism: The Coming Generation,*" *Review of Religious Research* 31 (March 1990): 268–79.

5. ACROSS A GREAT SPIRITUAL DIVIDE

1. Peter L. Berger, *The Heretical Imperative* (Garden City, NY: Doubleday, 1980).

2. For further discussion of the types of moral language, see Steven M. Tipton, *Getting Saved from the Sixties* (Berkeley: University of California Press, 1982).

3. Robert Wuthnow, *The Consciousness Reformation* (Berkeley: University of California Press, 1976).

4. Tipton, *Getting Saved from the Sixties.* See also his essay, "The Moral Logic of Alternative Religions," in Mary Douglas and Steve M. Tipton, eds., *Religion and America* (Boston: Beacon Press, 1982), 79–107.

5. For further discussion of the two types of spirituality, see Roland A. Delattre, "Supply-Side Spirituality: A Case Study in the Cultural Interpretation of Religious Ethics in America," in Rowland A. Sherrill, ed., *Religion and the Life of the Nation* (Urbana: University of Illinois Press, 1990), 84–107. "Letting go" has its spiritual roots in new thought and positive thinking; "mastery and control" arises out of Puritan Christianity.

6. David Martin, "Revived Dogma and New Cult," in Douglas and Tipton, *Religion and America,* 111.

7. Carol S. Pearson, *The Hero Within* (New York: Harper & Row, 1986).

8. Wuthnow found a moderately positive correlation between his measures of theism and individualism. He describes people who hold to both meaning systems as "traditional." Mystical and social scientific meanings systems also correlated positively. Because both meaning systems are of recent vintage, he labeled people who adhere to both as "modern." See *The Consciousness Reformation* (Berkeley: University of California Press, 1976), 144–45. The intellectual and religious roots accounting for the links between theism and individualism, and between mysticism and science, are discussed in many places. See, for example, on theism and individualism, Steven Lukes, *Individualism* (New York: Harper & Row, 1973), and on mysticism and science, Ernst Troeltsch, *The Social Teachings of the Christian Churches* (New York: Harper & Row, 1961).

9. Theodore Roszak, *The Making of a Counter Culture* (Garden City, NY: Doubleday, 1969), chapter 2.

10. See John Murray Cuddihy, *No Offense: Civil Religion and Protestant Taste* (New York: Seabury Press, 1978) for an elaboration of the argument that in America, religion for the most part assumes a posture of "no offense," of tolerance and civility toward religious differences.

11. Louise L. Hay, *You Can Heal Your Life* (Carson, CA: Hay House, 1984).

12. James Davison Hunter, *American Evangelicalism: Conservative Religion and the Quandary of Modernity* (New Brunswick, NJ: Rutgers University Press, 1983), 74–75.

13. Catherine L. Albanese, "Religion and the American Experience: A Century After," *Church History* 57 (September 1988): 337–51. Also see Robert S. Ellwood, *One Way: The Jesus Movement and Its Meaning* (Englewood Cliffs, NJ: Prentice-Hall, 1973) for an early discussion of the similarities between the hippie and Pentecostal worlds; and Joseph B. Tamney, *The Resilience of Christianity in the Modern World* (Albany: SUNY Press, 1992), chapter 4, on the Christian accommodation of the counterculture.

14. Albanese, "Religion and the American Experience: A Century After," 349–50.

15. Andrew M. Greeley, *The Catholic Myth* (New York: Charles Scribner's Sons, 1990).

16. See Wade Clark Roof, Jackson W. Carroll, and David A. Roozen, eds., *The Post-War Generation and Religious Establishments,* forthcoming.

17. See Michael H. Ducey, *Sunday Morning: Aspects of Urban Ritual* (New York: Free Press, 1977).

18. See Sharon Parks, *The Critical Years* (San Francisco: HarperCollins, 1991), chapter 3.

19. This argument is put forth by Richard Quebedeaux in his *By What Authority: The Rise of Personality Cults in American Christianity* (San Francisco: Harper & Row, 1982), chapter 4. Earlier, Sydney A. Ahlstrom made a quite similar claim. See his *A Religious History of the American People* (New Haven: Yale University Press, 1972), chapter 60 on "Harmonial Religion since the Later Nineteenth Century," 1021–1036. Both Ahlstrom and Quebedeaux see the 1960s as a crucial period of religious amalgamation. Also see Albanese, "Religion and the American Experience: A Century After."

20. Quebedeaux, *By What Authority,* 80.

21. See Joseph Veroff, Elizabeth Douvan, and Richard Kulka, *The Inner American: A Self-Portrait from 1957–1976* (New York: Basic Books, 1981). They argued that three types of changes were occurring in people's responses to questions of their well-being and coping styles: (1) the diminution of role standards as the basis for defining adjustment; (2) the increased focus on self-expressiveness and self-direction in social life; and (3) a shift in concern from social organizational integration to interpersonal intimacy.

22. Neil Postman, *Amusing Ourselves to Death: Public Discourse in the Age of Show Business* (New York: Penguin Books, 1985). Also see Walter Ong, *Orality and Literacy* (New York: Methuen, 1982); and his essay "Literacy and the Future of Print," *Journal of Communication* 30:1 (Winter 1980).

23. See Catherine L. Albanese, "From New Thought to New Vision: The Shamanic Paradigm in Contemporary Spirituality," unpublished paper. She argues that because of the ubiquitousness of electromagnetically derived images in

contemporary society and the cultural authority they have over our lives, individuals find it easy to turn to shamanic spirituality.

24. Daniel Yankelovich, *New Rules: Searching for Self-Fulfillment in a World Turned Upside Down* (New York: Random House, 1981).

25. Delattre, "Supply-Side Spirituality," 105.

26. Annie Gottlieb, *Do You Believe in Magic? The Second Coming of the 60s Generation* (New York: Times Books, 1987), 223.

27. Mary Jo Neitz, "In Goddess We Trust," in Thomas Robbins and Dick Anthony, eds., *In Gods We Trust* (New Brunswick, NJ: Transaction, 1990), 353–72.

28. Sam Keen, *Fire in the Belly* (New York: Bantam Books, 1991). Another book that has received a great deal of attention in the burgeoning men's movement is Robert Bly's *Iron John: A Book About Men* (Lexington: Addison-Wesley, 1991).

29. Carol Gilligan, *In A Different Voice* (Cambridge: Harvard University Press, 1982).

30. Michael McAteer, "To Pluck a Flower Is to Trouble a Star," *The Toronto Star* (June 30, 1990).

31. Gottlieb, *Do You Believe in Magic?*, 225. Also see Meredith B. McGuire, "Religion and the Body: Rematerializing the Human Body in the Social Sciences of Religion," *Journal for the Social Scientific Study of Religion* 29 (September 1990): 283–96.

6. RETURNING TO THE FOLD

1. For a discussion of "analogical" religious imagination, see David Tracy, *The Analogical Imagination: Christian Theology and the Culture of Pluralism* (New York: Crossroad, 1981). Also see Andrew M. Greeley, *The Catholic Myth* (New York: Charles Scribners's Sons, 1990), chapter 3.

2. Men and women born between 1936 and 1945, the immediate pre-boomer cohort, dropped out at the average age of 25.1; those born between 1926 and 1935 dropped out even later, at the average of 29.4.

3. David A. Roozen, "Church Dropouts: Changing Patterns of Disengagement and Re-Entry," *Review of Religious Research* 21 (Supplement, 1980): 427–50.

4. Obviously, there is a methodological artifact here. Younger boomers have not had as many years as older boomers in which to return.

5. Craig Dykstra, Editorial, *Theology Today* 46 (July 1989), 127.

6. A Princeton Religious Research Center study reports that 15% of American Catholics have attended a religious home group apart from the parish church in the previous two years. See William V. D'Antonio, "Faith, Autonomy, and Community: The Changing American Catholic Laity," in Nancy Tatom Ammerman and Wade Clark Roof, eds., *Work, Family, and Religion,* forthcoming.

7. There is some convergence among American Protestants and Catholics in child-rearing orientations. See Duane Alwin, "Religion and Parental Child-Rearing

Orientations: Evidence of a Catholic-Protestant Convergence," *American Journal of Sociology* 92 (September 1986): 412–20.

8. This argument is put forth, in the case of political socialization, backed up by data from the University of Michigan on the "Class of 1965" by Paul C. Light in his *Baby Boomers* (New York: W. W. Norton and Company, 1988), 185–86.

9. See the discussion and review of studies in Robert Wuthnow, *The Consciousness Reformation* (Berkeley: University of California Press, 1976), 184–88.

10. For an elaboration of the life-cycle theory, see Widich Schroeder, "Age Cohorts, the Family Life Cycle, and Participation in the Voluntary Church in America: Implications for Membership Patterns, 1950–2000," *Chicago Theological Seminary Register* 65 (Fall 1975).

11. Much evidence suggests that school-age children often lead their parents to church and synagogue. For an analysis of the postwar increase in churchgoing, see Dennison Nash and Peter Berger, "The Child, the Family, and the 'Religious Revival' in Suburbia," *Journal for the Scientific Study of Religion* 2 (October 1962): 85–93. Three decades later *Newsweek* magazine would report that baby boomers were returning to church, now led by their children. See "And the Children Shall Lead Them: Young Americans Return to God," *Newsweek* (December 17, 1990).

12. See Wuthnow's early analysis of "life-cycle" versus "generational" religious patterns of the sixties generation in *The Consciousness Reformation,* 154–64. For a similar conclusion to ours about the greater importance of generational change over life-cycle factors for boomers, see Ronald Inglehart, *Culture Shift in Advanced Industrial Society* (Princeton: Princeton University Press, 1990), chapter 2. For a general review of the literature on religion bearing on these competing interpretations, see Wade Clark Roof and Karen Walsh, "Life Cycle, Generation, and Participation in Religious Groups," in David Bromley and Jeffrey K. Hadden, eds., *Handbook on Religious Movements,* forthcoming.

13. Kenneth A. Briggs, "Baby Boomers: Boom or Bust for the Churches?" *Progressions* 2, no. 1 (January 1990): 5.

14. For an extended argument about the shift from a linear to a cyclical conception of adult development and its institutional implications generally, see Frederic M. Hudson, *The Adult Years* (San Francisco: Jossey-Bass Publishers, 1991).

15. For reviews of this literature, see Wade Clark Roof and William McKinney, *American Mainline Religion* (New Brunswick, NJ: Rutgers University Press, 1987), 107–17; and Robert Wuthnow, *The Restructuring of American Religion* (Princeton: Princeton University Press, 1988), 153–64.

16. See Wuthnow, *The Restructuring of American Religion,* 158.

17. For a detailed analysis of the insecurities of the middle class, see Barbara Ehrenreich, *Fear of Falling* (New York: Harper Perennial, 1990).

18. The combined set of variables mentioned in this paragraph "explains" remarkably little of the variance in whether a dropout returns to religion or not.

19. Here I draw on Robert Wuthnow's insightful distinction between coherence and consistency. Whereas the latter is a feature of an individual's belief set, the

former is an attribute ascribed to reality. Coherence has to do with how elements, even those that are inconsistent, come together in some meaningful way, as they often do in people's narrative accounts. See his *Meaning and Moral Order* (Berkeley: University of California Press, 1987), chapter 2.

20. See Roof and McKinney, *American Mainline Religion,* chapter 5. The extent of switching depends, of course, on the typology of religious groups that is used. With narrow denominational boundaries, or intra-Protestant switching, switching is higher than in the case of interfaith boundaries, such as switching among Protestants, Catholics, and Jews.

21. See Jon R. Stone, "The New Voluntarism and Presbyterian Affiliation," 122–49, in Milton J. Coalter, John M. Mulder, and Louis B. Weeks, *The Mainstream Protestant "Decline"* (Louisville: Westminster/John Knox Press, 1990).

7. CULTURES AND CONGREGATIONS

1. Dan Wakefield, *Returning: A Spiritual Journey* (New York: Doubleday, 1988), ix.

2. On the importance of Vatican II and *Humanae Vitae,* the birth-control encyclical letter, as factors contributing to the decline of authority and the rise of greater reliance on individual conscience among young Catholics, see Patrick H. McNamara, *Conscience First, Tradition Second* (Albany: SUNY Press, 1992).

3. The proportion of those reared as nonaffiliates is quite small—only 4% in our survey. On virtually all cultural profile items, dropouts and the nonaffiliated are very similar.

4. See Peter Berger, *The Sacred Canopy* (Garden City, NY: Doubleday, 1967), 133–34, for an analysis of how the term "religious preference" is used. On religious individualism, see the discussion of "Sheilaism" in Robert N. Bellah, Richard Madsen, William M. Sullivan, Ann Swidler, and Steven M. Tipton, *Habits of the Heart* (Berkeley: University of California Press, 1985), 221–27. For a review of empirical studies on religious individualism and recent findings from national surveys, see Bruce A. Greer and Wade Clark Roof, "Desperately Seeking Sheila: Locating Religious Privatism in American Society," *Journal for the Scientific Study of Religion,* 31 (September 1992): 346–52.

5. A huge body of research on ethnicity and religion in the American context exists. Relative to the Irish, the Germans, or the Poles, Italians have lower levels of church attendance, involvement in religious activities, and financial support of the church. See Andrew M. Greeley, *The Denominational Society* (Glencoe, IL: Scott, Foresman, and Company, 1972), 122. In our study Italian-American baby boomers had an above-average level (among Catholics) of dropping out, and a below-average level of returning to religious involvement after dropping out.

6. The term belongs to Andrew M. Greeley. See his "American Catholics Going Their Own Way," *New York Times Magazine* (October 10, 1982).

7. For a review of the literature on American culture since the time of de Tocqueville up until Will Herberg, see William Lee Miller, "American Religion

and American Political Attitudes," in James W. Smith and A. Leland Jamison, eds., *Religious Perspectives in American Culture* (Princeton: Princeton University Press, 1961), 81–118.

8. The term is found in many post-modernist writings, and especially among the French theorists.

9. Carl S. Dudley, *Where Have All Our People Gone?* (New York: Pilgrim Press, 1979), 41.

10. The term "thick gathering" and the perspective developed here is that of James F. Hopewell. See his accounts in *Congregation: Stories and Structures,* edited by Barbara G. Wheeler (Philadelphia: Fortress Press, 1987). Also see Barbara G. Wheeler, "Uncharted Territory: Congregational Identity and Mainline Protestantism," in Milton J. Coalter, John M. Mulder, and Louis B. Weeks, eds., *The Presbyterian Predicament* (Louisville: Westminster/John Knox Press, 1990), 67–89.

11. This figure was reported in an article on the parish in *The Los Angeles Times* (February 23, 1992): Section E, 1.

8. "IT'S HARD TO FIND A RELIGION YOU CAN BELIEVE TOTALLY IN"

1. Taken from Fr. Leo Booth, *Breaking the Chains* (Long Beach, CA: Emmaus Publications).

2. See *The Denver Post* (June 12, 1989): 29.

3. Frances Fitzgerald observed the role of laughter in the lives of fundamentalist women in Jerry Falwell's Thomas Road Church. She speaks of Jackie Gould, who "had ordered a new set of kitchen cabinets and had them installed without—she said, giggling—consulting her husband." See her *Cities on a Hill* (New York: Simon and Schuster, 1981), 135.

4. Arlie Hochschild (with Anne Machung), *The Second Shift: Working Parents and the Revolution at Home* (New York: Viking, 1989), 24.

5. Working appears to have a greater impact on the religious lives of boomer women than on nonboomer women. An analysis of the 1988 General Social Survey suggests that for American women as a whole, labor force participation seems not to have much effect on their religious involvement. See Lyn Gesch, M.A. Thesis, University of California at Santa Barbara, 1991.

6. The responses to three items were used to create an index: (1) "More needs to be done to advance equal opportunities for women"; (2) "Some equality in marriage is a good thing, but by and large the husband ought to have the main say-so in family matters"; and (3) "Having a job outside the home is good for a married woman because it gives her more of a chance to develop as a person." Responses to the second item were recoded for compatibility with the other two items.

7. The results of the poll were published in the *San Francisco Examiner* (June 8, 1989): A12.

8. See Judith Stacey, *Brave New Families: Stories of Domestic Upheaval in Late Twentieth Century America* (New York: Basic Books, 1990). Stacey describes in some detail the functionality of these extended families for working-class Americans.

9. Results from this survey conducted by the City University of New York are reported in the *Los Angeles Times* (December 21, 1991): 51.

10. *Los Angeles Times* (December 21, 1991): 55.

11. Garry Wills, *Bare Ruined Choirs: Doubt, Prophecy, and Radical Religion* (Garden City, NY: Doubleday, 1972), 21.

12. Andrew M. Greeley and his collaborators have argued that the declines of the period are accounted for "almost entirely by a change in sexual attitudes and in attitudes toward the papacy among American Catholics." See Andrew M. Greeley, William C. McCready, and Kathleen McCourt, *Catholic Schools in a Declining Church* (Kansas City: Sheed and Ward, 1976), 304.

13. William D'Antonio, James Davidson, Dean Hoge, and Ruth Wallace, *American Catholic Laity in a Changing Church* (Kansas City: Sheed and Ward, 1989), chapter 4.

14. See Denise Lardner Carmody, *The Double Cross* (New York: Crossroad Publishing, 1986); Mary Jo Weaver, *New Catholic Women* (San Francisco: Harper & Row, 1985); and Ruth A. Wallace, "Catholic Women and the Creation of a New Social Reality," *Gender and Society* 2 (March 1988): 24–38.

15. Also see the results from the *National Catholic Reporter*/Gallup poll, which corroborates many of our findings, in the *National Catholic Reporter* (September 11, 1987): 9.

16. Peter J. Henriot, Edward P. DeBerri, and Michael J. Schultheis, *Catholic Social Teaching: Our Best Kept Secret* (Maryknoll, NY: Orbis Books, 1990).

17. In an unpublished paper, Sister Mary Johnson found that the gender differences on abortion are not statistically significant. All the other relationships are statistically significant at the 0.05 level.

18. The *National Catholic Reporter*/Gallup poll found that younger Catholics were more likely to view church attendance and contributions as less important in defining a "good Catholic," while donating time and money to the poor was slightly more valued. In that poll large proportions of Catholics of all ages said they should have a say in church matters.

19. Peter L. Berger, *The Sacred Canopy* (New York: Doubleday, 1967), 95–101.

20. Roger G. Betsworth, *Social Ethics: An Examination of American Moral Traditions* (Louisville: Westminster/John Knox Press, 1990), chapter 6.

9. TRANSFORMING AMERICA'S RELIGIOUS LANDSCAPE

1. Martin E. Marty, "The Spirit's Holy Errand: The Search for a Spiritual Style in Secular America," *Daedalus* 96, no. 1 (Winter 1967): 99–115.

2. Quoted in Marty, "The Spirit's Holy Errand."

3. Marty, "The Spirit's Holy Errand,"101.

4. For an elaboration of how fluid and flexible, indeed syncretistic, popular faith was in colonial America, see Jon Butler, *Awash in a Sea of Faith* (Cambridge: Harvard University Press, 1990). Butler's description of the mix of Christian and eclectic spiritualities, including witchcraft, magic, folk medicines, miracles, and other forms of supernatural interventionism, differs greatly from the standard interpretation of New England Puritanism.

5. See Butler, *Awash in a Sea of Faith,* chapter 8. He points to the antebellum period in the United States as a "spiritual hothouse," a time of popular outbursts of spiritual syncretism associated with movements such as Methodism, Mormonism, African-American Christianity, and spiritualism.

6. Daniel Yankelovich, *New Rules: Searching for Self-Fulfillment in a World Turned Upside Down* (New York: Random House, 1981), 256–64.

7. Robert Wuthnow, *Acts of Compassion* (Princeton: Princeton University Press, 1991), 116.

8. See Leon F. Bouvier, "America's Baby Boom Generation: The Fateful Bulge," *Population Bulletin* 35, no. 1 (April 1980): 5.

9. Lynn Smith, "Oh Grow Up!" *Los Angeles Times Magazine* (November 17, 1991): 15.

10. Quoted in Smith, "Oh Grow Up!" 16.

11. For a witty yet scathing critique of the self-help movement, see Wendy Kaminer, *I'm Dysfunctional, You're Dysfunctional: The Recovery Movement and Other Self-Help Fashions* (Reading, MA: Addison-Wesley, 1992).

12. The study was carried out by Anthropologist Thomas S. Weisner, director of the Family Lifestyles Project. See the report in *The Los Angeles Times* (December 6, 1991): A3.

13. Ronald Inglehart, *Culture Shift in Advanced Industrial Society* (Princeton: Princeton University Press, 1990).

14. A cross-cultural analysis of the postwar generation in nine European countries and Australia finds remarkable similarities in institutional religious declines combined with many new spiritual quests. See Wade Clark Roof, Jackson W. Carroll, and David A. Roozen, eds., *The Post-War Generation and Religious Establishments,* forthcoming.

15. Inglehart, *Culture Shift,* 192.

16. Robert N. Bellah, Richard Madsen, William M. Sullivan, Ann Swidler, and Steven M. Tipton, *Habits of the Heart* (Berkeley: University of California Press, 1985).

17. Christopher Lasch, *The True and Only Heaven* (New York: W. W. Norton, 1991), 83.

18. M. Scott Peck, *The Different Drum: Community-Making and Peace* (New York: Simon and Schuster, 1987), 59.

19. See Gail Unterberger, "Twelve Steps for Women Alcoholics," *The Christian Century* (December 6, 1989).

20. For a discussion of special purpose groups, see Robert Wuthnow, *The Restructuring of American Religion* (Princeton: Princeton University Press, 1988), 153–72.

21. George Barna, *User Friendly Churches* (Ventura, CA: Regal Books, 1991).

22. Quoted in Ellen M. Umansky, "Finding God: Women in the Jewish Tradition," *Cross Currents: Religion and Intellectual Life* 41, no. 4 (Winter 1991): 532.

23. Catherine L. Albanese, *America: Religion and Religions,* 2d ed. (Belmont, CA: Wadsworth, 1991), 369.

24. See Harold Bloom, *The American Religion* (New York: Simon and Schuster, 1992). Even if one rejects his interpretation of a post-Christian nation, his argument about American spirituality and its self-assertive qualities is compelling.

25. Bloom, *The American Religion,* 33.

26. Here we rely upon Donald Capps's argument in his essay "Religion and Psychological Well-Being," in Phillip E. Hammond, ed., *The Sacred in a Secular Age* (Berkeley: University of California Press, 1985), 237–56.

27. Heinz Kohut, "Forms and Transformations of Narcissism," in Paul H. Ornstein, ed., *The Search for the Self: Selected Writings of Heinz Kohut 1950–1978,* vol. 1 (New York: International Universities Press, 1978).

28. Peter L. Berger, *A Rumor of Angels* (Garden City, NY: Anchor Books, 1970).

29. Robert Wuthnow, *Acts of Compassion* (Princeton: Princeton University Press, 1991), 116.

30. Penny Long Marler and David A. Roozen, "From Church Tradition to Consumer Choice: The Gallup Surveys of the Unchurched American," in C. Kirk Hadaway and David A. Roozen, eds., *Church and Denominational Growth* (Nashville: Abingdon Press, 1993), 258. The discussion in this section draws from their insightful analysis of the consequences of greater choice for institutional religion as well as from my earlier collaboration with William McKinney. See Wade Clark Roof and William McKinney, *American Mainline Religion: Its Changing Shape and Future* (New Brunswick, NJ: Rutgers University Press, 1987), 184-85.

31. See Jerry Gerber, Janet Wolff, Walter Klores, and Gene Brown, *Lifetrends: The Future of Baby Boomers and Other Aging Americans* (New York: Stonesong Press, 1989), 238.

32. Gerber, *et al., Lifetrends,* 233.

33. Louise Bernikow, *Alone in America: The Search for Companionship* (Boston: Faber and Faber, 1987).

Index

Abortion: conservative Christian views on, 94, 111, 112; current views on, 15, 36, 111, 285n17; prevalence of in 1960s, 33; and Roman Catholic church, 232, 233–34

Abundance, and spiritual power, 131, 137–40

Abuse, religious, 214–17; support groups for, 215

Addictions, 69–70, 130, 138. *See also* Twelve-Step programs; Alcoholics Anonymous

Adulthood, of boomers, 3–4, 5. *See also* Midlife

Advertising, 42–43

Affluence: of 1960s, 36, 42–48; and salvation, 134

African-American heritage: and education, 51; and Exodus story, 29; and family of origin, 19–21; and progressive church, 210–11

African Methodist Episcopal Church, in family of origin, 19, 21

Age-cohort factor: and countercultural experience, 34–35; and distrust of institutions, 41, 259; and dropping out of church, 154–55; and religious universalism, 72; and returning to church, 155, 164; and spiritual seekers, 81, 136–37. *See also* Birth cohorts

Aging, 248, 261. *See also* Midlife

Agnosticism: extent of, 73, 126; and being religious, 77–78, 193; and religious community, 160. *See also* God

AIDS, 50, 248

Albanese, Catherine L., 131

Alcoholics Anonymous (AA), 19, 23, 69. *See also* Twelve-Step programs

Alienation, 41

Ambiguity, in conservative Christianity, 101–2

Ambivalence, about institutional religion, 237–38

America: civil religion of, 15, 40; and covenant with God, 95, 217; mission to world of, 29; moral superiority of, 40–41

American culture, 5–7; changing of, 27–28; and conceptions of human nature, 68; moral decline of, 95–99

American Dream, in 1950s–1960s, 38, 42

"Analogical imagination," 173, 197

Antiwar protests, 39. *See also* Demonstrations; Vietnam war

Apocalyptic vision, 132

Assassinations, effects of, 22, 35, 36, 37, 38, 39

Astrology, belief in, 71, 72

Atheism, extent of, 73, 126. *See also* God

Attendance, weekly, 171; by gender, 233. *See also* Churches; Congregations

Authority: Bible as, 94, 95; and commitment, 97; distrust of, 31, 153; in evangelical *vs.* alternative spirituality, 119–20, 131; patriarchal, 113, 218–19; reclaiming of, 147; and women, 218–19. *See also* Institutional religion

Baby boomers: culture of, 7–8; definition of, 1; as generation of seekers, 8; individualism of, 28; influence of on American culture, 3–4; older *vs.* younger, 34–35, 41; peak of, 248; population size of, 1, 2; reasons for study of, 2–4; shared experiences of, 26; span in years of, 269n1; stereotypes of, 1–2; unifying themes of, 128–33

Baby bust, 2

Baptism, views on, 17

Baptist church, 14

Baritz, Loren, 38

"Barry Johnson," 11–13; epilogue of, 263; and Kennedy assassination, 37; and life-cycle theory, 163; and "new class," 166–67; return to church of, 151–54, 169, 172–74, 189, 191–92, 196–97; religious commitment of, 257; and Vietnam war, 29, 40

Barry, Dave, 4

Beatles, The, 33, 70

Beatniks, 38

Bellah, Robert, 6, 251

Berger, Peter, 258

Bible, 19, 21; and cultural narratives, 29; and literalism, 102; as moral guidebook, 13, 15, 94, 95